The Collected Short Works of Thorstein Veblen

Volume III

Thorstein Veblen

VERNON PRESS

www.vernonpress.com

In the Americas:
Vernon Press
1000 N West Street,
Suite 1200, Wilmington,
Delaware 19801
United States

In the rest of the world
Vernon Press
C/Sancti Espiritu 17,
Malaga, 29006
Spain

ISBN 978-1-62273-216-6

Contents

Publisher's Note

This three-volume collection contains Veblen's publications in academic journals and other scholarly press. The articles are organized under major chapters covering Veblen's pioneering thoughts on social organization; economic theory; social theory; institutions, social organization and economic performance; contemporary policies and social movements; social applications of evolutionary reasoning. The original outlets and years of publication are listed below.

- Böhm-Bawerk's Definition Of Capital And The Source Of Wages (Quarterly Journal of Economics, 1892)
- Gustav Schmoller's Economics (Quarterly Journal of Economics, 1901)
- The Use Of Loan Credit In Modern Business (The Decennial Publications Of The University Of Chicago, 1903)
- Credit and Prices (The Journal of Political Economy, 1905)
- The Overproduction Fallacy (The Quarterly Journal of Economics, 1892)

SOCIAL THEORY

- The Barbarian Status of Women (American Journal of Sociology, 1899)
- The Economic Theory of Women's Dress (Popular Science Monthly, 1894)
- The Beginnings of Ownership (American Journal of Sociology, 1898)
- The Instinct of Workmanship and the Irksomeness of Labor (American Journal of Sociology, 1898)

INSTITUTIONS, SOCIAL ORGANIZATION AND ECONOMIC PERFORMANCE

- Christian Morals and the Competitive System (International Journal of Ethics, 1910)
- The Intellectual Pre-Eminence of Jews in Modern Europe (Political Science Quarterly, 1919)
- The Opportunity of Japan (The Journal of Race Development, 1915)

VOLUME III

COMMENTARY ON CONTEMPORARY POLICIES AND SOCIAL MOVEMENTS

- The Industrial System and the Captains of Industry (DIAL. A Fortnightly, 1919)
- The Captains of Finance and the Engineers (DIAL. A Fortnightly, 1919)
- The Country Town (The Freeman, 1923)
- The Army of the Commonweal (Journal of Political Economy, 1894)
- The Price of Wheat Since 1867 (Journal of Political Economy, 1892)
- The Food Supply And The Price Of Wheat (The Journal of Political Economy, 1893)
- The Later Railway Combinations (The Journal of Political Economy, 1901)
- On the General Principles of a Policy of Reconstruction (Journal of the National Institute of Social Sciences, 1918)

PHILOSOPHY

- Kant's Critique of Judgment (The Journal of Speculative Philosophy, 1884)

SOCIAL APPLICATIONS OF EVOLUTIONARY REASONING

- The Evolution of the Scientific Point of View (The University of California Chronicle, 1908)
- The Place of Science in Modern Civilisation (American Journal of Sociology, 1906)
- The Mutation Theory and the Blond Race (The Journal of Race Development, 1913)
- The Blond Race and the Aryan Culture (University of Missouri Bulletin, 1913)
- An Early Experiment in Trusts (The Journal of Political Economy, 1904)
- As to a Proposed Inquiry into Baltic and Cretan Antiquities (The American Journal of Sociology, 1910)

COMMENTARY
ON CONTEMPORARY POLICIES
AND SOCIAL MOVEMENTS

Chapter 1

The Industrial System
and the Captains of Industry

IT HAS BEEN USUAL, and indeed it still is not unusual, to speak of three coordinate "factors of production": land, labor, and capital. The reason for this threefold scheme of factors in production is that there have been three recognized classes of income: rent, wages, and profits; and it has been assumed that whatever yields an income is a productive factor. This scheme has come down from the eighteenth century. It is presumed to have been true, in a general way, under the conditions which prevailed in the eighteenth century, and it has therefore also been assumed that it should continue to be natural, or normal, true in some eminent sense, under any other conditions that have come on since that time.

Seen in the light of later events this threefold plan of coordinate factors in production is notable for what it omits. It assigns no productive effect to the industrial arts, for example, for the conclusive reason that the state of the industrial arts yields no stated or ratable income to any one class of persons; it affords no legal claim to a share in the community's yearly production of goods. The state of the industrial art is a joint stock of knowledge derived from past experience, and is held and passed on as an indivisible possession of the community at large. It is the indispensable foundation of all productive industry, of course, but except for certain minute fragments covered by patent rights or trade secrets, this joint stock is no man's individual property. For this reason it has not been counted in as a factor in production. The unexampled advance of technology during the past one hundred and fifty years has now begun to call attention to its omission from the threefold plan of productive factors handed down from that earlier time.

Another omission from the scheme of factors, as it was originally drawn, was the business man. But in the course of the nineteenth century the business -man came more and more obtrusively to the front and came in for a more and more generous portion of the country's yearly income which was taken to argue that he also contributed increasingly to the yearly production of goods. So a fourth factor of production has provisionally been added to the threefold scheme, in the person of the "entrepreneur," whose wages of management are considered to measure his creative share in the production of goods, although there still is some question as to the precise part of the entrepreneur in productive industry.

"Entrepreneur" is a technical term to designate the man who takes care of the financial end of things. It covers the same fact as the more familiar "business man," but with a vague suggestion of big business rather than small. The typical entrepreneur is the corporation financier. And since the corporation financier has habitually come in for a very substantial share of the community's yearly income he has also been conceived to render a very substantial service to the community as a creative force in that productive industry out of which the yearly income arises. Indeed it is nearly true that in current usage "producer" has come to mean "financial manager," both in the standard economic theory and in everyday speech.

There need of course be no quarrel with all this. It is a matter of usage. During the era of the machine industry which is also the era of the commercial democracy business men have controlled production and have managed the industry of the commonwealth for their own' ends, so that the material fortunes of all the civilized peoples have continued to turn on the financial management of their business men. And during the same period not only have the conditions of life among these civilized peoples continued to be fairly tolerable on the whole, but it is also true that the industrial system which these business men have been managing for their own private gain all this time has continually been growing more efficient on the whole.

Its productive capacity per unit of equipment and man power has continually grown larger. For this very creditable outcome due credit should be, as indeed it has been, given to the business community which has had the oversight of things. The efficient enlargement of industrial capacity has, of course, been due to a continued advance in technology, to a continued increase of the available natural resources, and to a continued increase of population. But the business community have also had a part in bringing all this to pass; they have always been in a position to hinder this growth, and it is only by their consent and advice that things have been enabled to go forward so far as they have gone. This sustained advance in productive capacity, due to the continued advance in technology and in population, has also had another notable consequence. According to the Liberal principles of the eighteenth century any legally defensible receipt of income is a sure sign of productive work done.

Seen in the light of this assumption, the visibly increasing productive capacity of the industrial system has enabled all men of a liberal and commercial mind not only to credit the businesslike captains of industry with having created this productive capacity, but also to overlook all that the same captains of industry have been doing in the ordinary course of business to hold productive industry in check. And it happens that all this time things have been moving in such a direction and have now gone so far that it is today quite an open question whether the businesslike management of the captains is not more occupied with checking industry than with increasing its productive capacity.

This captain of industry, typified by the corporation financier, and latterly by the investment banker, is one of the institutions that go to make up the new order of things, which has been coming on among all the civilized peoples ever since the Industrial Revolution set in. As such, as an institutional growth, his life history hitherto should be worth looking into for anyone who proposes to understand the recent growth and present drift of this new economic order. The beginnings of the captain of industry are to be seen at their best among those enterprising Englishmen who made it their work to carry the industrial promise of the -Revolution out into tangible performance, during the closing decades of the eighteenth and the early decades of the nineteenth century. These captains of the early time are likely to be rated as inventors, at least in a loose sense of the word. But it is more to the point that they were designers and builders of factory, mill, and mine equipment, of engines, processes, machines, and .machine tools, as well as shop managers, at the same time that they took care, more or less effectually, of the financial end. Nowhere do these beginnings of the captain of industry stand out so convincingly as among the English toolbuilders of that early time, who designed, tried out, built, and marketed that series of indispensable machine tools that has made the practical foundation of" the mechanical industry. Something to much the same effect is due to be said for the pioneering work of the Americans along the same general lines of mechanical design and performance at a slightly later period. To men of this class the new industrial order owes much of its early success as well as of its later growth.

These men were captains of industry, entrepreneurs, in some such simple and comprehensive sense of the word as that which the economists appear to have had in mind for a hundred years after, when they have spoken of the wages of management that are due the entrepreneur for productive work done. They were a cross between a business man and an industrial expert, and the industrial expert appears to have been the more valuable half in their composition. But factory, mine, and ship owners, as well as merchants and bankers, also made up a vital part of that business community out of whose later growth and specialization the corporation financier of the nineteenth and twentieth centuries has arisen. His origins are both technological and commercial, and in that early phase of his life history which has been taken over into the traditions of economic theory and of common sense he carried on both of these lines of interest and of work in combination. That was before the large scale, the wide sweep, and the profound specialization of the advanced mechanical industry had gathered headway. But progressively the cares of business management grew larger and more exacting, as the scale of things in business grew larger, and so the directive head of any such business concern came progressively to give his attention more and more exclusively to the "financial end." At the same time and driven by the same considerations the businesslike management of industry has progressively been shifting to the footing of corporation finance. This has brought on a further division, dividing the ownership of the industrial equipment and resources from their management. But also at the same time the industrial system, on its technological side, has been progressively growing greater and going- farther in scope, diversity, specialization, and complexity, as well as in productive capacity per unit of equipment and man power.

The last named item of change, the progressive increase of productive capacity, is peculiarly significant in this connection. Through the earlier and pioneering decades of the machine era it appears to have been passably true that the ordinary routine of management in industrial business was taken up with reaching out for new ways and means and speeding up production to maximum capacity. That was before standardization of processes and of unit products, and fabrication of parts had been carried far, and therefore before quantity production had taken on anything like its later range and reach. And, partly because of that fact because quantity production was then still a slight matter and greatly circumscribed, as contrasted with its later growth the ordinary volume of output in the mechanical industries was still relatively slight and manageable. Therefore those concerns that were engaged in these industries still had a fairly open market for whatever they might turn out, a market capable of taking up any reasonable increase of output. Exceptions to this general rule occurred; as, for example, in textiles. But the general rule stands out obtrusively through the early decades of the nineteenth century so far as regards English industry, and even more obviously in the case of America. Such an open market meant a fair chance for competitive production, without too much risk of overstocking. And running to the same effect, there was the continued increase of population and the continually increasing reach and volume of the means of transport, serving to maintain a free market for any prospective increase of output, at prices which offered a fair prospect of continued profit. In the degree in which this condition of things prevailed a reasonably-free competitive production would be practicable.

The industrial situation so outlined began visibly to give way toward the middle of the nineteenth century in England, and at a correspondingly later period in America. The productive capacity of the mechanical industry was visibly overtaking the capacity of the market, so that free competition without afterthought was no longer a sound footing on which to manage production. Loosely, this critical or transitional period falls in and about the second quarter of the nineteenth century in England; elsewhere at a correspondingly later date. Of course the critical point, when business exigencies began to dictate a policy of combination and restriction, did not come at the same date in all or in most of the mechanical industries; but it seems possible to say that, by and large, the period of transition to a general rule of restriction in industry comes on at the time and for the reason so indicated. There were also other factors engaged in that industrial situation, besides those spoken of above, less notable and less sharply defined, but enforcing limitations of the same character. Such were, for example, a rapidly gaining obsolescence of industrial plant, due to improvements and extensions, as also the partial exhaustion of the labor supply by persistent overwork, under-feeding, and unsanitary conditions but this applies to the English case rather than elsewhere.

In point of time this critical period in the affairs of industrial business coincides roughly with the coming in of corporation finance as the ordinary and typical method of controlling the industrial output. Of course the corporation, or company, has other uses besides the restrictive control of the output with a view to a profitable market, but it should be sufficiently obvious that the combination of ownership and centralization of control which the corporation brings about is also exceedingly convenient for that purpose. And when it appears that the general resort to corporate organization of the larger sort sets in about the time when business exigencies begin to dictate an imperative restriction of output, it is not easy to avoid the conclusion that this was one of the ends to be served by this reorganization of business enterprise. Business enterprise may fairly be said to have shifted from the footing of free-swung competitive production to that of a conscientious withholding of efficiency, so soon and so far as corporation finance on a sufficiently large scale had come to be the controlling factor in industry. At the same time and in the same degree the discretionary control of industry, and of other business enterprise in great part, has passed into the hands of the corporation financier.

Corporate organization has continually gone forward to a larger scale and a more comprehensive coalition of forces, and at the same time, and more and more visibly, it has become the ordinary duty of the corporate management to adjust production to the requirements of the market by restricting the output to what the traffic will bear, that is to say, what will yield the largest net earnings. Under corporate management it rarely happens that production is pushed to the limit of capacity. It happens, and can happen, only rarely and intermittently. This has been true, increasingly, ever since the ordinary productive capacity of the mechanical industries seriously began to overtake and promised to exceed what the market would carry off at a reasonably profitable price. And ever since that critical turn in the affairs of industrial business somewhere in the middle half of the nineteenth century it has become increasingly imperative to use a wise moderation and stop down the output to such a rate and volume as the traffic will bear. The cares of business have required an increasingly undivided attention on the part of the business men, and in an ever increasing measure their day's work has come to center about a running adjustment of sabotage on production. And for this purpose, evidently, the corporate organization of this business, on an increasingly large scale, is very serviceable, since the requisite sabotage on productive industry can be effectually administered only on a large plan and with a firm hand." The leaders in business are men who have studied and thought all their lives. They have thus learned to decide big problems at once, basing their decisions upon their knowledge of fundamental principles." Jeremiah W. Jenks.

That is to say, the surveillance of this financial end of industrial business, and the control of the requisite running balance of sabotage, have been reduced to a routine governed by settled principles of procedure and administered by suitably trained experts in corporation finance. But under the limitations to which all human capacity is subject it follows from this increasingly exacting discipline of business administration that the business men are increasingly out of touch with that manner of thinking and those elements of knowledge that go to make up the logic and the relevant facts of the mechanical technology. Addiction to a strict and unremitting valuation of all things in terms of price and profit leaves them, by settled habit, unfit to appreciate those technological facts and values that can be formulated only in terms of tangible mechanical performance; increasingly so with every further move into a stricter addiction to businesslike management and with every further advance of the industrial system into a still wider scope and a still more diversified and more delicately balanced give and take among its interlocking members.

They are experts in prices and profits and financial maneuvers, and yet the final discretion in all questions of industrial policy continues to rest in their hands. They are by training and interest captains of finance, and yet, with no competent grasp of the industrial arts, they continue to exercise a plenary discretion as captains of industry. They are unremittingly engaged in a routine of acquisition, in which they habitually reach their ends by a shrewd restriction of output, and yet they continue to be entrusted with the community's industrial welfare, which calls for maximum production.

Such has been the situation in all the civilized countries since corporation finance has ruled industry, and until a recent date. Quite recently this settled scheme of business management has shown signs of giving way, and a new move in the organization of business enterprise has come in sight, whereby the discretionary control of industrial production is shifting still farther over to the side of finance and still farther out of touch with the requirements of maximum production. The new move is of a twofold character: (a) the financial captains of industry have been proving their industrial incompetence in a progressively convincing fashion, and (b) their own proper work of financial management has progressively taken on a character of standardized routine such as no longer calls for or admits any large measure of discretion or initiative. They have been losing touch with the management of industrial processes, at the same time that the management of corporate business has, in effect, been shifting into the hands of a bureaucratic clerical staff. The corporation financier of popular tradition is taking on the character of a chief of bureau.

The changes which have brought the corporation financier to this somewhat inglorious position of a routine administrator set in along with the early growth of corporation finance, somewhere around the middle of the nineteenth century, and they have come to a head somewhere about the passage to the twentieth century, although it is only since the latter date that the outcome is becoming at all clearly defined. When corporate organization and the consequent control of output came into bearing there were two lines of policy open to the management: (a) to maintain profitable prices by limiting the output, and (b) to maintain profits by lowering the production cost of an increased output. To some extent both of these lines were followed, but on the whole the former proved the more attractive; it involved less risk, and it required less acquaintance with the working processes of industry. At least it appears that in effect the preference was increasingly given to the former method during this half-century of financial management. For this there were good reasons. The processes of production were continually growing more extensive, diversified, complicated, and more difficult for any layman in technology to comprehend and the corporation financier was such a layman, necessarily and increasingly so, for reasons indicated above. At the same time, owing to a continued increase of population and a continued extension of the industrial system, the net product of industry and its net earnings continued to increase independently of any creative effort on the part of the financial management. So the corporation financier, as a class, came in for an "un-earned increment" of income on the simple plan of "sitting tight." That plan is intelligible to any layman. All industrial innovation and all aggres-sive economy in the conduct of industry not only presumes an insight into the ' technological details of the industrial process, but to any other than the technological experts, who know the facts intimately, any move of that kind will appear hazardous. So the business men who have controlled in-dustry, being laymen in all that concerns its management, have increas-ingly been content to let well enough alone and to get along with an ever increasing overhead charge of inefficiency, so long as they have lost noth-ing by it. The result has been an ever increasing volume of waste and mis-direction in the use of equipment, resources, and man power throughout the industrial system.

In time, that is to say within the last few years, the resulting lag, leak, and friction in the ordinary working of this mechanical industry under busi-ness management have reached such proportions that no ordinarily intel-ligent outsider can help seeing them wherever he may look into the facts of the case. But it is the industrial experts, not the business men, who have finally begun to criticize this businesslike mismanagement and neglect of the ways and means of industry. And hitherto their efforts and advice have met with no cordial response from the business men in charge, who have, on the whole, continued to let well enough alone that is to say, what is well enough for a short-sighted business policy looking to private gain, howev-er poorly it may serve the material needs of the community. But in the meantime two things have been happening which have deranged the re-gime of the corporation financier: industrial experts, engineers, chemists, minerologists, technicians of all kinds have been drifting into more re-sponsible positions in the industrial system and have been growing up and multiplying within the system, because the system will no longer work at all without them; and on the other hand, the large financial interests on whose support the corporation financiers have been leaning have gradual-ly come to realize that corporation finance can best be managed as a comprehensive bureucratic routine, and that the two pillars of the house of corporate business enterprise of the larger sort are the industrial ex-perts and the large financial concerns that control the necessary funds; whereas the corporation financier is little more than a dubious intermedi-ate term between these two.

One of the greater personages in American business finance took note of this situation in the late nineties and set about turning it to account for the benefit of himself and his business associates, and from that period dates a new era in American corporation finance. It was for a time spoken of loosely as the Era of Trust-Making, but that phrase does not describe it at all adequately. It should rather be called the Era of the Investment Banker, and it has come to its present stage of maturity and stability only in the course of the past quarter-century.

The characteristic features and the guiding purpose of this improved method in corporation finance are best shown by a showing of the meth-ods and achievements of that great pioneer by whom it was inaugurated.

As an illustrative case, then, the American steel business in the nineties was suffering from the continued use of out-of-date processes, equipment, and locations, from wasteful management under the control of stubbornly ignorant corporation officials, and particularly from intermittent haphazard competition and mutual sabotage between the numerous concerns which were then doing business in steel. It appears to have been the last-named difficulty that particularly claimed the attention and supplied the opportunity of the great pioneer. He can by no stretch of charity be assumed to have had even a slight acquaintance with the technological needs and shortcomings of the steel industry. But to a man of commercial vision and financial sobriety it was plain that a more comprehensive, and therefore more authoritative, organization and control of the steel business would readily obviate much of the competition which was deranging prices. The apparent purpose and the evident effect of the new and larger coalition of business interests in steel was to maintain profitable prices by a reasonable curtailment of production. A secondary and less evident effect was a more economical management of the industry, which involved some displacement of quondam corporation financiers and some introduction of industrial experts. A further, but unavowed, end to be served by the same move in each of the many enterprises in coalition undertaken by the great pioneer and by his competitors was a bonus that came to these enterprising men in the shape of an increased capitalization of the business. But the notable feature of it all as seen from the point of view of the public at large was always the stabilization of prices at a reasonably high level, such as would always assure reasonably large earnings on the increased capitalization.

Since then this manner of corporation finance has been further perfected and standardized, until it will now hold true that no large move in the field of corporation finance can be made without the advice and consent of those large funded interests that are in a position to act as investment bankers; nor does any large enterprise in corporation business ever escape from the continued control of the investment bankers in any of its larger transactions ; nor can any corporate enterprise of the larger sort now continue to do business except on terms which will yield something appreciable in the way of income to the investment bankers, whose continued supply is necessary to its success. The financial interest here spoken of as the investment banker is commonly something in the way of a more or less articulate syndicate of financial houses, and it is to be added that the same financial concerns are also commonly, if not invariably, engaged or interested in commercial banking of the usual kind. So that the same well-established, half-syndicated ramification of banking houses that have been taking care of the country's commercial banking, with its center of credit and of control at the country's financial metropolis, is ready from beforehand to take over and administer the country's corporation finance on a unified plan and with a view to an equitable distribution of the country's net earnings among themselves and their clients. The more inclusive this financial organization is, of course, the more able it will be to manage the country's industrial system as an inclusive whole and prevent any hazardous innovation or experiment, as well as to limit production of the necessaries to such a volume of output as will yield the largest net return to itself and its clients. Evidently the improved plan which has thrown the discretion and responsibility into the "hands of the investment banker should make for a safe and sound conduct of business, such as will avoid fluctuations of price, and more particularly avoid any unprofitable speeding-up of productive industry.

Evidently, too, the initiative has hereby passed out of the hands of the corporation financier, who has fallen into the position of a financial middleman or agent, with limited discretion and with a precariously doubtful future. But all human institutions are susceptible of improvement, and the course of improvement may now and again, as in his case, result in supersession and displacement. And doubtless it is all for the best, that is to say, for the good of business, more particularly for the profit of big business.

But now as always corporation finance is a traffic in credit; indeed, now more than ever before. Therefore to stabilize corporate business sufficiently in the hands of this inclusive quasi-syndicate of banking interests 'it is necessary that the credit system of the country should as a whole be administered on a unified plan and inclusively. All of which is taken care of by the same conjunction of circumstances; the same quasi-syndicate of banking interests that makes use of the country's credit in the way of corporation finance is also the guardian of the country's credit. From which it results that, as regards those large-scale credit extensions which are of substantial consequence, the credits and debits are, in effect, pooled within the syndicate, so that no substantial derangement of the credit situation can take effect except by the free choice of this quasi-syndicate of investment banking houses; that is to say, not except they see an advantage to themselves in allowing the credit situation to be deranged, and not beyond the point which will best serve their collective purpose as against the rest of the community. With such a closed system no extension of credit obligations or multiplication of corporate securities, with the resulting inflation of values, need bring any risk of a liquidation, since credits and debits are in effect pooled within the system. By way of parenthesis it may also be remarked that under these circumstances "credit" has no particular meaning except as a method of accounting. Credit is also one of the timeworn institutions that are due to suffer obsolescence by improvement.

This process of pooling and syndication that is remaking the world of credit and corporation finance has been greatly helped on in America by the establishment of the Federal Reserve system, while somewhat similar results have been achieved elsewhere by somewhat similar devices. That system has greatly helped to extend, facilitate, simplify, and consolidate the unified control of the country's credit arrangements, and it has very conveniently left the substantial control in the hands of those larger financial interests into whose hands the lines of control in credit and industrial business were already being gathered by force of circumstances and by sagacious management of the interested parties. By this means the substantial core of the country's credit system is gathered into a self-balanced

whole, closed and unbreakable, self-insured against all risk and derangement. All of which converges to the definitive stabilization of the country's
business; but since it reduces financial traffic to a riskless routine it also
converges to the conceivable obsolescence of corporation finance and
eventually, perhaps, of the investment banker.

Chapter 2

The Captains of Finance
and the Engineers

IN MORE THAN ONE RESPECT the industrial system of today is notably different from anything that has gone before. It is eminently a system, self-balanced and comprehensive; and it is a system of interlocking mechanical processes, rather than of skilful manipulation. It is mechanical rather than manual. It is an organization of mechanical powers and material resources, rather than of skilled craftsmen and tools; although the skilled workmen and tools are also an indispensable part of its comprehensive mechanism. It is of an impersonal nature, after the fashion of the material sciences, on which it constantly draws.

It runs to "quantity production" of specialized and standardized goods and services. For all these reasons it lends itself to systematic control under the direction of industrial experts, skilled technologists, who may be called "production engineers," for want of a better term.

This industrial system runs on as an inclusive organization of many and diverse interlocking mechanical processes, interdependent and balanced among themselves in such a way that the due working of any part of it is conditioned on the due working of all the rest. Therefore it will work at its best only on condition that these industrial experts, production engineers, will work together on a common understanding; and more particularly on condition that they must not work at cross purposes. These technological specialists whose constant supervision is indispensable to the due working of the industrial system constitute the general staff of industry, whose work it is to control the strategy of production at large and to keep an oversight of the tactics of production in detail.

Such is the nature of this industrial system on whose due working depends the material welfare of all the civilized peoples. It is an inclusive system drawn on a plan of strict and comprehensive interdependence, such that, in point of material welfare, no nation and no community has anything to gain at the cost of any other nation or community. In point of material welfare, all the civilized peoples have been drawn together by the state of the industrial arts into a single going concern. And for the due working of this inclusive going concern it is essential that that corps of technological specialists who by training, insight, and interest make up the general staff of industry must have a free hand in the disposal of its available resources, in materials, equipment, and man power, regardless of any national pretensions or any vested interests. Any degree of obstruction, diversion, or withholding of any of the available industrial forces, with a view to the special gain of any nation or any investor, unavoidably brings on a dislocation of the system; which involves a disproportionate lowering of its working efficiency and therefore a disproportionate loss to the whole, and therefore a net loss to all its parts.

And all the while the statesmen are at work to divert and obstruct the working forces of this industrial system, here and there, for the special advantage of one nation and another at the cost of the rest; and the captains of finance are working, at cross purposes and in collusion, to divert whatever they can to the special gain of one vested interest and another, at any cost to the rest. So it happens that the industrial system is deliberately handicapped with dissension, misdirection, and unemployment of material resources, equipment, and man power, at every turn where the statesmen or the captains of finance can touch its mechanism; and all the civilized peoples are suffering privation together because their general staff of industrial experts are in this way required to take orders and submit to sabotage at the hands of the statesmen and the vested interests. Politics and investment are still allowed to decide matters of industrial policy which should plainly be left to the discretion of the general staff of production engineers driven by no commercial bias.

No doubt this characterization of the industrial system and its besetting tribulations will seem overdrawn. However, it is not intended to apply to any date earlier than the twentieth century, or to any backward community that still lies outside the sweep of the mechanical industry. . Only gradually during the past century, while the mechanical industry has progressively been taking over the production of goods and services, and going over to quantity production, has the industrial system taken on this character of an inclusive organization of interlocking processes and interchange of materials; and it is only in the twentieth century that this cumulative progression has come to a head with such effect that this characterization is now, visibly becoming true. And even now it will hold true, visibly and securely, only as applies to the leading mechanical industries, those main lines of industry that shape the main conditions of life, and in which quantity production has become the common and indispensable rule. Such are, for examples: transport and communication, the production and industrial use of coal, oil, electricity and water power, the production of steel and other metals; of wood pulp, lumber and other building materials; of textiles and rubber, as also grain-milling and much of the grain-growing, together with meat-packing and a good share of the stock-raising industry.

There is, of course, a large volume of industry in many lines which has not, or only in part and doubtfully, been drawn into this network of mechanical processes and quantity production, in any direct and conclusive fashion. But these other lines of industry that still stand over on another and older plan of operation are, after all, outliers and subsidiaries of the mechanically organized industrial system, dependent on or subservient to those greater underlying industries which make up the working body of the system, and which therefore set the pace for the rest. And in the main, therefore, and as regards these greater mechanical industries on whose due working the material welfare of the community depends from day to day, this characterization will apply without material abatement.

But it should be added that even as regards these greater, primary and underlying, lines of production the system has not yet reached a fatal degree of close-knit interdependence, balance, and complication ; it will still run along at a very tolerable efficiency in the face of a very appreciable amount of persistent derangement. That is to say, die industrial system at large has not yet become so delicately balanced a mechanical structure and process that the ordinary amount of derangement and sabotage necessary to the ordinary control of production by business methods will paralyze the whole outright. The industrial system is not yet sufficiently close-knit for that. And yet, that extent and degree of paralysis from which the civilized world's industry is suffering just now, due to legitimate business-like sabotage, goes to argue that the date may not be far distant when the interlocking processes of the industrial system shall have become so closely interdependent and so delicately balanced that even the ordinary modicum of sabotage involved in the conduct of business as usual will bring the whole to a fatal collapse.

The derangement and privation brought on by any well-organized strike of the larger sort argues to the same effect. In effect, the progressive advance of this industrial system towards an all-inclusive mechanical balance of interlocking processes appears to be approaching a critical pass, beyond which it will no longer be practicable to leave its control in the hands of business men working at cross purposes for private gain, or to entrust its continued administration to others than suitably trained technological experts, production engineers without a commercial interest. What these men may then do with it all is not so plain; the best they can do may not be good enough; but the negative proposition is becoming sufficiently plain, that this mechanical state of the industrial arts will not long tolerate the continued control of production by the vested interests under the current businesslike rule of incapacity by advisement. In the beginning, that is to say during the early growth of the machine industry, and particularly in that new growth of mechanical industries which arose directly out of the Industrial Revolution, there was no marked division between the industrial experts and the business managers.

That was before the new industrial system had gone far on the road of progressive specialization and complexity, and before business had reached an exactingly large scale; so that even the business men of that time, who were without special training in technological matters, would still be able to exercise something of an intelligent oversight of the whole, and to understand something of what was required in the mechanical conduct of the work which they financed and from which they drew their income. Not unusually the designers of industrial processes and equipment would then still take care of the financial end, at the same time that they managed the shop. But from an early point in the development there set in a progressive differentiation, such as to divide those who designed and administered the industrial processes from those others who designed and managed the commercial transactions and took care of the financial end. So there also set in a corresponding division of powers between the business management and the technological experts. It became the work of the technologist to determine, on technological grounds, what could be done in the way of productive industry, and to contrive ways and means of doing it; but the business management always continued to decide, on commercial grounds, how much work should be done and what kind and quality of goods and services should be produced; and the decision of the business management has always continued to be final, and has always set the limit beyond which production must not go.

With the continued growth of specialization the experts have necessarily had more and more to say in the affairs of industry, but always their findings as to what work is to be done and what ways and means are to be employed in production have had to wait on the findings of the business managers as to what will be expedient for the purpose of commercial gain. This division between business management and industrial management has continued to go forward, at a continually accelerated rate, because the special training and experience required for any passably efficient organization and direction of these industrial processes has continually grown more exacting, calling for special knowledge and abilities on the part of those who have this work to do and requiring their undivided interest and their undivided attention to the work in hand. But these specialists in technological knowledge, abilities, interest, and experience, who have increasingly come into the case in this way inventors, designers, chemists, mineralogists, soil experts, crop specialists, production managers and engineers of many kinds and denominations have continued to be employees of the captains of industry, that is to say, of the captains of finance, whose work it has been to commercialize the knowledge and abilities of the industrial experts and turn them to account for their own gain.

It is perhaps unnecessary to add the axiomatic corollary that the captains have always turned the technologists and their knowledge to account in this way only so far as would serve their own commercial profit, not to the extent of their ability or to the limit set by the material circumstances or by the needs of the community. The result has been, uniformly and as a matter of course, that the production of goods and services has advisedly been stopped short of productive capacity, by curtailment of output and by derangement of the productive system. There are two main reasons for this, and both have operated together throughout the machine era to stop industrial production increasingly short of productive capacity, (a)' The commercial need of maintaining a profitable price has led to an increasingly imperative curtailment of the output, as fast as the advance of the industrial arts has enhanced the productive capacity.

And (b) the continued advance of the mechanical technology has called for an ever-increasing volume and diversity of special knowledge, and so has left the businesslike captains of finance continually farther in arrears, so that they have been less and less capable of comprehending what is required in the ordinary way of industrial equipment and personnel. They have therefore, in effect, maintained prices at a profitable level by curtailment of output rather than by lowering production-cost per unit of output, because they have not had such a working acquaintance with the technological facts in the case as would enable them to form a passably sound judgment of suitable ways and means for lowering production-cost ; and at the same time, being shrewd business men, they have been unable to rely on the hired-man's-loyalty of technologists whom they do not understand. The result has been a somewhat distrustful blindfold choice of processes and personnel and a consequent enforced incompetence in the management of industry, a curtailment of output below the needs of the community, below the productive capacity of the industrial system, and below what an intelligent control of production would have made commercially profitable. Through the earlier decades of the machine era these limitations imposed on the work of the experts by the demands of profitable business and by the technical ignorance of the business men, appears not to have been a heavy handicap, whether as a hindrance to the continued development of technological knowledge or as an obstacle to its ordinary use in industry. That was before the mechanical industry had gone far in scope, complexity, and specialization; and it was also before the continued' work of the technologists had pushed the industrial system to so high a productive capacity that it is forever in danger of turning out a larger product than is required for a profitable business. But gradually, with the passage of time and the advance of the industrial arts to a wider scope and larger scale, and to an increasing specialization and standardization of processes, the technological knowledge that makes up the state of the industrial arts has called for a higher degree of that training that makes industrial specialists; and at the same time any passably efficient management of industry has of necessity drawn on them and their special abilities to an ever-increasing extent.

At the same time and by the same shift of circumstances, the captains of finance, driven by an increasingly close application to the affairs of business, have been going farther out of touch with the ordinary realities of productive industry; and, it is to be admitted, they have also continued increasingly to distrust the technological specialists, whom they do not understand, but whom they can also not get along without. The captains have per force continued to employ the technologists, to make money for them, but they have done so only reluctantly, tardily, sparingly, and with a shrewd circumspection ; only because and so far as they have been persuaded that the use of these technologists was indispensable to the making of money.

One outcome of this persistent and pervasive tardiness and circumspection on the part of the captains has been an incredibly and increasingly uneconomical use of material resources, and an incredibly wasteful organization of equipment and man power in those great industries where the technological advance has been most marked. In good part it was this discreditable pass, to which the leading industries had been brought by these one-eyed captains of industry, that brought the regime of the captains to an inglorious close, by shifting the initiative and discretion in this domain out of their hands into those of the investment bankers. By custom the investment bankers had occupied a position between or overlapping the duties of a broker in corporate securities and those of an underwriter of corporate floatations such a position, in effect, as is still assigned them in the standard writings on corporation finance. The increasingly large scale of corporate enterprise, as well as the growth of a mutual understanding among these business concerns, also had its share in this new move. But about this time, too, the "consulting engineers" were coming notably into evidence in many of those lines of industry in which corporation finance has habitually been concerned.

So far as concerns the present argument the ordinary duties of these consulting engineers have been to advise the investment bankers as to the industrial and commercial soundness, past and prospective, of any enterprise that is to be underwritten. These duties have comprised a painstaking and impartial examination of the physical properties involved in any given case, as well as an equally impartial auditing of the accounts and appraisal of the commercial promise of such enterprises, for the guidance of the bankers or syndicate of bankers interested in the case as underwriters. On this ground working arrangements and a mutual understanding presently arose between the consulting engineers and those banking houses that habitually were concerned in the underwriting of corporate enterprises.

The effect of this move has been two-fold: experience has brought out the fact that corporation finance, at its best and soundest, has now become a matter of comprehensive and standardized bureaucratic routine, necessarily comprising the mutual relations between various corporate concerns, and best to be taken care of by a clerical staff of trained accountants; and the same experience has put the financial houses in direct touch with the technological general staff of the industrial system, whose surveillance has become increasingly imperative to the conduct of any profitable enterprise in industry. But also, by the same token, it has appeared that the corporation financier of nineteenth-century tradition is no longer of the essence of the case in corporation finance of the larger and more responsible sort. He has, in effect, come to be no better than an idle wheel in the economic mechanism, serving only to take up some of the lubricant.

Since and so far as this shift out of the nineteenth century into the twentieth has been completed, the corporation financier has ceased to be a captain of industry and has become a lieutenant of finance; the captaincy having been taken over by the syndicated investment bankers and administered as a standardized routine of accountancy, having to do with the flotation of corporation securities and with their fluctuating values, and having also something to do with regulating the rate and volume of output in those industrial enterprises which so have passed under the hand of the investment bankers.

By and large, such is the situation of the industrial system today, and of that financial business that controls the industrial system. But this state of things is not so much an accomplished fact handed on out of the recent past; it is only that such is the culmination in which it all heads up in the immediate present, and that such is the visible drift of things into the calculable future. Only during the last few years has the state of affairs in industry been obviously falling into the shape so outlined, and it is even yet only in those larger and pace-making lines of industry which are altogether of the new technological order that the state of things has reached this finished shape. But in these larger and underlying divisions of the industrial system the present posture and drift of things is unmistakable. Meantime very much still stands over out of that regime of rule-of-thumb, competitive sabotage, and commercial log-rolling, in which the businesslike captains of the old order are so altogether well at home, and which has been the best that the captains have known how to contrive for the management of that industrial system whose captains they have been. So that wherever the production experts are now taking over the management, out of the dead hand of the self-made captains, and wherever they have occasion to inquire into the established conditions of production, they find the ground cumbered with all sorts of incredible make-shifts of waste and inefficiency such makeshifts as would perhaps pass muster with any moderately stupid elderly layman, but which look like blind-fold guess-work to these men who know something of the advanced technology and its working-out.

Hitherto, then, the growth and conduct of this industrial system presents this singular outcome. The technology the state of the industrial arts which takes effect in this mechanical industry is in an eminent sense a joint stock of knowledge and experience held in common by the civilized peoples. It requires the use of trained and instructed workmen born, bred, trained, and instructed at the cost of the people at large. So also it requires, with a continually more exacting insistence, a corps of highly trained and specially gifted experts, of divers and various kinds. These, too, are born, bred, and trained at the cost of the community at large, and they draw their requisite special knowledge from the community's joint stock of accumulated experience. These expert men, technologists, engineers, or whatever name may best suit them, make up the indispensable General Staff of the industrial system; and without their immediate and unremitting guidance and correction the industrial system will not work. It is a mechanically organized structure of technical processes designed, installed, and conducted by these production engineers. Without them and their constant attention the industrial equipment, the mechanical appliances of industry, will foot up to just so much junk. The material welfare of the community is unreservedly bound up with the due working of this industrial system, and therefore with its unreserved control by the engineers, who alone are competent to manage it. To do their work as it should be done these men of the industrial general staff must have a free hand, unhampered by commercial considerations and reservations; for the production of the goods and services needed by the community they neither need nor are they in any degree benefited by any supervision or interference from the side of the owners. Yet the owners, now represented, in effect, by the syndicated investment bankers, continue to control the industrial experts and limit their discretion arbitrarily, for their own commercial gain, regardless of the needs of the community.

Hitherto these men who so make up the general staff of the industrial system have not drawn together into anything like a self-directing working force; nor have they been vested with anything more than an occasional, haphazard, and tentative control of some disjointed sector of the industrial equipment, with no direct or decisive relation to that personnel of productive industry that may be called the officers of the line and the rank and file. It is still the unbroken privilege of the financial management and its financial agents to "hire and fire." The final disposition of all the industrial forces still remains in the hands of the business men, who still continue to dispose of these forces for other than industrial ends. And all the while it is an open secret that with a reasonably free hand the production experts would today readily increase the ordinary output of industry by several fold, variously estimated at some 300 per cent to 1200 per cent of the current output. And what stands in the way of so increasing the ordinary output of goods and services is business as usual.

Right lately these technologists have begun to become uneasily "class-conscious" and to reflect that they together constitute the indispensable General Staff of the industrial system. Their class consciousness has taken the immediate form of a growing sense of waste and confusion in the management of industry by the financial agents. They are beginning to take stock of that all-pervading mismanagement of industry that is inseparable from its control for commercial ends. All of which brings home a realization of their own shame and of damage to the common good. So the engineers are beginning to draw together and ask themselves, "What about it?"

This uneasy movement among the technologists set in, in an undefined and fortuitous way, in the closing years of the nineteenth century; when the consulting engineers, and then presently the "efficiency engineers," began to make scattered corrections in detail, which showed up the industrial incompetence of those elderly laymen who were doing a conservative business at the cost of industry. The consulting engineers of the standard type, both then and since then, are commercialized technologists, whose work it is to appraise the industrial value of any given enterprise with a view to its commercial exploitation. They are a cross between a technological specialist and a commercial agent, beset with the limitations of both and commonly not fully competent in either line. Their normal position is that of an employee of the investment bankers, on a stipend or a retainer, and it has ordinarily been their fortune to shift over in time from a technological footing to a frankly commercial one. The case of the efficiency engineers, or scientific-management experts, is somewhat similar. They too have set out to appraise, exhibit, and correct the commercial shortcomings of the ordinary management of those industrial establishments which they investigate, to persuade the business men in charge how they may reasonably come in for larger net earnings by a more closely shorn exploitation of the industrial forces at their disposal. During the opening years of the new century a lively interest centered on the views and expositions of these two groups of industrial experts; and not least was the interest aroused by their exhibits of current facts indicating an all-pervading lag, leak, and friction in the industrial system, due to its disjointed and one-eyed management by commercial adventurers bent on private gain.

During these few years of the opening century the members of this informal guild of engineers at large have been taking an interest in this question of habitual mismanagement by ignorance and commercial sabotage, even apart from the commercial imbecility of it all. But it is the young rather than the old among them who see industry in any other light than its commercial value. Circumstances have decided that the older generation of the craft have become pretty well commercialized. Their habitual outlook has been shaped by a long and unbroken apprenticeship to the corporation financiers and the investment bankers; so that they still habitually see the industrial system as a contrivance for the round-about process of making money. Accordingly, the established official Associations and Institutes of Engineers, which are officered and engineered by the elder engineers, old and young, also continue to show the commercial bias of their creators, in what they criticize and in what they propose. But the new generation which has been coming on during the present century are not similarly true to that tradition of commercial engineering that makes the technological man an awestruck lieutenant of the captain of finance.

By training, and perhaps also by native bent, the technologists find it easy and convincing to size up men and things in terms of tangible performance, without commercial afterthought, except so far as their apprenticeship to the captains of finance may have made commercial afterthought a second nature to them. Many of the younger generation are beginning to understand that engineering begins and ends in the domain of tangible performance, and that commercial expediency is another matter. Indeed, they are beginning to understand that commercial expediency has nothing better to contribute to the engineer's work than so much lag, leak, and friction. The four years' experience of the war has also been highly instructive on that head. So they are beginning to draw together on a common ground of understanding, as men who are concerned with the ways and means of tangible performance in the way of productive industry, according to the state of the industrial arts as they know them at their best; and there is a growing conviction among them that they together constitute the sufficient and indispensable general staff of the mechanical industries, on whose unhindered team-work depends the due working of the industrial system and therefore also the material welfare of the civilized peoples. So also, to these men who are trained in the stubborn logic of technology nothing is quite real that cannot be stated in terms of tangible performance; and they are accordingly coming to understand that the whole fabric of credit and corporation finance is a tissue of make-believe.

Credit obligations and financial transactions rest on certain principles of legal formality which have been handed down from the eighteenth century, and which therefore antedate the mechanical industry and carry no secure conviction to men trained in the logic of that industry. Within this technological system of tangible performance corporation finance and all its works and gestures are completely idle; it all comes into the working scheme of the engineers only as a gratuitous intrusion which could be barred out without deranging the work at any point, provided only that men made up their mind to that effect that is to say, provided the make-believe of absentee ownership were discontinued. Its only obvious effect on the work which the engineers have to take care of is waste of materials and retardation of the work. So the next question which the engineers are due to ask regarding this timeworn fabric of ownership, finance, sabotage, credit, and unearned income is likely to be : Why cumbers it the ground? And they are likely to find the scriptural answer ready to their hand.

It would be hazardous to surmise how, how soon, on what provocation, and with what effect the guild of engineers are due to realize that they constitute a guild, and that the material fortunes of the civilized peoples* already lie loose in their hands. But it is already sufficiently plain that the industrial conditions and the drift of conviction among the engineers are drawing together to some such end. Hitherto it has been usual to count on the interested negotiations continually carried on and never concluded between capital and labor, between the agents of the investors and the body of workmen, to bring about whatever readjustments are to be looked for in the control of productive industry and in the distribution and use of its product. These negotiations have necessarily been, and continue to be, in the nature of business transactions, bargaining for a price, since both parties to the negotiation continue to stand on the consecrated ground of ownership, free bargain, and self-help; such as the commercial wisdom of the eighteenth century saw, approved and certified it all, in the time before the coming of this perplexing industrial system. In the course of these endless negotiations between the owners and their workmen there has been some loose and provisional syndication of claims and forces on both sides; so that each of these two recognized parties to the industrial controversy has come to make up a loose-knit vested interest, and each speaks for its own special claims as a party in interest. Each is contending for some special gain for itself and trying to drive a profitable bargain for itself, and hitherto no disinterested spokesman for the community at large or for the industrial system as a going concern has cut into this controversy between these contending vested interests. The outcome has been businesslike concession and compromise, in the nature of bargain and sale. It is true, during the war, and for the conduct of the war, there were some half-concerted measures taken by the Administration in the interest of the nation at large, as a belligerent; but it has always been tacitly agreed that these were extraordinary war measures, not to be countenanced in time of peace. In time of peace the accepted rule is still business as usual; that is to say, investors and workmen wrangling together on a footing of business as usual.

These negotiations have necessarily been inconclusive. So long as ownership of resources and industrial plant is allowed, or so long as it is allowed any degree of control or consideration in the conduct of industry, nothing more substantial can come of any readjustment than a concessive mitigation of the owners' interference with production. There is accordingly nothing subversive in these bouts of bargaining between the federated workmen and the syndicated owners. It is a game of chance and skill played between two contending vested interests for private gain, in which the industrial system as a going concern enters only as a victim of interested interference. Yet the material welfare of the community, and not least of the workmen, turns on the due; working of this industrial system, without interference. Concessive mitigation of the right to interfere with production, on the part of either one of these vested interests, can evidently come to nothing more substantial than a concessive mitigation.

But owing to the peculiar technological character of this industrial system, with its specialized, standardized, mechanical, and highly technical inter-locking processes of production, there has gradually come into being this corps of technological production specialists, into whose keeping the due functioning of the industrial system has now drifted by force of circumstance. They are, by force of circumstance, the keepers of the community's material welfare; although they have hitherto been acting, in effect, as keepers and providers of free income for the kept classes. They are thrown into the position of responsible directors of the industrial system, and by the same move they are in a position to become arbiters of the community's material welfare. They are becoming class-conscious, and they are no longer driven by a commercial interest, in any such degree as will make them a vested interest in that commercial sense in which the syndicated owners and the federated workmen are vested interests. They are, at the same time, numerically and by habitual outlook, no such heterogeneous and unwieldy body as the federated workmen, whose numbers and scattering interest has left all their endeavors substantially nugatory. In short, the engineers are in a position to make the next move.

By comparison with the population at large, including the financial powers and the kept classes, the technological specialists which come in question here are a very inconsiderable number; yet this small number is indispensable to the continued working of the productive industries. So slight are their numbers, and so sharply defined and homogeneous is their class, that a sufficiently compact and inclusive organization of their forces should arrange itself almost as a matter of course, so soon as any appreciable proportion of them shall be moved by any common purpose. And the common purpose is not far to seek, in the all-pervading industrial confusion, obstruction, waste, and retardation which business as usual continually throws in their face. At the same time they are the leaders of the industrial personnel, the workmen, the officers of the line and the rank and file; and these are coming into a frame of mind to follow their leaders in any adventure that holds a promise of advancing the common good.

To those men, soberly trained in a spirit of tangible performance and endowed with something more than an even share of the sense of workmanship, and 'endowed also with the common heritage of partiality for the rule of Live and Let Live, the disallowance of an outworn and obstructive right of absentee ownership is not likely to seem a shocking infraction of the sacred realities. That customary right of ownership by virtue of which the vested interests continue to control the industrial system for the benefit of the kept classes, belongs to an older order of things than the mechanical industry. It has come out of a past that was made up of small things and traditional make-believe. For all the purposes of that scheme of tangible performance that goes to make up the technologist's world, it is without form and void. So that, given time for due irritation, it should by no means come as a surprise if the guild of engineers are provoked to put their heads together and, quite out of hand, disallow that large ownership that goes to make the vested interests and unmake the industrial system. And there stand behind them the massed and rough-handed legions of the industrial rank and file, ill at ease and looking for new things. The older commercialized generation among them would, of course, ask themselves: Why should we worry? What do we stand to gain? But the younger generation, not so hard-bitten by commercial experience, will be quite as likely to ask themselves: What do we stand to lose? And there is the patent fact that such a thing as a general strike of the technological specialists in industry need involve no more than a minute fraction of one per cent of the population; yet it would swiftly bring a collapse of the old order and sweep the timeworn fabric of finance and sabotage into the discard for good and all.

Such a catastrophe would doubtless be deplorable. It would look something like the end of the world to all those persons who take their stand with the kept classes, but it may come to seem no more than an incident of the day's work to the engineers and to the rough-handed legions of the rank and file. It is a situation which may well be deplored. But there is no gain in losing patience with a conjunction of circumstances. And it can do no harm to take stock of the situation and recognize that, by force of circumstance, it is now open to the Council of Technological Workers' and Soldiers' Deputies to make the next move, in their own way and in their own good time. When and what this move will be, if any, or even what it will be like, is not something on which a layman can hold a confident opinion. But so much seems clear, that the industrial dictatorship of the captain of finance is now held on sufferance of the engineers and is liable at any time to be discontinued at their discretion as a matter of convenience.

Chapter 3

The Country Town

The country town of the great American farming-region is the perfect flower of self-help and cupidity standardized on the American plan. Its name may be Spoon River or Gopher Prairie, or it may be Emporia or Centralia or Columbia. The pattern is substantially the same, and is repeated several thousand times with a faithful perfection which argues that there is no help for it, that it is worked out by uniform circumstances over which there is no control, and that it wholly falls in with the spirit of things and answers to the enduring aspirations of the community. The country town is one of the great American institutions; perhaps the greatest, in the sense that it has had and continues to have a greater part than any other in shaping public sentiment and giving character to American culture.

The location of ally given town has commonly been determined by collusion between "interested parties" with a view to speculation in real estate, and it continues through its life-history (hitherto) to be managed as a real-estate "proposition." Its municipal affairs, its civic pride, its community interest, converge upon its real-estate values, which are invariably of a speculative character, and which all its loyal citizens are intent on "booming" and "boosting" - that is to say, lifting still farther off the level of actual ground-values as measured by the uses to which the ground is turned. Seldom do the current (speculative) values of the town's real estate exceed the use-value of it by less than 100 per cent; and never do they exceed the actual values by less than 200 per cent, as shown by the estimates of the tax-assessor, nor do the loyal citizens ever cease their endeavours to lift the speculative values to something still farther out of touch with the material facts. A country town which does not answer to these specifications is "a dead one," one that has failed to "make good," and need not be counted with, except as a warning to the unwary "boomer[1] .Real estate is the one community-interest that binds the townsmen with a common bond; and it is highly significant - perhaps it is pathetic, perhaps admirable - that those inhabitants of the town who have no holdings of real estate and who never hope to have any, will commonly also do their little best to inflate the speculative values by adding the clamour of their unpaid chorus to the paid clamour of the professional publicity-agents, at the cost of

---

[1] "The great American game," they say, is Poker. Just why Real Estate should not come in for honourable mention in that way is not to be explained offhand. And an extended exposition of the reasons why would be tedious and perhaps distasteful, besides calling for such expert discrimination as quite exceeds the powers of a layman in these premises. But even persons who are laymen on both heads will recognize the same family traits in both.

so adding a little something to their own cost of living in the enhanced rentals and prices out of which the expenses of publicity are to be met.

Real estate is an enterprise in "futures," designed to get something for nothing from the unwary, of whom it is believed by experienced persons that "there is one born every minute." So farmers and townsmen together throughout the great farming-region are pilgrims of hope looking forward to the time when the community's advancing needs will enable them to realize on the inflated values of their real estate, or looking more immediately to the chance that one or another of those who are "born every minute" may be so ill-advised as to take them at their word and become their debtors in the amount which they say their real estate is worth. The purpose of country-town real estate, as of farm real estate in a less extreme degree, is to realize on it. This is the common bond of community-interest which binds and animates the business-community of the country town. In this enterprise there is concerted action and a spirit of solidarity, as well as a running business of mutual manoeuvring to get the better of one another. For eternal vigilance is the price of country-town real estate, being an enterprise in salesmanship.

Aside from this common interest in the town's inflated real estate, the townsmen are engaged in a vigilant rivalry, being competitors in the traffic carried on with the farm-population. The town is a retail trading-station, where farm-produce is bought and farm-supplies are sold, and there are always more traders than are necessary to take care of this retail trade. So that they are each and several looking to increase their own share in this trade at the expense of their neighbours in the same line. There is always more or less active competition, often underhand. But this does not hinder collusion between the competitors with a view to maintain and augment their collective hold on the trade with their farm-population.

From an early point in the life-history of such a town, collusion habitually becomes the rule, and there is commonly a well recognized ethical code of collusion governing the style and limits of competitive manoeuvres which any reputable trader may allow himself, In effect, the competition among business-concerns engaged in any given line of traffic is kept well in hand by a common understanding, and the traders as a body direct their collective efforts to getting what can be got out of the underlying farm-population. It is on this farm-trade also, and on the volume and increase of it, past and prospective, that the real-estate values of the town rest. As one consequence, the volume and profit of the farm-trade is commonly overstated, with a view to enhancing the town's real-estate values.

Quite as a matter of course, the business of the town arranges itself under such regulations and usages that it foots up to a competition, not between the business-concerns, but between town and country, between traders and customers. And quite as a matter of, course, too, the number of concerns doing business in any one town greatly exceeds what is necessary to carry on the traffic; with the result that while the total profits of the business in any given town are inordinately large for the work done, the profits of any given concern are likely to be modest enough. The more successful ones among them commonly do very well and come in for large returns on their outlay, but the average returns per concern or per man are quite modest, and the less successful ones are habitually doing business within speaking-distance of bankruptcy. The number of failures is large, but they are habitually replaced by others who still have something to lose. The conscientiously habitual overstatements of the real-estate interests continually draw new traders into the town; for the retail trade of the town also gets its quota of such persons as are born every minute, who then transiently become supernumerary retail traders. Many fortunes are made in the country towns, of-tell fortunes of very respectable proportions; but many smaller fortunes are also lost.

Neither the causes nor the effects of this state of things have been expounded by the economists, nor has it found a place in the many formulations of theory that have to do with the retail trade; presumably because it is all, under the circumstances, so altogether "natural" and unavoidable. Exposition of the obvious is a tedious employment, and a recital of commonplaces does not hold the interest of readers or audience. Yet, for completeness of the argument, it seems necessary here to go a little farther into the details and add something on the reasons for this arrangement. However obvious and natural it may be, it is after all serious enough to merit the attention of anyone who is interested in the economic situation as it stands, or in finding a way out of this situation; which is just now quite perplexing, as the futile endeavours of the statesmen will abundantly demonstrate.

However natural and legitimate it all undoubtedly may be, the arrangement as it runs to-day imposes on the country's farm-industry an annual overhead charge which runs into ten or twelve figures, and all to the benefit of no one. This overhead charge of billions, due to duplication of work, personnel, equipment, and traffic, in the country towns is, after all, simple and obvious waste. Which is perhaps to, be deprecated, although one may Well hesitate to find fault with it all, inasmuch as it is all a simple and obvious outcome of those democratic principles of self-help and cupidity on which the commonwealth is founded. These principles are fundamentally and eternally right and good - so long as popular sentiment runs to that effect - and they are to be accepted gratefully, with the defects of their qualities. The whole arrangement is doubtless all right and worth its cost; indeed it is avowed to be the chief care and most righteous solicitude of the constituted authorities to maintain and cherish it all.

To an understanding of the country town and its place in the economy of American farming, it should he noted that in the great farming-regions any given town has a virtual monopoly of the trade within the territory tributary to it. This monopoly is neither complete nor indisputable; it does not cover all lines of traffic equally, nor is outside competition completely excluded in any line. But the broad statement is quite sound, that within its domain any given country town in the farming-country has a virtual monopoly of trade in those main lines of business in which the townsmen are chiefly engaged. And the townsmen are vigilant in taking due precautions that this virtual monopoly shall not be broken in upon. It may be remarked by the way that this characterization applies to the country towns of the great farming-country, and only in a less degree to the towns of the industrial and outlying sections.

Under such a (virtual) monopoly, the charge collected on the traffic adjusts itself, quite as a matter of course, to what the traffic will bear. It has no other relation to the costs or the use-value of the service rendered. But what the traffic will bear is something to be determined by experience and is subject to continued readjustment and revision, with the effect of unremittingly keeping the charge close up to the practicable maximum. Indeed, there is reason to believe that the townsmen are habitually driven by a conscientious cupidity and a sense of equity to push the level of charges somewhat over the maximum; that is to say, over the rate which would yield them the largest net return, Since there are too many of them, they are so placed as habitually to feel that they come in for something short of their just deserts, and their endeavour to remedy this state of things is likely to lead to overcharging rather than the reverse.

What the traffic will bear in this retail trade is what the farm-population will put up with, without breaking away and finding their necessary supplies and disposing of their marketable products elsewhere, in some other town, through itinerant dealers, by recourse to brokers at a distance, through the mail-order concerns, and the like. The two dangerous outside channels of trade appear to be the rival country towns and the mail-order houses, and of these the mail-order houses are apparently the more real menace as well as the more dreaded. Indeed they are quite cordially detested by right-minded country-town dealers. The rival country towns are no really grave menace to the usurious charges of any community of country-town business man, since they are all and several in the same position and none of them fails to charge all corners all that the traffic will bear.

There is also another limiting condition to be considered in determining what the traffic will bear in this retail trade, though it is less, or at least less visibly, operative, namely: the point beyond which the charges can not enduringly be advanced without discouraging the farm-population unduly; that is to say, the point beyond which the livelihood of the farm-population will be cut into so severely by the overcharging of the retail trade that they begin to decide that they have nothing more to lose, and so give up and move out. , This critical point appears not commonly to be reached in the ordinary retail trade - as, e.g., groceries, clothing, hardware - possibly because there still remains, practicable in an extremity, the recourse to outside dealers of one sort and another. In the business of country-town banking, however, and similar money-lending by other persons than the banks, the critical point is not infrequently reached and passed. Here the local monopoly is fairly complete and rigorous, which brings on an insistent provocation to overreach.

Then, too, the banker deals in money-values, and money-values are for ever liable to fluctuate, at the same time that the fortunes of the banker's farm-clients are subject to the vicissitudes of the seasons and of the markets; and competition drives both banker and client to base their habitual rates, not on a conservative anticipation of what is likely to happen, but on the lucky chance of what may come to pass barring accidents and the acts of God. And the banker is under the necessity - "inner necessity," as the Hegelians would say - of getting all he can and securing himself against all risk, at the cost of any whom it may concern, by such charges and stipulations as will ensure his net gain in any event. It is the business of the country-town business-community, one with another, to charge what the traffic will bear; and the traffic will bear charges that are inordinately high as counted on the necessary cost or the use-value of the work to be done. It follows, under the common-sense logic of self-help, cupidity, and business-as-usual, that men eager to do business on a good margin will continue to drift in and cut into the traffic until the number of concerns among whom the gains are to be divided is so large that each one's share is no more than will cover costs and leave a "reasonable" margin of net gain. So that while the underlying farm-population continues to yield inordinately high charges on the traffic, the business-concerns engaged, one with another, come in for no more than what will induce them to go on; the reason being that in the retail trade as conducted on this plan of self-help and equal opportunity, the stocks, equipment and man-power employed will unavoidably exceed what is required for the work, by some 200 to 1000 per cent, those lines of the trade being the more densely over-populated which enjoy the nearest approach to a local monopoly, as e. g., groceries, or banking[2].

It is perhaps not impertinent to call to mind that the retail trade throughout, always and everywhere, runs on very much the same plan of inordinately high charges and consequently extravagant multiplication of stocks, equipment, work, personnel, publicity, credits, and costs, It runs to the same effect in city, town and country. And in city, town or country it is in all of these several respects the country's largest business-enterprise in the aggregate; and always something like three-fourths to nine-tenths of it is idle waste, to be cancelled out of the community's working-efficiency as lag, leak and friction. When the statesmen and the newspapers - and other publicity-agencies - speak for the security and the meritorious work of the

---

[2] The round numbers named above are safe and conservative, particularly so long as the question concerns the staple country towns of the great farming-regions, as has already been remarked, they are only less securely applicable in the case of similar towns in the industrial and outlying parts of the country. To some they may seem large and loose. They are based on a fairly exhaustive study of statistical materials gathered by special inquiry in the spring of 1918 for the Statistical Division of the Food Administration but not published hitherto. There has been little detailed or concrete discussion of the topic. See, however, a very brief paper by Isador Lubin on "The Economic Costs of Retail Distribution," published in the Twenty-second Report of the Michigan Academy of Science, which runs in great part on the same material. It is, or should be, unnecessary to add that the retail trade of the country-towns is neither a unique nor an extravagant development of business as usual. It is in fact very much the sort of thing that is to be met with in the retail trade anywhere, in America and elsewhere.

country's business men, it is something of this sort they are talking about. The bulk of the country's business is the retail trade, and in an eminent sense the retail trade is business-as-usual.

The retail trade, and therefore in its degree the country town, have been the home ground of American culture and the actuating centre of public affairs and public sentiment throughout the nineteenth century, ever more securely and unequivocally as the century advanced and drew towards it close. In American parlance "The Public," so far as it can be defined, has meant those persons who are engaged in and about the business of the retail trade, together with such of the kept classes as draw their keep from this traffic. The road to success has run into and through the country town, or its retail-trade equivalent in the cities, and the habits of thought engendered by the preoccupations of the retail trade have shaped popular sentiment and popular morals and have dominated public policy in what was to be done and what was to be left undone, locally and at large, in political, civil, social, ecclesiastical, and educational concerns. The country's public men and official spokesmen have come up through and out of the country-town community, on passing the test of fitness according to retail-trade standards, and have carried with them into official responsibility the habits of thought induced by these interests and these habits of life.

This is also what is meant by democracy in American parlance, and it was for this country-town pattern of democracy that the Defenders of American Faith once aspired to make the world safe. Meantime democracy, at least in America, has moved forward and upward to a higher business-level, where larger vested interests dominate and bulkier margins of net gain are in the hazard. It has come to be recognized that the country-town situation of the nineteenth century is now by way of being left behind; and so it is now recognized, or at least acted on, that the salvation of twentieth-century democracy is best to be worked out by making the world safe for Big Business, and then letting Big Business take care of the interests of the retail trade and the Country town, together with much else. But it should not be overlooked that in and through all this it is the soul of the country town that goes marching on

.Towards the close of the century, and increasingly since the turn of the century, the trading-community of the country towns has been losing its initiative as a maker of charges and has by degrees become tributary to the great vested interests that move in the background of the market. In a way the country towns have in an appreciable degree fallen into the position of toll-gate keepers for the distribution of goods and collection of customs for the large absentee owners of the business. Grocers, hardware-dealers, meat-markets, druggists, shoe-shops, are more and more extensively falling into the position of local distributors for jobbing houses and manufacturers. They increasingly handle "package goods" bearing the brand of some (ostensible) maker, whose chief connexion with the goods is that of advertiser of the copyright brand which appears on the label. Prices, and margins, are made for the retailers, which they can take or leave. But leaving, in this connexion, will commonly mean leaving the business - which is not included in the premises. The bankers work by affiliation with and under surveillance of their correspondents in the sub-centres of credit, who are similarly tied in under the credit-routine of the associated banking-houses in the great centres. And the clothiers duly sell garments under the brand of "Cost-Plus," or some such apocryphal token of merit.

All this reduction of the retailers to simpler terms has by no means lowered the overhead charges of the retail trade as they bear upon the underlying farm-population; rather the reverse, Nor has it hitherto lessened the duplication of stocks, equipment, personnel and work, that goes into the retail trade; rather the reverse, indeed, whatever may yet happen in that connexion. Nor has it abated the ancient spirit of self-help and cupidity that has always animated the retail trade and the country town; rather the reverse ; inasmuch as their principals back in the jungle of Big Business cut into the initiative and the margins of the retailers with "package goods," brands, advertising, and agency-contracts; which irritation the retailers and provokes them to retaliate and recoup where they see an opening; that is, at the cost of the underlying farm-population. It is true, the added overcharge which so can effectually be brought to rest on the farm-population may well be a negligible quantity; there never was much slack to be taken upon that side.

The best days of the retail trader and the country town are past. The retail trader is passing under the hand of Big Business, and so is ceasing to be a masterless man ready to follow the line of his own initiative and help to rule his corner of the land in collusion with his fellow-townsmen. Circumstances are prescribing for him. The decisive circumstances that hedge him about have been changing in such a way as to leave him no longer fit to do business on his own, even in collusion with his fellow-townsmen. The retail trade and the country town are an enterprise in salesmanship, of course, and salesmanship is a matter of buying cheap and selling dear; all of which is simple and obvious to any retailer, and holds true all around the circle from grocer to banker and back again. During the period while the country town has flourished and grown into the texture of the economic situation, the salesmanship which made the outcome was a matter of personal qualities, knack and skill that gave the dealer an advantage in meeting his customers man to man, largely a matter of tact, patience and effrontery; those qualities, in short, which have qualified the rustic horse-trader and have cast a glamour of adventurous enterprise over American country life. In this connexion it is worth recalling that the personnel engaged in the retail trade of the country towns has in the main been drawn by self-selection from the farm-population, prevailingly from the older settled sections where this traditional animus of the horse-trader is of older growth and more untroubled.

All this was well enough, at least during the period of what may be called the masterless country town, before Big Business began to come in its own in these premises. But this situation has been changing, becoming obsolete, slowly, by insensible degrees. The factors of change have been such as: increased facilities of transport and communication; increasing use of advertising, largely made possible by facilities of transport and communication; increased size and combination of the business-concerns engaged in the wholesale trade, as packers, jobbers, warehouse-concerns handling farm-products; increased resort to package-goods, brands, and trade-marks, advertised on a liberal plan which runs over the heads of the retailers; increased employment of chain-store methods and agencies; increased dependence of local bankers on the greater credit-establishments of the financial centres. It will be seen, of course, that this new growth finally runs back to and rests upon changes of a material sort in the industrial arts, and more immediately on changes in the means of transport and communication.

In effect, salesmanship, too, has been shifting to the wholesale scale and plan, and the country-town retailer is not in a position to make use of the resulting wholesale methods of publicity and control. The conditioning circumstances have outgrown him. Should he make the shift to the wholesale plan of salesmanship lie will cease to be a country-town retailer and take on the character of a chain-store concern, a line-yard lumber-syndicate, a mail-order house, a Chicago packer instead of a meat market, a Reserve Bank instead of a county-seat banker, and the like; all of which is not contained in the premises of the country-town retail trade.

The country town, of course, still has its uses, and its use so far as bears on the daily life of the underlying farm-population is much the same as ever; but for the retail trade and for those accessory persons and classes who draw their keep from its net gains, the country-town is no longer what it once was. It has been falling into the position of a way station in the distributive system, instead of a local habitation where a man of initiative and principle might reasonably hope to come in for a "competence" - that is a capitalized free livelihood - and bear his share in the control of affairs without being accountable to any master-concern "higher up" in the hierarchy of business. The country town and the townsmen are by way of becoming ways and means in the hands of Big Business. Barring accidents, bolshevism, and the acts of God or the United States Congress, such would appear to be the drift of things in the calculable future, that is to say, in the absence of disturbing causes.

This does not mean that the country town is on the decline in point of population or the volume of its traffic; but only that the once masterless retailer is coming in for a master, that the retail trade is being standardized and re-parcelled by and in behalf of those massive vested interests that move obscurely in the background, and that these vested interests in the background now have the first call on the "income strewn that flows from the farms through the country town. Nor does it imply that that spirit of self-help and collusive cupidity that made and animated the country town at its best, has faded out of the mentality of this people. It has only moved upward and onward to higher duties and wider horizons. Even if it should appear that the self-acting collusive storekeeper and banker of the nineteenth-century country town "lies a-mouldering in his grave," yet "his soul goes marching on." It is only that the same stock of men with the same traditions and ideals are doing Big Business on the same general plan on which the country town was built. And these men who know the country town "from the ground up" now find it ready to their hand, ready to be turned to account according to the methods and principles bred in their own bone. And the habit of mind induced by and conducive to business-as-usual is much the same whether the balance-sheet runs in four figures or in eight.

It is an unhappy circumstance that all this plain speaking about the country town, its traffic, its animating spirit, and its standards of merit, unavoidably has an air of finding fault. But even slight reflection will show that this appearance is unavoidable even where there is no inclination to disparage. It lies in the nature of the case, unfortunately. No unprejudiced inquiry into the facts can content itself with anything short of plain speech, and in this connexion plain speech has an air of disparagement because it has been the unbroken usage to avoid plain speech touching these things, these motives, aims, principles, ways and means and achievements of these substantial citizens and their business and fortunes. But for all that, all these substantial citizens and their folks, fortunes, works, and opinions are no less substantial and meritorious, in fact. Indeed one can scarcely appreciate the full measure of their stature, substance and achievements, and more particularly the moral costs of their great work in developing the country and taking over its resources, without putting it all in plain terms, instead of the salesmanlike parables that have to be employed in the make-believe of trade and politics.

The country town and the business of its substantial citizens are and have ever been an enterprise in salesmanship; and the beginning of wisdom in salesmanship is equivocation. There is a decent measure of equivocation which runs its course on the hither side of prevarication or duplicity, and an honest salesman - such "an honest man as will bear watching" - will endeavour to confine his best efforts to this highly moral zone where stands the upright man who is not under oath to tell the whole truth. But "self-preservation knows no moral law"; and it is not to be overlooked that there habitually enter into the retail trade of the country towns many competitors who do not falter at prevarication and who even do not hesitate at outright duplicity; and it will not do for an honest man to let the rogues get away with the best - or any - of the trade, at the risk of too narrow a margin of profit on his own business-that is to say a narrower margin than might be had in the absence of scruple. And then there is always the base line of what the law allows; and what the law allows can not be far wrong. Indeed, the sane presumption will be that whoever lives within the law has no need to quarrel with his conscience. And a sound principle will be to improve the hour to-day and, if worse comes to worst, let the courts determine to-morrow, under protest, just what the law allows, and therefore what the moral code exacts. And then, too, it is believed and credible that the courts will be wise enough to see that the law is not allowed to apply with such effects as to impede the volume or narrow the margins of business-as-usual.

He either fears his fate too much, or his deserts are small, Who dare not put it to the touch" and take a chance with the legalities and moralities for once in a way, when there is easy money in sight and no one is looking, particularly in case his own solvency - that is his life as a business-concern - should be in the balance. Solvency is always a meritorious work, however it may be achieved or maintained; and so long as one is quite sound on this main count one is sound on the whole, and can afford to forget pec-cadilloes, within reason. The country-town code of morality at large, as well as its code of business-ethics, is quite sharp, meticulous; but solvency always has a sedative value in these premises, at large and in personal de-tail. And then, too, solvency not only puts a man in the way of acquiring merit, but it makes him over into a substantial citizen whose opinions and preferences have weight and who is therefore enabled to do much good for his fellow-citizens - that is to say, shape them somewhat to his own pattern. To create mankind in one's own image is a work that partakes of the divine, and it is a high privilege which the substantial citizen common-ly makes the most of. Evidently this salesmanlike pursuit of the net gain has a high cultural value at the same time that it is invaluable as a means to a competence.

The country-town pattern of moral agent and the code of morals and proprieties, manners and customs, which come -up out of this life of salesmanship, are such as this unremitting habituation is fit to produce. The scheme of conduct for the business man and for "his sisters and his cousins and his aunts" is a scheme of salesmanship, seven days in the week. And the rule of life of country-town salesmanship is summed up in what the older logicians have called *suppressio veri and suggestio falsi.* The dominant note of this life is circumspection[3] .

One must avoid offence, cultivate good will, at any reasonable cost, and continue unfailing in taking advantage of it; and, as a corollary to this axi-om, one should be ready to recognize and recount the possible shortcom-ings of one's neighbours, for neighbours are (or may be) rivals in the trade, and in trade one man's loss is another's gain, and a rival's disabilities count in among one's assets and should not be allowed to go to waste. One must be circumspect, acquire merit, and avoid offence. So one must eschew opinions, or information, which are not acceptable to the com-mon run of those whose good will has or may conceivably come to have any commercial value. The country-town system of knowledge and belief can admit nothing that would annoy the prejudices of any appreciable number of the respectable townsfolk. So it becomes a system of intellectu-al, institutional, and religious hold-overs. The country town is conserva-tive; aggressively and truculently so, since any assertion or denial that runs counter to any appreciable set of respectable prejudices would come in for some degree of disfavour, and any degree of disfavour is intolerable to men whose business would presumably suffer by it, Whereas there is no (business) harm done in assenting to, and so in time coming to believe in, any or all of the commonplaces of the day before yesterday. In this sense the country town is conservative, in that it is by force of business-expediency intolerant of anything but holdovers. Intellectually, institu-

---

[3] It might also be called salesmanlike pusillanimity.

tionally, and religiously, the country towns of the great farming-country are "standing pat" on the ground taken somewhere about the period of the Civil War; or according to the wider chronology, somewhere about Mid-Victorian times. And the men of affairs and responsibility in public life, who have passed the test of country-town fitness, as they must, are men who have come through and made good according to the canons of faith and conduct imposed by this system of hold-overs.

Again it seems necessary to enter the caution that in so speaking of this system of country-town holdovers and circumspection there need be no hint of disparagement. The colloquial speech of our time, outside of the country-town hives of expedient respectability, carries a note of disallowance and disclaimer in all that it has to say of hold-overs; which is an unfortunate but inherent defect of the language, and which it is necessary to discount and make ones peace with. It is only that outside of the country towns, where human intelligence has not yet gone into abeyance and where human speech accordingly is in continued process of remaking, sentiment and opinion to the unhappy effect which this implicit disparagement of these hold-overs discloses. Indeed, there is much, or at least something, to be said to the credit of this country-town system of holdovers, with its canons of salesmanship and circumspection. It has to its credit many deeds of Christian charity and Christian faith. It may be - as how should it not? - that many of these deeds of faith and charity are done in the businesslike hope that they will have some salutary effect on the doer's balance-sheet; but the opaque fact remains that these business men do these things, and it is to be presumed that they would rather not discuss the ulterior motives.

It is a notorious commonplace among those who get their living by promoting enterprises of charity and good deeds in general, that no large enterprise of this description can be carried through to a successful and lucrative issue without due appeal to the country towns and due support by the businesslike townsmen and their associates and accessory folks. And it is likewise notorious that the country-town community of business men and substantial households will endorse, and contribute to virtually any enterprise of the sort, and ask few questions. The effectual interest which prompts the endorsement of and visible contribution to these enterprises is a salesmanlike interest in the "prestige value" that comes to those persons who endorse and visibly contribute; and perhaps even more insistently, there is the loss of "prestige value" that would come to anyone who should dare to omit due endorsement of and contribution to any ostensibly public-spirited enterprise of this kind that has caught the vogue and does not violate the system of prescriptive hold-overs.

Other interest there may well be, as, e.g., human charity or Christian charity - that is to say solicitude for the salvation of one's soul - but without due appeal to salesmanlike respectability the clamour of any certified solicitor of these good deeds will be but as sounding brass and a tinkling cymbal. One need only try to picture what would be the fate, e.g., of the campaigns and campaigners, for Red Cross, famine-relief, Liberty Bonds, foreign missions, Interchurch fund, and the like, in the absence of such

appeal and of the due response. It may well be, of course, that the salesmanlike townsman endorses with the majority and pays his contribution
as a mulct, under compunction of expediency, as a choice between evils,
for fear of losing good will. But the main fact remains. It may perhaps all
foot up to this with the common run, that no man who values his salesmanlike well-being will dare follow his own untoward propensity in dealing with these certified enterprises in good deeds, and speak his profane
mind to the certified campaigners. But it all comes to the same in the upshot. The substantial townsman is shrewd perhaps, or at least he aims to
be, and it may well be that with a shrewd man's logic he argues that two
birds in the bush are worth more than one in the hand; and so pays his
due peace-offering to the certified solicitor of good deeds, somewhat in
the spirit of those addicts of the faith who once upon a time bought Papal
indulgences. But when all is said, it works; and that it does so, and that
these many adventures and adventurers in certified mercy and humanity
are so enabled to subsist in any degree of prosperity and comfort is to be
credited, for the major part, to the salesmanlike tact of the substantial citizens of the country towns.

One hesitates to imagine what would be the fate of the foreign missions,
e.g., in the absence of this salesmanlike solicitude for the main chance in
the country towns. And there is perhaps less comfort in reflecting on what
would be the terms of liquidation for those many churches and church-
men that now adorn the land, if they were driven to rest their fortunes on
unconstrained gifts from de facto worshippers moved by the first-hand
fear of God, in the absence of that more bounteous subvention that so
comes in from the quasi-consecrated respectable townsmen who are so
constrained by their salesmanlike fear of a possible decline in their prestige.

Any person who is seriously addicted to devout observances and who
takes his ecclesiastical verities at their face might be moved to deprecate
this dependence of the good cause on these mixed motives. But there is no
need of entertaining doubts here as to the ulterior goodness of these businesslike incentives. Seen in perspective from the outside - as any economist must view these matters - it should seem to be the part of wisdom, for
the faithful and for their businesslike benefactors alike, to look steadfastly
to the good end and leave ulterior questions of motive on one side. There
is also some reason to believe that such a view of the whole matter is not
infrequently acted upon. And when all is said and allowed for, the main
fact remains, that in the absence of this spirit of what may without offence
be called salesmanlike pusillanimity in the country towns, both the glory
of God and the good of man would be less bountiful served, on all these
issues that engage the solicitors of good deeds.

This system of innocuous hold-overs, then, makes up, what may be
called the country-town profession of faith, spiritual and secular. And so it
comes to pass that the same general system of hold-overs imposes its bias
on the reputable organs of expression throughout the community - pulpit,
public press, courts, schools - and dominates the conduct of public affairs;
inasmuch as the constituency of the country-town, in the main and the

everyday run, shapes the course of reputable sentiment and conviction for the American community at large. Not because of any widely prevalent aggressive preference for that sort of thing, perhaps, but rather because it would scarcely be a "sound business proposition" to run counter to the known interests of the ruling class; that is to say, the substantial citizens and their folks. But the effect is much the same and will scarcely be denied. It will be seen that in substantial effect this country-town system of hold-overs is of what would be called a "salutary" character; that is to say, it is somewhat intolerantly conservative. It is a system of professions and avowals, which may perhaps run to no deeper ground than a salesmanlike pusillanimity, but the effect is much the same. In the country-town community and its outlying ramifications, as in any community of men, the professions made and insisted on will unavoidably shape the effectual scheme of knowledge and belief.

Such is the known force of inveterate habit. To the young generation the prescriptive hold-overs are handed down as self-evident and immutable principles of reality, and the (reputable) schools can allow themselves no latitude and no question. And what is more to the point, men and women come to believe in the truths which they profess, on whatever ground, provided only that they continue stubbornly to profess them. Their professions may have come out of expedient make-believe, but, all the same, they serve as premises in all the projects, reflections, and reverie of these folks who profess them. And it will be only a provocation of harsh and protracted exposure to material facts running unbroken to the contrary, that the current of their sentiments and convictions can he brought to range outside of the lines drawn for them by these professed articles of truth.

The case is illustrated, e. g., by the various and widely varying systems of religious verities current among the outlying peoples, the peoples of the lower cultures, each and several of which are indubitably and immutably truthful to their respective believers, throughout all the bizarre web of their incredible conceits and grotesqueries, none of which will bear the light of alien scrutiny[4] .

Having come in for these professions of archaic make-believe, and continuing stubbornly to profess implicit faith in these things as a hopeful

---

[4] There is, of course, no call in this Christian land to throw up a doubt or question touching any of the highly remarkable verities of the Christian confession at large. While it will be freely admitted on all hands that many of the observances and beliefs current among the "non-Christian tribes" are grotesque and palpable errors of mortal mind; it must at the same time, and indeed by the same token, be equally plain to any person of cultivated tastes in religious superstition, and with a sound bias, that the corresponding convolutions of unreason in the Christian faith are in the nature of a divine coagulum of the true, the beautiful, and the good, as it was in the beginning, is now, and ever shall be; world without end! But all the while it evident that all these "beastly devices of the heathen," just referred to, are true, beautiful and good to their benighted apprehension only because their apprehension has been benighted by their stubborn profession of these articles of misguides make-believe, through the generations; which is the point of the argument.

sedative of the wrath to come, these things come to hedge about the scheme of knowledge and belief as well as the scheme of what is to be done or left undone. In much the same way the country-town system of prescriptive hold-overs has gone into action as the safe and, sane body of American, common sense, until it is now self-evident to American public sentiment that any derangement of these hold-overs, would bring the affairs of the human race to a disastrous collapse. And all the while the material conditions are progressively drawing together into such shape that this plain country-town common sense will no longer work.

Chapter 4

The Army of the Commonweal

THE ostensible purpose of the "Army of the Commonweal" has been the creation of a livelihood for a great number of people by means of a creation of employment, to be effected by a creation of capital through the creation of fiat money. That is to say, on the face of it, the heart of the "movement" is an articulate hallucination. In this its elaborate form the hallucination probably holds a secure lodgement only in the minds of a small number of people, including a large part of those who have enrolled themselves in the Army on ground of a serious conviction. By those who have sympathized with and furthered this new-fashioned excursion into the field of economic reform the hallucination probably is rarely harbored in this painstakingly absurd shape. Among the common run of its sympathisers the sentiment with which assent is given to the demonstrations of the Army seems to go no farther, either in its scope or in its elaboration of details, than a general conviction that society owes every honest man a living; but a sentiment going that length certainly has obtained some considerable vogue. How, or under what circumstances, or precisely why "society" is to afford the honest man a livelihood is a thoroughly unprofitable question. The answer, so far, does not go much beyond the general proposition that it is to afford it. To the extent to which such a sentiment prevails, even in the vaguest form, it is certainly a sufficiently serious accession to the public sentiment of the community, and a sufficiently striking innovation in the American attitude toward economic questions.

No doubt much of the disturbance is due to demagogism, perhaps more is due to a taste for picturesque adventure and a distaste for serious application to unfamiliar work, and much of the countenance accorded it by outsiders may be less disinterested than would appear at first glance. But the sentiment on which it proceeds must not be conceived to be entirely, or even mainly spurious. The Army of the Commonweal is a new departure in American methods, whether it is to be considered a departure of grave import or not, and a new departure in any people's manner of life and of looking at things does not come about altogether gratuitously; there must be something more vital than a feigned sentiment behind it. After all deduction is made for the spectacular and the meretricious in this "movement," after allowing for the attraction which it exerts on idlers as a temporary means of subsistence and entertainment, and on the friends of humanity as a means of martyrdom, after allowing for the elements of blackmail and of business shrewdness in the enthusiasm with which these straggling bands have sometimes, especially in the middle West, been speeded on their way, and for the promptings of discontent that have mingled in the sympathy expressed by outsiders remote from the scene and without personal interest in the demands put forth, there is still left a broad substratum of honest sentiment shared in by an appreciable fraction of the community. What is the economic import of this sentiment?

As near as the bizarre characters in which it is written can yet be deciphered, the message of the Army of the Commonweal says that certain economic concepts are not precisely the same to many people today that they have been to the generation which is passing. "Capital," to this new popular sense, is the "capital" of Karl Marx rather than that of the old-school economists or of the market place. The concept of "property" or of "ownership" is in process of acquiring a flexibility and a limitation that would have puzzled the good American citizen of a generation ago. By what amounts to a subconscious acceptance of Hegelian dialectic it has come about that an increase of a person's wealth, beyond a certain ill-defined point, should not, according to the new canon of equity, be permitted to increase his command over the means of production or the processes which those means serve. Beyond an uncertain point of aggregation, the inviolability of private property, in the new popular conception, declines. In Hegelian phrase, a change in quantity, if it is considerable enough, amounts to a change in kind. A man - still less a corporation - must no longer do what he will with his own, if what is classed as his own appreciably exceeds the average. It is competent for his neighbors to appeal for his guidance to the corporate will of the community, and ill default of an expression of the corporate will the neighbors in question may properly act vicariously for the community.

But the content of the new accession to popular sentiment is not exhausted by this question of detail alone. Its scope is more magnificent than petty property relations between one individual and the next. There is a class, shown by the Army of the Commonweal to be larger than was previously apprehended, which is, or has been, drifting away from the old-time holding ground of the constitution. The classic phrase is no longer to read, "life, liberty, and the pursuit of happiness"; what is to be insured to every free-born American citizen under the new dispensation is "life, liberty, and the means of happiness." The economic significance of this change of attitude, if the new habit of mind should spread so far as to become the dominant attitude of an effective majority of the American people, is tremendous. It means the difference between the civil republic of the nineteenth century and the industrial republic of the socialists, with the gradual submergence of private initiative under the rising claims of industrial solidarity. But whether any sweeping change of this nature will, or can, come, is extremely doubtful. In order to a continued growth of the sentiment it is necessary that experience should prove the feasibility of paternalism, or socialism, on a scale that is not borne out by the experience of the past.

And the appeal from individual initiative and responsibility is not taken to the local civil body, as would have been expected to happen if an analogous disturbance had occurred at any time in the past. The industrial solidarity that is assumed is not a solidarity and autonomy of the local unit. The movement does not contemplate an application of the principle of the town-meeting to solve an economic difficulty. It is not an appeal to local self-help; it is an appeal to Caesar. These individual unemployed men, whether out of employment by preference or by force of circumstances, are acting on "a wild surmise" that they individually stand in some direct, vital economic relation to the general government, and through the general government to all the rest of the community, without intermediation of any lower or local body. These men disregard the fact of local units and local relations with a facility which bespeaks their complete emancipation from the traditions of local self-government. If the industrial republic is to be floated in on the wave of sentiment which has carried the Army of the Commonweal, it will not be the anarchist republic of autonomous communes held together in a lax and dubious federation.

It may seem a sweeping generalization to say that this attitude is but an expression of the fact latterly emerging into popular consciousness, that the entire community is a single industrial organism, whose integration is advancing day by day, regardless of any traditional or conventional boundary lines or demarkations, whether between classes or between localities. The biologist might, perhaps, name the process "economic cephalization." The aberrations, in which this consciousness - or half-consciousness - of an increasing industrial coherence is expressing itself, must not be allowed to mask the significance of the great substantial fact whose distorted expression they are. That the expression of the fact has taken a form so nearly farcical is something for which society may be indebted to the influence of protectionism, or populism, or to the ethical and the clerical economists and sociologists, or to any other of the ramifications of the paternalistic tree of life; but the substance, upon which these deft artificers may have imposed a vicious form, has been furnished by the situation. This substratum of sentiment is, as popular sentiment must be, the product of the environment acting upon the average intelligence available in the community at the time. An intellectually undisciplined populace, especially when under the guidance of leaders whose prime qualification for leadership in an intellectual crusade in an intense and comprehensive sympathy, may not, at the first stroke, achieve what will prove a tenable theory of the facts whose presence has stimulated the movement of their brain; but in no community does an appreciably large class take a new attitude toward a question of public concern without the provocation of a change in the situation of the community, or of some considerable portion of it.

The result, in the way of public sentiment, wrought out by the action of the environment upon the average intelligence may, within limits, be readily shaped by well-meaning advocates of any doctrine which purports to solve all new questions that arise and remedy all defects that come into view as the economic structure of society grows and changes form. The spell of the bearer of a universal solvent is irresistible, at least until his nostrum has repeatedly failed in the test, or until the generation which has given it credence is dead. Now, we have had at least three lines of professedly infallible hortatory instruction converging upon this point in popular belief. As between these three, the priority in point of the date of its advent into popular teaching, as well as in point of naiveté, belongs to the column which upholds the two-fold principle of fiat money (greenbackism, bimet-allism) and of flat prosperity (protectionism). Second, there is a cloud of witnesses, the gentler-mannered spokesmen of the pulpit, whose dis-course runs upon the duties of the rich toward the poor, and of rulers to-ward their subjects - the duty of a "superior" towards an "inferior" class; these bear testimony to the strength and beauty of the patriarchal relation - the Spencerian relation of status. Third, there is the cisatlantic line of the Socialists of the Chair, whose point of departure is the divine right of the State; whose catch-word is: "Look to the State;" whose maxim of political wisdom is: "The State can do no wrong." A few decades ago these phrases read, "The King," where they now read, "The State." This change of phra-seology marks a step in the evolution of language, *et praetera nihil.* The spirit remains the same as ever. It is the spirit of loyalty, petition, and sub-mission to a vicarious providence. This position has been euphemistically termed State Socialism, but it is, in principle, related to socialism as the absolute monarchy is to the republic. These three variants of paternalism have had the public ear, and have constituted themselves guides and in-terpreters to the public intelligence during the period in which the in-creasing coherence and interdependence within the economic organism has been coming into view, and the result is what we see. The ingrained sense and practical tact of the American people (or rather of a fraction of it) have been blurred into reflecting an uncertain image of industrial pa-ternalism. But with it all goes a valuable acquisition in the shape of a crude appreciation of the most striking and characteristic fact in modern indus-trial evolution.

The changed attitude on an economic question, of which many occur-rences connected with the Army of the Commonweal are an evidence, is in substance due to a cumulative organic change in the constitution of the industrial community - a change which may, or may not be considered to have reached serious proportions, which may, in itself considered, be a change for better or for worse, which may still be in its initial stage or may already have nearly run its course, but in any case it is a change of suffi-cient magnitude to seek expression, now that the occasion offers. To use a Spencerian phrase, advancing "industrial integration" has gone far enough to obtrude itself as a vital fact upon the consciousness of an ap-preciable fraction of the common people of the country.

Chapter 5

The Price of Wheat Since 1867

The year 1867 marks the highest point reached by the annual average price of wheat since wheat production on a considerable scale for the foreign market became a recognized feature of American farming5 .The immediate cause of this high price was the occurrence of two successive bad seasons in 1866 and 1867[6] .

The wheat harvests of 1866 and 1867 gave an unusually low yield both in Europe and America; the former being worse in America and the latter in Europe[7].The American corn crop was also deficient in yield for both years, especially 1867, and of low grade. The acreage sown to wheat in America increased greatly these years, and the result was a larger aggregate production of wheat in 1867 than for some years previous. (See Chart IV.) Such was the situation of the wheat supply after the harvest of 1867. The situation of American farming generally, so far as concerns the prices obtainable for staple products, was fairly good; but prices were better, relatively, for grains than for meat products. The average for wheat, corn, oats, beef, pork, lard, butter, in the New York market was higher for the two years 1867 and 1868 than it has been since that time[8]

---

[5] No. 2 Spring Wheat in the Chicago market averaged $1.43 (gold) for the year. In New York, Milwaukee Club averaged $1.75.

[6] It is to be noted by way of orientation that the wheat crops available for the general market had been, on the whole, very good in 1863 and 1864; especially the former year, which was, in the United Kingdom particularly, and to a good extent in Continental Europe, the most satisfactory wheat harvest for a long series of years. Much the same is true of other grains for those years. In America the wheat crop was good in 1863, and had been excellent for two or three years previous; while in 1864 the American wheat crop was over average yield, but the acreage was smaller than the previous year, and the output was consequently somewhat short. The harvest of 1865, both in Europe and America, fell slightly short of an average yield. The harvests of the years 1863-7, taking into account the total available product, form a decreasing series, beginning with one of the very best grain crops of the century and closing with one of the worst.

[7] 1866, therefore, will be memorable as a year of pestilence, war, scarcity, Irish discontent, and as a year in which occurred the most extensive and severe financial crisis of the present century;" (London Economist, 'Commercial History and Review,' 1867) "The harvest of 1867 was almost universally bad or indifferent. The winter of 1866-7 was exceptionally severe-especially in this country. Over the whole north of Europe and a considerable part of Germany, the grain crops of 1867 were alarmingly deficient. The maize also failed to the extent of a third, or even a half. The potato crop is reckoned the worst since 1845-6. The only really great crops have been in Hungary and along the lower Danube." (Ibid. 1868)

[8] The prices referred to here and elsewhere in this paper, unless otherwise indicated, are gold prices averaged for the calendar year.

1867-8 marks the summit of the price movement in farm products gen-erally[9]. The trend of prices for agricultural staples in this country-and to a slightly less extent in England and on the continent of Europe-for some years previous had been up-wards; from about 1863 it had been pretty strongly upwards. Since this time it has been generally downwards, broken only by an occasional temporary recovery, until the last few years. Some-thing similar is true of the price movement of staple commodities general-ly, taking the period as a whole[10].

But the temporary movement of general prices for the time being, at this precise point (1867-8), was not in the same direction as that of staple farm products. General prices were declining. 1867-8 was a period of depres-sion in business generally. The industries that are not immediately de-pendent on the seasons had reached their highest activity, for the time, earlier than this; the speculative movement had culminated in 1866, and business was now dull. But farming did not share in the general feeling of depression that prevailed in other industries in 1867-8, nor had it shared appreciably in the buoyant, not to say feverish, activity of the years imme-diately preceding. In short, the forces which controlled the situation for American farming were not the same that went to make the general indus-trial situation. It mattered little whether general business was brisk or dull so long as the seasons favored American crops and prices. And, deter-mined by the character of the seasons, the tone of American farming was markedly depressed in 1865-6, when other industries were buoyant, and distinctly active in 1867-8, when times generally were dull[11]

With respect to methods and appliances directly affecting wheat produc-tion and wheat prices, the following facts may serve to characterize the situation at the point (1867-8) selected as the beginning of the period un-

---

[9]This applies to what is known in Northern and Eastern markets as Farm Pro-duce, and takes no account of cotton, tobacco, sugar or rice. These products of Southern farming, as well as wool and fruits, are hardly to be classed with grains and meat products in any discussion of prices from the standpoint of the wheat producer.

[10] See the tables of Mr. AUGUSTUS SAUERBECK; journal of the Statistical Society, September, 1886, and those of Dr. A. SOETBEER, in his Materialien.

[11] The reason for this course of things seems to have been partly that the foreign demand for American farm produce was not specially urgent immediately after the war (relatively large surpluses of grain having been carried over from previous good years in Europe), partly that American crops in 1865 and 1866 were very moderate or deficient, and partly that the premium on gold was rapidly declining, so as to mask the actual advance that was taking place in agricultural staples (which for some purposes practically amounted to a decline in price). By the summer of 1866 the first and last of these causes had ceased to act. The crops for the next two years were under average, but the foreign demand increased greatly in urgency and the premium on gold remained nearly stationary. At the same time there was a marked decline in the prices of other staples-which was to the advantage of the farmer-and when 1868 proved a fair average, or at the worst a slightly deficient season, with no obtrusive ill-fortune to offset the favorable state of the markets, the farmers of the wheat producing sections had reason to be well content.

der discussion: The latest great advance in wheat-farming machinery was the self-rake reaper, which was rapidly being adopted during and immediately after the war. In ocean transportation, the iron steamship was fast replacing the sailing vessels of earlier years. Inland, from western markets to the seaboard, grain was carried by water wherever that was practicable. Shipments of grain from Chicago eastward were by lake-and-canal, with virtually no all-rail or lake-and-rail competition[12]

Ocean freights in 1867-8 were low as compared with what they usually were both before and after that time[13].

Chart I (Part a): Annual average price of wheat (cents per bushel)

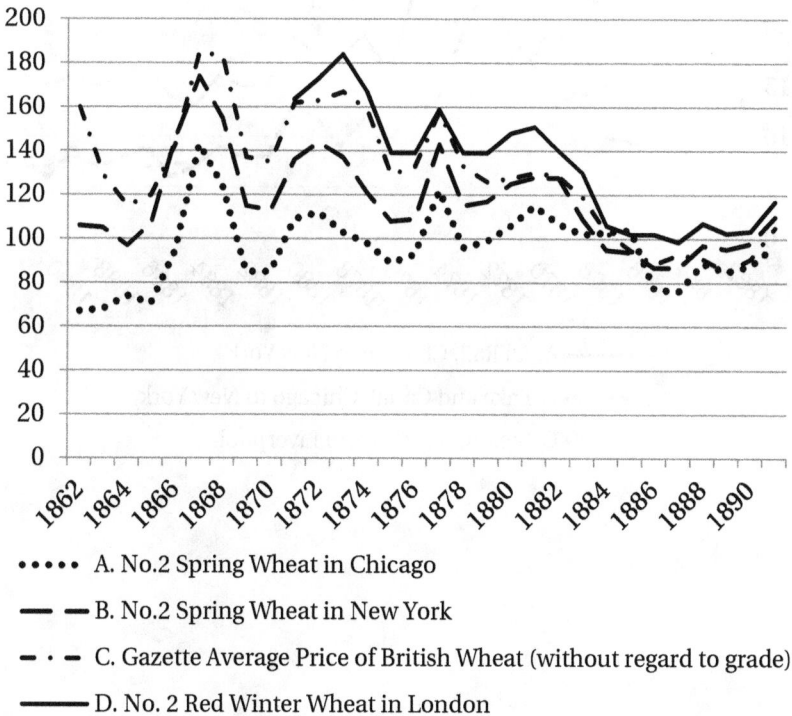

••••• A. No.2 Spring Wheat in Chicago

— — B. No.2 Spring Wheat in New York

— · — C. Gazette Average Price of British Wheat (without regard to grade)

———— D. No. 2 Red Winter Wheat in London

---

[12] Both wheat and corn had been received in New York from the West by rail before 1870, and, indeed, in some appreciable quantity, but these shipments were accounted a temporary and anomalous diversion rather than a serious competition with the water route.

[13] There had been an "over-production " of steam tonnage during the years immediately preceding, and freights were recognized to be ruling unduly low in consequence.

Chart I (Part b): Annual average freight rates of wheat (cents per bushel)

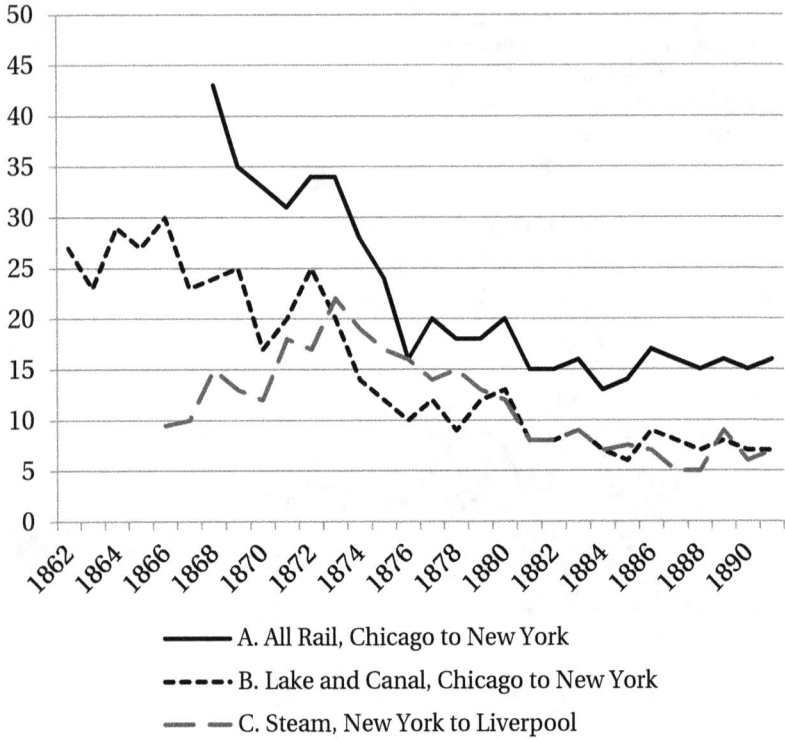

——— A. All Rail, Chicago to New York

- - - - B. Lake and Canal, Chicago to New York

— — C. Steam, New York to Liverpool

Chart II: Annual average prices in Chicago (average of 1867-77= 100)

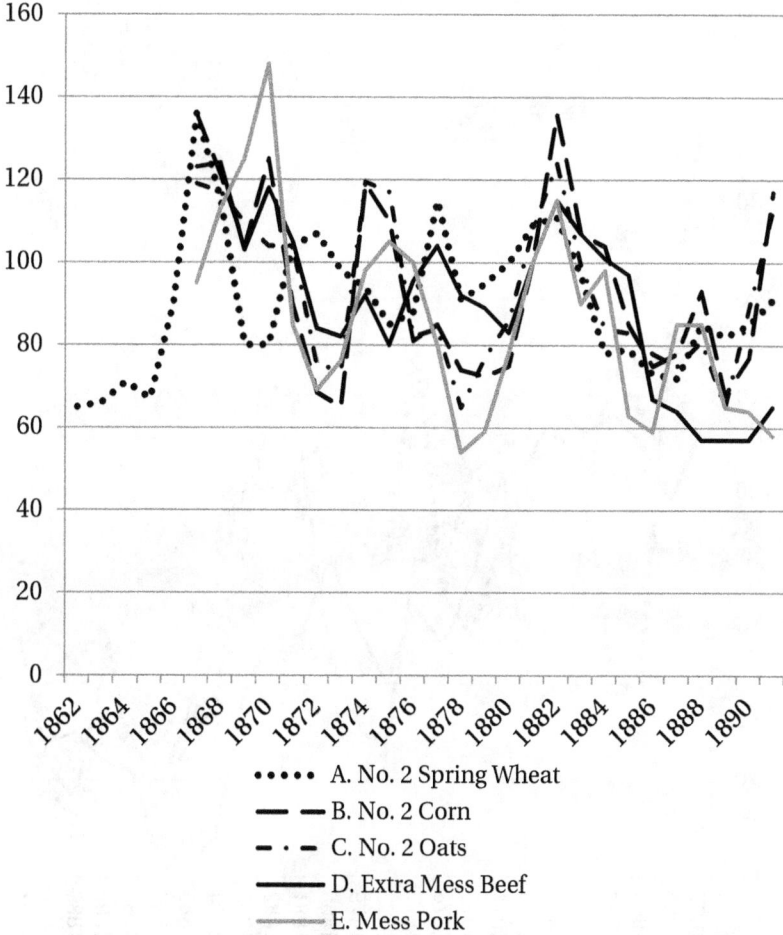

- ••••• A. No. 2 Spring Wheat
- — — B. No. 2 Corn
- — · — C. No. 2 Oats
- ——— D. Extra Mess Beef
- ——— E. Mess Pork

Chart III: Annual Average Prices (Average of 1867-77= 100)

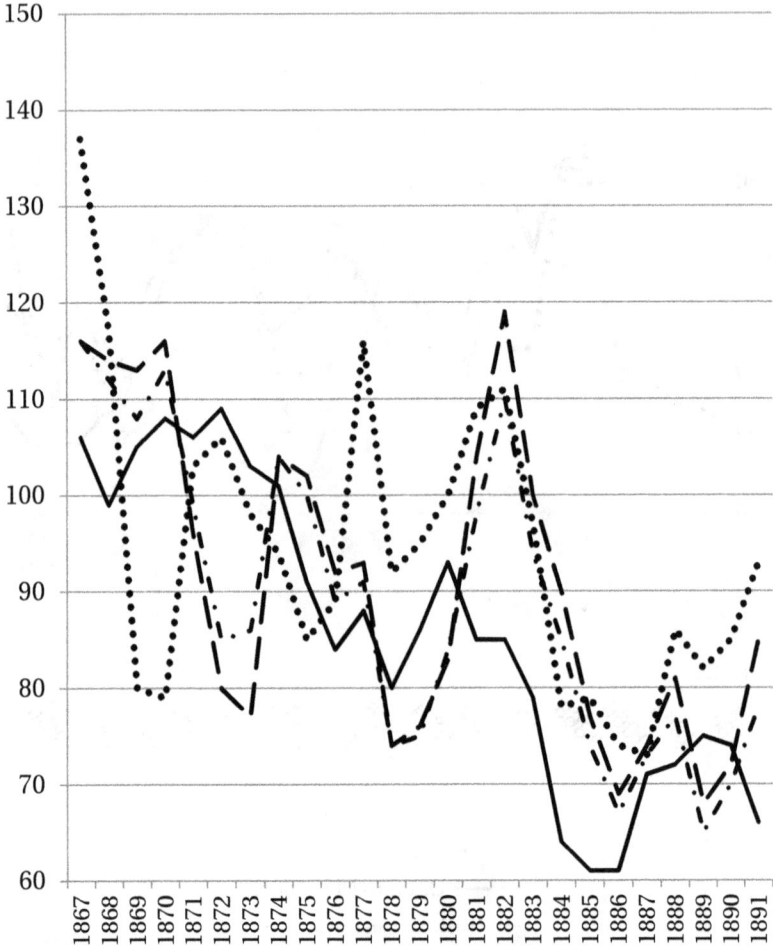

••••• A. No. 2 Spring Wheat in Chicago

— — B. Average of Wheat, Corn, Oats, Beef, Pork, Lard in Chicago

— · — C. Average of Wheat, Corn, Oats, Beef, Pork, Lard in New York

——— D. Average of Ten Staples (Iron, Wool, Standard Sheetings,
Leather, Linseed, Oil, Salt, Fish, Sugar, Coffee, Molasses) in
American Wholesale Markets

Chart IV: Annual Acreage and Production of Wheat

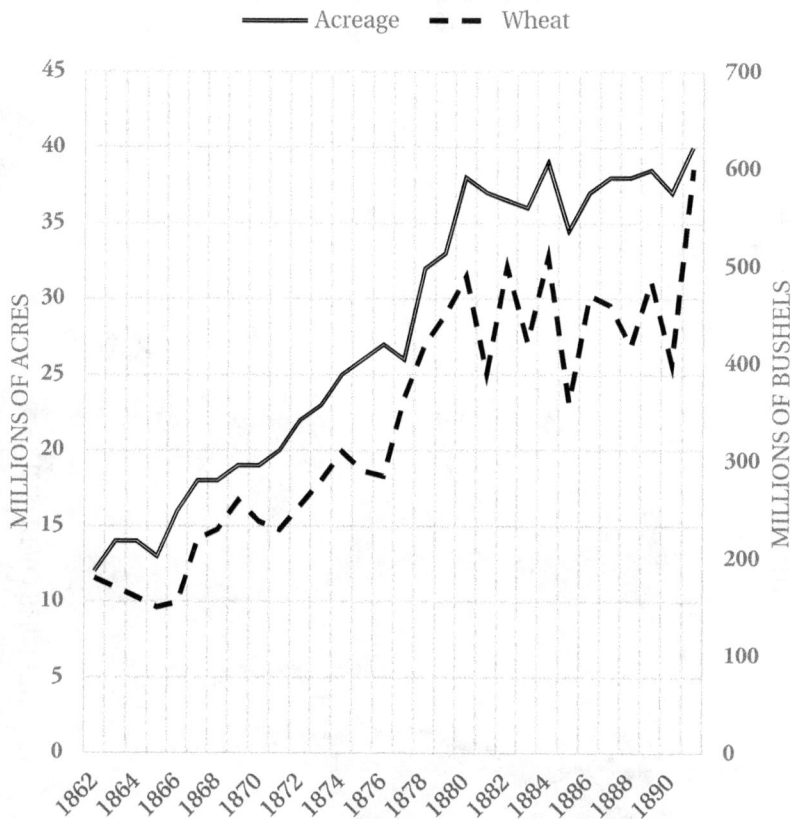

Chart V: I. Maryland, Pennsylvania, New York; II.Illinois, Indiana, Kentucky, Michigan, Ohio, Tennessee, Wisconsin; III. Dakota (after 1882), Iowa, Kansas, Minnesota, Missour, Nebraska, Texas; IV. California (after 1868), Oregon, (after 1869), Washington (after 1882).

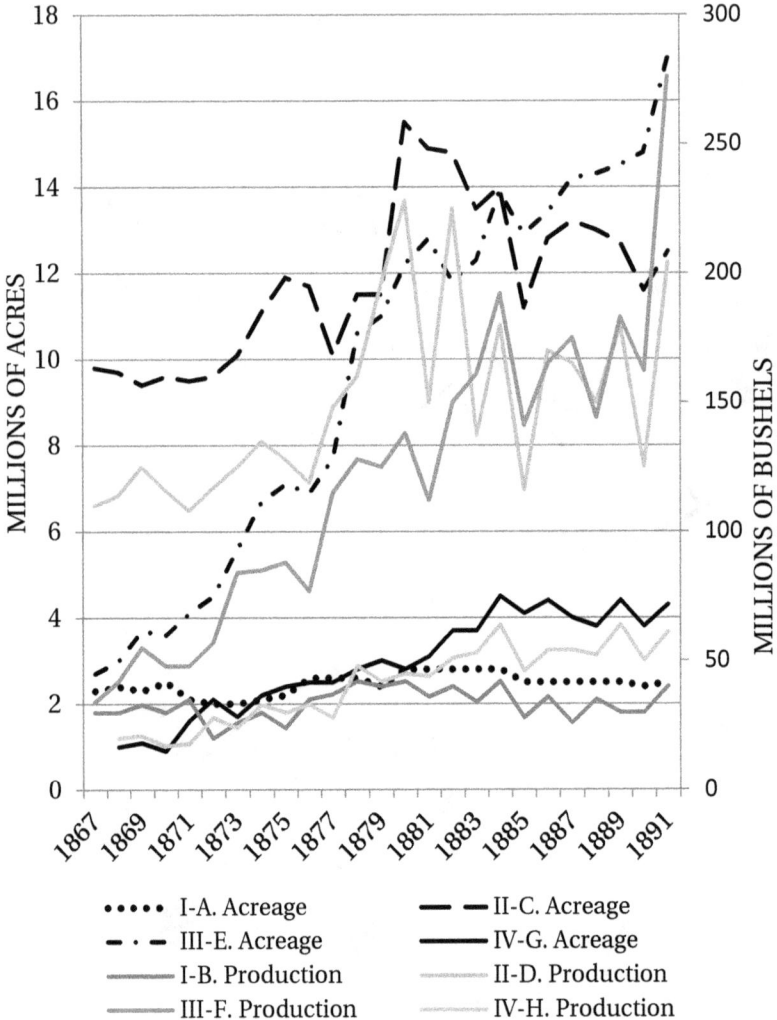

Inland freights and local charges were high, as measured by standards since grown familiar to the grain trade. Lake-and-canal freights to New York were rather high even as compared with what they had been immediately before the war[14] (See Chart 1. B.) The "center line of production" of wheat in 1867 was very close to the eastern boundary of Illinois. (For the movement of the acreage sown to wheat at this time see Charts IV. and V.) that year was of under average quality. Grade for grade, British wheat at that time was preferred to American. During the later years-from about 1880-the great and permanent decline of British wheat relatively to No. 2 Red Winter is due to the fact that with the adoption of the most modern methods of milling the harder and stronger American wheats have come

---

The lines for wheat in Chicago and in New York are, as near as may be, for the same grade down to 1889, and therefore afford a fairly accurate comparison of the course of prices in those two markets. For 1890 and 1891 the New York price is that of No. 2 Red Winter, which at those dates was very nearly coincident with No. 2 Spring - perhaps a trifle over the latter. The line traced by American wheat in the London market is, therefore, not avail-able for a precise comparison with the American price. In comparing the lines it should be borne in mind that No. 2 Red Winter wheat ruled from one or two cents to ten or twelve cents above No. 2 Spring during the earlier years covered by the chart - (down to about 1881-2; and that during the later years the difference has been slight and shifting-sometimes in favor of one, sometimes of the other. On this account, the rate of approach of the American price to the English price during the period appears greater on the chart than it has been in fact. The line for British wheat represents the actual average of the selling price of wheat in the towns of the United Kingdom from which returns are collected. It therefore indicates price without regard to grade, and any comparison of this line with the other lines of the chart can be of value only as suggesting the relative course of prices, rather than as furnishing anything in the nature of a demonstration. Wherever-during the earlier years -the line for British wheat falls considerably below that for No. 2 Red Winter in London, it is to be taken, generally, as indicating that the British crop of transporting a bushel of wheat from the Mississippi river to New York as follows:

Freight by rail to Chicago (200 miles)	20 cents
Inspection (in and out)	¼ cent
Storage	2 ½ cents
Commissions	1 ½ cents
Freight, Chicago to Buffalo, by Lake	6 ½ cents
Insurance	1 ¼ cents
Elevator at Buffalo	2 cents
Handling	¼ cent
Commissions at Buffalo	1 ½ cent
Freight, canal to New York	13 ½ cents
Expenses in New York	3 cents
Total Expenses	52 ½ cents

to be preferred to British wheat that may be otherwise of unexceptionable character. B. The lines traced on the chart by freight rates from Chicago to New York are computed in currency, for the years of depreciated paper money. That for lake - and - canal represents the charges only for the months during which the canals were open each year, and is consequently not to be taken as a true yearly average. That for all - rail represents the yearly average, and after about 1876-77 it may be taken as an approximately true indication of freights. It is, however, to be noted that the figures it indicates are probably always, but not uniformly, too high; partly because little, or sometimes no grain was shipped at the highest rates quoted, and partly because there is no means of knowing how far the figures published were cut under. The making of special rates, sometimes very considerably below published tariffs, was always practiced, sometimes to a very great extent. These lines are, therefore, also not available for any precise comparison. In converting English quotations into American terms, the penny has been rated at two cents. Consequently these quotations, as traced on the chart, range lower than a more exact computation would make them. The figures for inland freights may be found in the Statistical Abstract of the United States, or in the reports of the New York Produce Exchange, or of the Chicago Board of Trade. Those for ocean freights in either of the two latter publications or in the reports of the Secretary of Agriculture. It appears on closer study of the price movement of wheat and the development of the forces which determined the movement during the years from 1867 to the present, that the course of development falls into three more or less clearly defined periods-1867-73, 1873-1882, and 1882-1891. The last four years, 1887-1891, may perhaps as properly be counted as the initial stage of a new phase of the development, but the nearness of this last change to the present, as well as the fact that the characteristic features of the change are not yet sufficiently defined for satisfactory discussion as a separate whole, will pre-vent these years from being taken up as a distinct   period.

I. 1867-1873.

From 1867 to 1870 the average of prices of staple farm products, as a whole, kept very much on a level. This was not due to a uniformity of movement of the whole, nor to a steadiness on part of the different items. Wheat declined during the latter half of 1868, and the decline continued in 1869. It remained low through 1870, and rose again in 1871. The course of prices in none of the other staples ran parallel with that of wheat, and the lines traced by the members of the group during these years do not show the presence of any single controlling force. The line for wheat runs boldly across that for the group as a whole in 1870-72, wheat prices rising very distinctly, while prices for all the rest of the group fall, strongly and unitedly (see Chart II.). In 1873 the line for wheat shares the general downward trend of the group as a whole; after which all parallelism between the course of wheat prices and prices of other staples apparently ceases, until

1877. In general, during the twelve years from 1867 to 1878, wheat prices run a course apparently independent of the prices of other staple farm products. Closer study of the causes which controlled wheat prices in those years will show that there were special forces acting on wheat sufficient to account for this apparent anomaly. Neither can it be said that wheat prices follow the general course of prices for other than agricultural products at the time. Wheat prices, and other agricultural prices as well, partook only in a superficial way of the general speculative advance of the years 1871 to 1873. Nor do agricultural prices enter on the decline that followed the break of the speculative movement, until it had been in progress for over a year in general prices. It is only when a considerable series of years is taken as a whole that the parallelism between the course of agricultural prices and of prices generally at this time becomes apparent. It is true of wheat and of other agricultural staples, as it is of commodities generally, that prices ruled higher during the closing years of the sixties than they did ten years later. As to the detailed movements by which this general course of prices was worked out. The year 1869 was one of depression in farming; the corn crop was short and of poor quality; the season had been cold and wet; wheat gave a large yield, and the winter wheat was of very fair quality, but much of the spring wheat was low grade. The crops of 1868 had depressed prices for the early part of the year, and the new crops did nothing towards a recovery. The British wheat crop was about an average, and altogether there was no large demand for American wheat abroad. Taken as a whole, 1870 was rather a featureless year for wheat. There was a medium crop, of moderate grade. Corn was a large crop and of high grade. The crop of the United Kingdom was slightly over average bulk, and distinctly over average quality. The outbreak of the French-German war brought prices to a higher level for short time; and later, when the fall of Paris and the close of the war was looked for, prices advanced again. Late in 1870 and during the early months of 1871 wheat advanced on the strength of an expected increased demand on the return of peace, and also on the strength of a considerable diminution of the stocks below what had been on hand a year or two earlier. Supplies had been unusually large in 1868 and 1869, and it may be set down that prices of wheat had been abnormally depressed for a year or two on that account. So that, independently of known facts as to the change in the size of the stocks on hand, the change in acreage during the years in question reflect the fact that prices were ruling "too low" in 1869 and 1870. In the normal course of things at the time, apart from fortuitous circumstances, the wheat area ought to have increased with some rapidity.

From 1867 to 1869 there is an increase in acreage of some magnitude, but in 1870 there is an absolute decrease, followed by an increase in 1871 of rather less than the average annual increase for the years 1867-73. But what is more significant still, than the figures for the aggregate wheat area, is the manner in which the figures for particular sections of the country vary. In the older sections (groups I. and II. of Chart V.) the acreage in wheat declined in 1869, apparently in con- sequence of the decline in price that had set in during the latter half of 1868, and of an advance in the prices of hog products, and perhaps in part because of a low yield. But 1869 was a year of exceptionally good yield, especially of winter wheat, which is grown in those older sections, and wheat-growing proved profitable for the year, in spite of low prices; and the following year the acreage sowed to wheat was about as large as it had been the previous year. In the new wheat country west of the Mississippi, and in California; where the cultivated area was increasing fast; where the farmers had virtually undertaken, on the strength of the prices of previous years, to increase their crops the coming year; and where wheat was practically the only available crop; there the change from an increase of wheat acreage to a standstill or a decrease was not easily carried out, and did not take place with the same promptness. The farming of that country was based on the increase of the wheat acreage as its vital principle, and it consequently took time to effect a change. A decrease in wheat acreage in those states would mean pretty much the same as a decrease in the total number of acres of cultivated land. The acreage in those sections, therefore, went on increasing strongly, especially in the trans-Mississippi states, in 1869; but, although the yield in 1869 had been good, there was a decrease in wheat area of some 500,000 acres in those sections for 1870. The decline in price seems to have acted as a distinct check to wheat-growing, from which the wheat states of the Northwest had to take time to recover; in fact, they had to wait for a fresh wave of immigration. The variation in acreage corresponding to the variation in price suggests that the price at which wheat could be profitably grown in 1868-73 was such a price as would be indicated in the Chicago market at that time by something between $1.25 and $0.85 gold, or $1.75 and $1 currency. Probably it is safe to say that an average price much below $1 gold for No. 2 Spring in the Chicago market, would not have been sufficient to induce any increase of the acreage cultivated in wheat during those years.

The years 1871-72 were years of slightly under average yield in America, and somewhat more below average in Great Britain, with a considerable demand for wheat on the Continent. The corn crop of both years was also a little short of the previous year, on account of a reduced acreage. The crops of 1870, 1871 and 1872 sold at good prices. Probably the prices obtained by the farmers at the local markets in the newer wheat regions of the West were very nearly as good as what they had realized for the crops of 1866 and 1867. The proximate cause which deter- mined the price of each successive crop of wheat down to 1873, was the same as since that time. It is the crop and the crop prospect of wheat. Second and subsidiary to it is the character of the harvest of other grains.[15] The crop, the available supply, is the immediate controlling factor in making the price of wheat.

---

[15] Mr. G. SHAW-LEFEVRE has shown (Journal of the Statistical Society, December, 1879) that from 1852 to 1872 the price of wheat had very generally varied inversely as the British crop. Since that time a like statement will hold true if, instead of the British crop alone, the entire available wheat harvest of the world is taken into account.

That has of course held true since 1873 as it did before. But the general causes that have operated to determine the course of the price of wheat, and, in some degree to determine the magnitude of the available supply, have not been altogether the same since that year as they were for the years immediately preceding.

Taken as a whole, these six years (1868-73) were a period of decline in wheat prices, both absolutely and relatively to prices of staples generally. (See Chart III.) It was a period, for the most part, of a sluggish condition of trade, though general prices as computed in gold were not on the whole declining after 1868. With that year began the movement in railroad building that afterward became the characteristic feature and gave the tone to the business situation down to 1873. The speculation and inflation of values which became perceptible in 1870 and reached a climax in 1873, did not affect farming in any appreciable degree. Its influence on agricultural prices is not exactly imperceptible, but to all appearances it had a very inconsiderable effect in the way of advancing prices of farm products. There is, in the nature of things, no reason why American agriculture, and especially wheat farming, should have shared greatly in the boom of those years. The boom did very little to increase the demand for farm products, and it did nothing at all to decrease their cost of production at the time. On the contrary it distinctly acted to increase their cost. Prices of what the farmers had to buy were advancing, through the action of causes that had but a remote and indirect influence on the prices of what the farmers had to sell. Improvements were being introduced in the production and transportation of grain and other products, but not at any greater rate than the use of like improved processes and methods was increasing in other branches of industry.

The main facts bearing on wheat prices in the years immediately previous to the crisis of 1873 are these: American wheat crops were fair or moderate; corn crops were above average after 1869; freights were high, and, on the whole tending to advance; commissions and charges for storage, handling, etc., were heavy, but they were in process of improvement; British crops, and European crops generally, were, on the whole, fair or moderately short, so that there was an active and growing, but for the most part not a very urgent export demand; there was a speculative movement of considerable intensity, especially in 1871-2, in the prices of other than agricultural products; and this last fact, on the whole, went to offset the favorable factors in a situation that would otherwise have been moderately advantageous to the wheat farmer. The result was that prices in the primary markets ranged too low to greatly stimulate wheat growing or to satisfy the farmers of the West, and there was a good deal of complaint. Compared with the industries that felt the direct impetus of the speculative movement, the profits of wheat farming, in the general run, were distinctly moderate.

II. 1873-1882.

With 1873 the movement of wheat prices and wheat production entered on a new phase. The commercial crash of that year was of course not felt at the time to be an auspicious change for wheat farming, but the farming community of the wheat-growing country did not long feel the effects of the shock, and they never realized that 1873-78 was a season of hard times.

These years are the most remarkable period that has been seen in American wheat growing. After 1872, or more precisely from the time when the prospect for the harvest of 1873 was falling into definite shape in the summer of that year, the price began to decline[16]. It receded steadily, with the ordinary fluctuations from month to month, until 1875, when it averaged $1.023, currency, or $0.889, gold, for the year in Chicago. Then it began to recover in the same manner, and, with the single break of the anomalous record of 1877, the yearly averages show a steady advance, one above another, until 1882. The turning point was early in August, 1882. As to the movement in acreage. In 1872 the area sown to wheat was 20,858,359 acres; in 1880 it was 37,986,717, an average annual increase of 2,141,044 acres, or something over 10 per cent a year for the whole eight years. The average annual increase in acreage during the years 1867-72, the period of greatest previous increase, was 905,644 acres, or something over five per cent. a year for the whole six years.

From 1873 to 1880 there was but one crop, that of 1876, that was distinctly poor, and one other that was below the normal average yield, taking the aggregate wheat crop of the country as a whole. The crop of 1881, again, was short, by an average of about two bushels per acre; but that of 1882 was nearly as much over the average. The crop of 1873 was a very good one in this country, and distinctly poor in England and Western Europe. The American crop of 1874 was over average in bulk, though much of the spring wheat was not very satisfactory in quality, and was also lower in yield than the winter wheat; the British crop was very good, both in bulk and grade, and that of Western Europe generally was very satisfactory. It was distinctly a year of abundance. The American corn crop of 1873 had been under average, and that of 1874 was poor[17]According to the government report the wheat crop of 1875 was a bushel short of the normal average yield per acre for the whole country, with an unusual proportion of the

---

[16] The beginning of the fall in the price of wheat preceded the failure of Jay Cooke & Co. by some three months, though there was a heavy drop in wheat also immediately after the crash which the failure of that firm initiated.

[17] The Chicago Board of Trade Report contradicts the statement of the Commissioner of Agriculture as to the corn crop of 1874, but the former seems to have allowed too much weight to the condition of the crop in the region tributary to the Chicago market, where the crop was good and fairly high grade, and so placed its estimates too high.

lower grades both in Winter and Spring Wheat[18]. The British crop was very deficient, and that of the Continent was also under average. It is to be noted as at least very probable that unusually large supplies were carried over this year from the previous harvest. Corn yielded much over average in 1875, but there seems to have been an unusually large proportion of soft, poor corn. A larger amount was exported of this than of any previous corn crop. In 1876 wheat was a poor crop-worse than any since 1866. The spring wheat crop was extremely disappointing in point of yield, but on the whole of fair quality. The British crop was worse than that of the previous year -26 per cent under average -and the like is true for the Continent. This year was the last of a series of four, during which the average yield per acre of wheat in America, as estimated by the Department of Agriculture, decreased regularly by about one-half bushel a year; while the last two of the four had also been years of very deficient crops abroad. The average (gold) price for the twelve months following the harvest of 1876 was probably higher in the local markets of the West than for any previous period of twelve months. This was due partly to the distinctly short crops, and partly to the Russo- Turkish war, which put a stop to exports from Eastern Russia in the spring of 1877. The prices of other grain, of which there was no shortage, seem to have been perceptibly influenced by the scarcity of wheat. Then follow four extraordinary wheat harvests in America, coupled with corn crops every one of which was considerably over average, and one of them very abundant, and with nearly every other crop ranging over average the greater part of the four years. It is to be added that, except in wheat, crops had been unusually good for a couple of years before 1877. A draw- back to this favorable showing was the poor crops in the spring wheat region of the Northwest in 1878 and 1879, amounting in some localities, in the former year, to a complete failure. The cause of this was very hot weather shortly before harvest. In grade, the crop of 1879 compared favorably with that of 1878, especially the spring wheat; which, however, was of low grade in both years. 1880 was a better year for the wheat growers of the Northwest, though the average yield for the whole country did not equal that of the previous year[19] .

---

[18] The Annual Report of the Chicago Board of Trade criticises the Government estimate as too high for the Northwest. "The crop of Minnesota and Iowa harvested in 1875 was estimated [in the Report of the Commissioner of Agriculture] at 57,000,000 bushels. This was, undoubtedly, considerably in excess of the actual yield of merchantable wheat, as no exhibit of deliveries appears in any record that would justify a conclusion of its correctness. That crop met the misfortune of wet weather in its harvesting and subsequent care, and probably a large amount was lost that under more favorable influences would have found its way to market." Annual Report, 1876. Secretary's Review.

[19] Altogether, the boast of the Commissioner in his report for that year seems well founded, that the four years of President Hayes's administration had been more productive and more prosperous years for American agriculture than " any other continuous four years in our history. They have been years of exceptionally good crops of all the different staples grown either for home consumption or export."

In the United Kingdom the crop was very deficient in 1877, but better on the Continent. 1878 was a fair average year, if not over average, in England, but under average on the Continent taken as a whole. For 1879 the Economist says: "The wheat crop, and the harvest generally of 1879, is not only the worst in fourteen years [since the failure of 1867], but the worst which has occurred, probably, for thirty years." It was a bad year for nearly all of Europe. Though not up to the ordinary average, 1880 was a much better year in Europe, and the two years following were each an improvement on the next before, until the harvest of 1882, which was reported to have been "of a fair average kind" for wheat. The grain harvest as a whole for that year was "under the average, or slightly under the average." As for the American crops of these two years- 1881-2-the run of luck of the wheat farmers came to an abrupt reversal in 1881[20] .Winter wheat, especially in the great winter wheat states of the Ohio valley and the Lake region, was very seriously deficient, both in bulk and grade. The spring wheat crop of the North- west was also deficient, but not to as great an extent. In 1882, however, there was another very good harvest, 35 per cent above that of 1881, and nearly equal to that of 1879. But only part of the winter wheat crop of that year was marketed at the high prices that had ruled in 1881 and early in 1882. The price broke suddenly at the time the spring wheat crop was being harvested, and never recovered. (See Chart I.)

The immediate relation between crops and price during these years, 1873-82, is a relation not simply between the American crop and the American price; it is a relation between the aggregate crop of the modern industrial countries and the price in the world's market. A short crop in America, as in 1875, acts to raise the price; the effect is perceptible in the line it traces. But the depressing effect of an extremely abundant American crop, as that of 1879, when coupled with a deficiency abroad, is not distinctly perceptible in the course of prices for the next twelve months. When, however, a deficiency in America coincides with a deficiency abroad, as in 1876, the effect on the course of prices for the succeeding year is very striking. During the years just reviewed, and since that time, the American price of wheat has not been governed, habitually or mainly, by the volume of the American crop, as was the case, in the main, down to the years immediately preceding the civil war; nor by the European, or British crop, as was pretty much the case during the sixties (more accurately the fifteen or twenty years, ending about 1872-3); but by the aggregate volume of the world's- crop, in which America's contribution has counted sufficiently to distinctly and greatly influence the course of prices in the world's market. Indeed, the American wheat crop counted for more

---

These four years were, in the main, much more favorable for Winter wheat than for Spring.

[20] In no season since the inauguration of crop reporting has there been so general disaster, involving corn, wheat, barley, buckwheat and rye, oats alone being exempted from loss." Report of the Statistician in the Report of the Commissioner of Agriculture, 1881.

as a factor in fixing the yearly price of grain during these years, from 1873 to 1881, than any other equally distinct single factor, and more than it has counted for, relatively, before or since.

The American crop during those years occupied a position of striking dramatic value. It nearly attained the point of a virtual monopoly control of prices. The forces which placed it in this commanding position were the fortuitous circumstances of the seasons, but the seasons were of so uniform a character as to make the position one of some permanence. There need be no doubt but that, taken as a whole, wheat growing during these years was distinctly profitable. How profitable is a question that does not admit of an intelligible answer, but there are indications that it was, perhaps, the most paying branch of American farming during a time when American farming paid unusually well. During the five or six years already spoken of above, 1867 to 1872-3, wheat farming must be held to have been moderately profitable, taking the period as a whole; though as much can hardly be said for the latter half of those half-dozen years. Neither can it be said that wheat farming during that period was on the whole a more profitable occupation than agriculture generally; still less can it be said that the inducements it offered were great as compared with the average of the country's industries. This is especially true of the years 1869-72. For the succeeding period of ten years, however, it may safely be asserted that both statements are true. Wheat farming compared favorably with other farming, and perhaps still more favorably with the average of other industries. Chart III. shows the course of prices of five representative staple farm products in comparison with the price of wheat. The lines of the chart show that the price of wheat ranged relatively higher during these years than the average of the prices of wheat, corn, oats, beef, pork and lard; and a further detailed comparison with prices of other staple farm products, some of which are given in the tables of the Appendix, goes to show that the like is true to at least as great an extent when wheat is compared with the whole range of farm products.

The same chart includes, also, the line traced by the course of prices of ten staple commodities, all of which are among those that go to make up the wheat farmer's expenditure, and most of them are products of industries with which wheat farming may fairly be compared. The line traced by these runs, relatively, still lower even than that for staple farm products during these years. A more detailed comparison with prices ruling in other goods during the same years does not by any means tend to vitiate the inference which the lines of the chart offer If the conditions of production, therefore, had remained the same throughout the period as they were during the years immediately preceding, both in wheat and other farming and in other industries, it would follow that wheat farming had gained in lucrativeness relatively to other occupations simply in consequence of an enhanced price for its product. But the conditions of production did not remain unchanged, either in wheat farming or any other industry. It was a period of very material advance in methods and appliances, and the advance was assuredly no less in those particulars that had to do, directly and indirectly, with wheat farming than in any other. The changes for the better in the implements actually in use by wheat farmers during the period was very great, both in cheapness and in efficiency. The case of the reaper may be taken as an example of the improvements by which wheat farming profited. During the early seventies the self-rake was in use, and had reached practically the same degree of efficiency as it has to-day. About 1872-75 the harvester came into pretty general use. The harvester was an advance over the self-rake such as anyone who has not seen both machines in use on the wheat fields of the West will scarcely appreciate. During the period from 1874 to 1878 the wire-binder was introduced, and proved itself in many respects superior to any harvesting machinery before in use. A great number of machines of different makes were sold, but the wire-binder never finally and decisively replaced the harvester. Down to the first extended and practically successful introduction of the twine-binder, 1879-80, no wire-binding machines had been offered that were entirely acceptable. The presence of the wire itself was a drawback; the machines were unsatisfactory and tantalizing, on the score of heavy draft or of inefficient work. From the time of the first successful introduction of the twine-binder, 1879, the wire-binder, as well as the harvester, was distinctly out of date.

The price at which each of these machines was successively introduced was always considerably higher than the price of the machine which it replaced. The prices were not sufficiently uniform to admit of giving satisfactory figures, but, in a general way, it may be said that, at its first introduction in the wheat lands west of the Mississippi, the harvester was perhaps of 50 per cent higher cost to the farmer than the self-rake. In a few years the price was very considerably reduced. Likewise, when the twine-binder began to replace the harvester, it was at a price something like a hundred per cent above that of the latter. This price also gradually declined, until it is possible to get a twine-binder to-day, more efficient than the machines that were sold at $320 in 1880, from $100 to $120[21] .The best twine binder now costs less than the common run of self-rake reapers did in 1872-3. A twine-binder cost more-perhaps nearly twice as much-in 1880 than a self-rake reaper in 1872. But that the twine-binder was distinctly better worth its price in 1880 than a self-rake reaper, which could then be bought for about a third of the price of the former, is sufficiently established by the fact that the binder replaced the reaper in spite of the disadvantage in price.

As to the work of which these machines were capable. In 1870-73, in the wheat country of the Western states, the ordinary self-rake reaper was drawn by two horses, sometimes three, with one man, or sometimes a boy or a woman, for driver. The machine would cut ten or twelve, sometimes fifteen acres of the common run of spring wheat, such as would yield in an

---

[21] Self-rake reapers of the standard makes were sold for about $200, currency, about 1870. From that time the price declined to $150 or $160 in 1875-6. Harvesters when first successfully and extensively introduced, about 1872-3, were sold for $200 and over. By 1878-9 the price had declined by nearly one-half.

ordinary year 15 or 20 bushels per acre, in a day of about twelve hours; the average day's work, on the wheat fields of Minnesota, say, was probably not far from eleven acres. Four, or sometimes five, men were required to bind the grain cut by one machine, and one man, not entirely without help from the binders, could shock the day's cut of grain. The harvester required the same number of horses, could cut the same or a little smaller amount of grain per day, and required two men to do the binding. The driver of the harvester was usually a boy, or some person of less value for heavy work than an able-bodied man.

The harvester saved a distinctly larger proportion of the grain than the self-rake. The twine-binder required at the time of its introduction-and not much improvement has been made in this respect-three horses, though four could and can be used to advantage with most machines of this class, wherever the fields are large and the ground not unusually firm. A binder may-sometimes with advantage-be operated with two animals; but that is the exception, not the rule. Such a machine, a six-feet-cut, would, with a full equipment of horses, cut and bind twelve acres and upwards in a day of twelve hours in ordinary average Minnesota grain. As high as twenty acres a day, on an average through the harvest season, have been cut and bound with one machine, and even as high as twenty-five acres of ordinary grain has been covered in a single day; but in these cases the binder has worked long hours, and almost invariably these very high records have been made by the use of more than three horses, or with a frequent change of teams. Fifteen acres of ordinary spring wheat on fairly level ground may perhaps be a little over the average of the day's work accomplished by the twine-binder the first few years after its introduction, and a little under the average of what the same class of machines will accomplish now. The machines are made to cut a wider swath, on an average, now than ten or twelve years ago. The self- binder dispenses with hand labor in binding the grain. The driver is usually, and profitably, a grown person, if not in physical development, at least in intelligence. One unusually efficient man will shock the grain cut and bound by a single machine. Usually it takes more than one man. Such are the main features in the development in reaping machinery since 1870. The greatest advance in efficiency was made during the period 1872-82. In no other particular that has to do directly with wheat production has the advance been as great as in reaping machinery, but the development elsewhere has been much the same in kind if not in degree. Threshing by steam-power came into general use in the wheat country during the same years. An item that marks a very distinct advance, so far as concerns the spring wheat country of the Northwest, is the introduction of a successful straw-burning engine, 1875-80. The barbed-wire fence is an invention of the first importance for American farming; and of greater value, perhaps, to the farmers of the great wheat states than to any others. The wire fence, too, developed gradually. It practically reached its highest efficiency by the end of the period under discussion; though prices of wire have fallen lower since than they had been down to that time, and so have increased the availability of the fence[22].

There are very many improvements in means and methods of work in other industries that affected the cost of wheat production during the years under discussion, and since that time. Their manner of operation has been by lowering the cost of what the wheat farmer has to buy, or by increasing his share of the final price paid by the consumer for his product. The line of Chart III, the resultant of ten staple commodities, suggests how far the wheat farmer was benefited by the first-mentioned effect of this class of causes. The second effect has been produced mainly by mechanical improvements in the handling and transportation of grain and other farm products. The details of the process of improvement in the shipment and sale of grain, are very numerous and complex; but for the present purpose they express themselves in a reduction of the expenses that must be borne by the grain during its transit from the farm to the consumer. The causes that underlie these changes in local and transit rates need not engage our attention here. Among the striking improvements in the direction of cheapening transportation, by which the wheat trade of this period was benefited, were the substitution of steel rails for iron, with the far-reaching consequences following from that innovation; the increase in size of the vessels carrying grain from Chicago to Buffalo (and the use of barges); the lowering and final abolition of tolls on the New York canals, together with an increase of the carrying capacity of the Erie canal. The decline in freights on grain between Chicago and New York from 1872 to 1876 was very great; after that date it was not pronounced. There was a pretty steady decline in annual average ocean freights on grain from 1873 to 1882; but ocean freights had advanced eleven cents from 1867 to 1873, so that the total decline in 1882 as compared with 1867 was only 2.62 cents. But freights are not the only charges the grain has to bear in its transit from the farm to the out-bound vessel in New York harbor.

It has sometimes happened that the local charges- commissions, storage, and the like-at the various points where the grain has to be handled have in the aggregate equaled the cost of carriage alone[23]. Local charges,

---

[22] The wire fence is practically a portable fence of very high efficiency. It is cheap, effective, durable, light, erected and removed with very little labor, occupies a minimum of space, and does not accumulate snow or weeds.

[23] The following statement by the Statistician of the New York Produce Exchange shows what was the character and importance of other than freight charges at the time rail shipments were becoming general and customary: "The lake insurance and transfer and shipping charges, added to the average lake and canal rate of 1876, make the cost about equal with the rail; but the latter, making better dispatch, resulting in a saving of interest on ventures, with less liability to damage by heating, has, at last season's rail rates, an advantage over the water route." (Annual Report, N.Y. Produce Exchange, 1875-6, p. 220.) The apparent difference in favor of the lake-and - canal route at this time was more than six cents a bushel (see Chart 1.13). The real difference was not quite so great, on account of special rates of varying amount having been made by the railroads during the year.

for storage, handling, commissions, and the like, in Chicago amounted to some two or three cents per bushel, and suffered no very pronounced decline during these years. In New York they ranged from 3-5 cents in 1872-3 to 1-2 cents in 1881-2. Charges for handling and commission at Liverpool were still higher, and remained much higher throughout the period[24]. In the charges for handling grain there was a great reduction made during the seventies at practically all the intermediate points through which grain had to pass on its way to the European markets. The beginning of serious competition between the railways and the lake-and-canal route for the carriage of wheat to the seaboard dates from about 1873-4, when all-rail shipments on a considerable scale were first made, under conditions that are not to be regarded as in any way abnormal.

By 1873-4 the carriage of grain by lake-and-rail and by all-rail was becoming a regular and ordinary feature of the trade. One result, and a very important one, of this change, was the adoption of the method of grading and bulking grain in eastern trade centers, after the fashion that was in use in Chicago and the railroad grain centers of the West. Down to 1874 no rules for the grading and handling of bulk grain, or for its sale and delivery ex-store, had been adopted in the New York market. Deliveries by canal-boat and by rail were made by special consignments and in distinct lots. It was the practice to preserve the identity of the lot of grain shipped, and deliver the particular boat or car-load to the consignee, as is the practice now with respect to most other goods than grain. The relatively small size of a car-load, and the consequent liability of any considerable consignments of grain shipped over a long distance to become divided up on the way, and to arrive at its destination in a scattering fashion, made the adoption of grading and bulking grain indispensable.

A lot of 15 or 20 car-loads might be delivered in fractions of one, two, or more cars, at odd times during a period of, perhaps, two or three weeks, or in extreme cases even more; the result being uncertainty, complaints, and demurrage. The method of bulking graded grain, together with the consequent development of railroad-owned grain elevators at New York, had an immediate effect, not only in facilitating handling and giving a definite and universal standard of quotations, but also in reducing the expense, and consequently the charges of handling, as well as the number and amounts of commissions and other like local charges. The period 1873-82 includes, also, the adoption and development of the system of railroad elevators at New York. This development of terminal facilities during the period reduced the total charges on grain received by rail in New York and delivered to ocean-going vessels from 4 or 5 cents to about 13 cents a bushel. Railroad competition with the Erie canal system threatened to

---

[24] Grain elevators began to be used in Liverpool only at the end of the seventies, and the reduction which had been effected in local charges previous to 1880 was, therefore, quite inconsiderable. They are stated by Messrs. Read and Pell, in their report to the Agricultural Interests Commission, 1880, to have been at that time about 2S. id. per quarter (about 6 cents per bushel).

divert the grain trade from that route to other ports, as Philadelphia and Baltimore, and this led to close scrutiny of local charges at Buffalo and New York, with a view to removing any abuses that burdened the traffic.

Criticism and recrimination ensued between the trade corporations of the two cities, in which some interesting developments, due to the virtual monopoly long possessed by the Erie Canal route, came to light. It was found that the charges, at Buffalo perhaps more elaborately than elsewhere, had been ingeniously arranged to take as high toll as might be on every bushel that passed through, without regard to ulterior effects on the traffic. The traffic, in fact, was treated as if its volume and value were a fixed quantity, which local charges could have no particular effect either to help or to hinder. This view was pretty near the truth down to the beginning of all - rail shipments on a considerable scale. Under the stress of necessity the middle-men, who drew their income from the traffic, gradually and reluctantly lowered their charges during the seventies to a point at which their amount would no longer work to the manifest detriment of the traffic. It may be added that since about 1880-82 the question of local charges has been less of a subject for recrimination between trade corporations, and no great reductions have been effected, probably because there has been little room for great or sudden reductions. Reference to the Chart (I. A.) will suggest, in the convergence of the lines for the Chicago and the New York prices during these years, how this reduction in transit charges worked to the benefit of the primary market. General changes in local charges and freights west of Chicago are more difficult to trace; not only from the difficulty of obtaining the figures, but also, because these local freights have been subject to local and temporary disturbances that vitiate the figures obtainable for any given place and route for purposes of any broad generalization. Figures are obtainable that go to show that a considerable, but very irregular process of reduction has been going on in rates on grain, but what has been the aggregate average result of the process is very hard to say. On the whole the reduction seems to have been no less pronounced-perhaps rather more pronounced--than the corresponding reduction in charges from Chicago to the seaboard.

The controlling fact which determined the price of wheat in the world's market during these years was a short supply. The seventies, especially after 1876, were a succession of poor harvests in Europe. The American harvests were large, and the annual output was increasing every year, but it did not overtake the demand until 1881, when the series of poor harvests in Europe had come to a close, and the draft on the American supply was no longer as great as it had been. The course of wheat prices was extraordinary, not to say anomalous, through the whole period. Owing to special, largely fortuitous causes, the price was extraordinarily high; and owing to other special causes, partly fortuitous, partly the result of systematic human effort, the high prices ruling were exceptionally remunerative to the American farmer. But while wheat farmers generally, even more than those mainly occupied with other lines of farming, had reason to rejoice in the good fortune of those years of high prices and large yields, the good fortune did not come to all in equal proportion. Winter wheat fared distinctly better in point of crops during the years of rising prices than spring wheat. Every crop from 1877 to 1880 gave an extraordinarily heavy yield in the great winter wheat states (Chart V, group II),[25] while the four years, 1878-81, were all either moderate or distinctly poor in the spring wheat states. To this is to be added that from 1873 to 1877 grass- hoppers visited portions of the states west of the Mississippi, and seriously diminished the aggregate output and the average remunerativeness of the wheat crop in those states.

Still, the acreage under wheat increased greatly, and without intermission, from year to year in the spring wheat group, while in the great winter wheat group the acreage barely held its own from 1875 to 1879. The line traced by beef on Chart II. sets forth the main fact that goes to explain this halt in the increase of the wheat acreage of these states, as well as the signal increase in 1880, and to some extent the decline that set in with 1881. The price of beef advanced strongly from 1875 onward, and the winter wheat states were in a peculiarly favorable position to take advantage of the advance. The halt in the advance of the wheat acreage in 1875 was due in great part to a diversion of the farming of those states from wheat to beef. The remoter cause which underlay the advance in the price of beef was the shipment of fresh meat to Europe. Fresh meat shipments, as a business undertaking, began in October, 1875. The reason for the peculiar movement of the wheat acreage in the winter wheat states during the best years for winter wheat, both as to crops and price, is accordingly not that wheat did not pay well in those states at that time, but that beef paid better.

The movement of the acreage in the spring wheat states is testimony to the fact that wheat-growing did pay well even under relatively adverse circumstances during these years. A change was in progress during these years in the relative prices of winter and spring wheat, a change which completed itself during the eighties. The tradition had been that winter wheat alone could make flour of the best quality, and the softer varieties of winter wheat were preferred to the harder. Spring wheat flour was inferior, according to the old standards and methods, to flour made from winter wheat. Hence winter wheat ruled several cents higher in the market (from 5 or 6 to 20 or 30, or even more) than spring wheat of a corresponding grade. The " new process " of milling that came into vogue in the seventies treated the hard wheats to better advantage than the old process had done, and the great difference in price was somewhat diminished. When

---

[25] The lines for production are drawn on a scale en of that of the lines for acreage; the normal average yield per acre of wheat for the whole country being a fraction over 12 bushels. The rise or fall of the line for production, relatively to that for acreage, indicates approximately the yield per acre for any given year. Wherever the line for production rises greatly above that for acreage, the yield per acre was over the normal average for the whole country, and wherever it falls below, the yield was under the average. The figures from which the lines of these two charts are plotted may be found in the Statistical Abstract of the United States.

the " roller process " and " gradual reduction " was introduced into the milling system of this country (late in the seventies), and the capabilities of that method came to be developed and appreciated, as to a good extent they were within the first half-dozen years after its introduction, it appeared that a more salable flour could be produced from the hard spring wheats of the Northwest than the best of winter wheat flour, at the same time that a bushel of the spring wheat of the prairies would grind into a larger quantity of flour.[26]

The result was that the relative desirability of the two classes of wheat for milling gradually changed. Down to about 1881-2, by which time the effect of the improved machinery and methods was making itself felt in England, and when the new-process flour had gained some popularity among British consumers, especially bakers, winter wheat, American and British, had customarily ruled somewhat higher than American Spring. The difference varied with the season, but generally the divergence for some years previous to 1880 would amount, on an average for the year, to something like 5 to 10 cents per bushel in favor of winter wheat. About 1880-81 this customary divergence begins to sensibly diminish. By 1884 the difference in favor of No. 2 Red Winter over No. 2 Spring had fallen to about 3 cents per bushel in the Liverpool market. In Chicago the average difference for the year in 1884 was 6.3 cents in favor of No. 2 Red Winter; a difference which afterwards decreased still further, and has practically disappeared. In 1887 winter ranged from I cent or less to 4 or 5 cents over spring in Liverpool; in Chicago, 1 or 2 cents over. In 1889 there was a difference the other way.

Winter wheat seems to have definitively lost its advantage over spring, the softer varieties of winter especially so. But it is also to be noted that spring wheat has not held the advantage which for a short time it gained over winter wheat. The latest improved methods and appliances seem to treat either, or rather both in due proportion, with the very best results. What advantage there is is in favor of the hard wheats as compared with the soft, and rests on the greater quantity and "strength" of the flour yielded by the hard wheat, rather than on its superior quality in any other respect. About the middle of the eighties the development of milling processes had successfully made a fresh movement in advance, in making use of a mixture of different varieties of wheat, with the very best results. The mixing of wheats with a view to getting a given result is now an established practice in milling, both in this country and in Europe, and as a consequence a shortage of one kind relatively to the other results in an advance on the part of the kind which is relatively scarce.

---

[26] A Minnesota Patent had attained great popularity by 1876, and the progress of introduction into popular favor of the flours which the gradual reduction process was especially fitted to turn out was therefore well under way before that process came into general use.

III. 1882-1891.

The years since 1882 have been eventful enough, in a way, as regards the course of the price of wheat, but they have been tame in comparison with the ten years that preceded them. The period is remarkable for a relatively close parallelism in the course of prices for all the staple farm products, as well as between the prices of farm products generally and those of other staples. As a whole it is a period from which anomalies are absent to an unusual extent. About 1881, the causes which had controlled the course of wheat prices during the years immediately preceding gave way to a new set of causes, in many respects of quite a different character. The supply of the western nations was no longer drawn from America and Western Europe entirely, or almost entirely, as had been the case.

The seasons in Europe were no longer regularly under the normal average. The American acre- age had increased until, with accessions that were beginning to come in from several new sources, the customary demand was fully met. The change that was at hand in 1881-2 in grain prices was not entirely unforeseen at the time, but the magnitude of the change of which we then witnessed the initial stage was by no means adequately appreciated by those who had most to do with wheat at the time the change set in. The yearly average for 1882 in Chicago was a little higher than that of the previous year.[27] Such was not the case with respect to the markets of New York and Liverpool. The price in Chicago, for the year as a whole, was "too high," so that wheat was not freely exported. The New York wheat trade saw that this was the case, and said so; but Chicago, especially through the early months of the year, held stiffly to prices that the course of the general wheat market did not warrant.[28]From 1882 the price sagged off heavily, with the usual fluctuations, till it reached a permanently lower level in 1884-some 30 or 35 cents below the prices of ten years

---

[27] Wheat opened in Chicago in 1882 at about $1.26- some 12 cents higher than any yearly average since 1877. It fluctuated unsteadily until early August, when it suddenly fell to $1.05; the distinctly, doggedly bullish tone of the Chicago market that had prevailed through the first seven or eight months of the year gave way for the time, and wheat ranged below $1 through the greater part of the remaining four months and closed at about 99 cents.

[28] After all allowance is made for cut and special rates, and for every other factor that may go to make the apparent cost of transit of grain from Chicago or any other speculative western grain market to the seaboard greater than the actually necessary cost, or greater than the expense actually borne by the grain in transit, it is scarcely possible to avoid the impression that the difference in the price of wheat between the western market and the market at the seaboard or in Europe was, and is, less than the cost of transit, including unavoidable commissions and insurance. The implication of the available figures for transit and local charges, even after they have been scaled down freely, is that the traders in the western markets pay more for wheat, on the average, than they realize from it. So anomalous a state of business is, of course, not easily credible, but it would not be easy to disprove its presence.

earlier. During this steep decline the Chicago operators were pretty constantly holding back, and holding prices relatively higher in Chicago than elsewhere.[29]

The years from 1884 to 1887 were, as a whole, rather feature- less in wheat. The market was prevailingly dull and heavy, and generally disappointing to Chicago operators. On the whole there was a decline during these years. There was scored in 1887 the lowest yearly average that wheat has reached, in Chicago, during the period since the Civil War. During these four years (1884-7) No. 2 wheat never rose to $1. It fluctuated with the seasons and the crop reports, generally between 70 and go cents, but without any sustained advance. 1888, or rather the later months of 1888 and the early part of 1889, was a season of high prices, as compared with immediately preceding years. It was also a period of high prices in Chicago and in the western markets generally, as compared with the course of prices in the Eastern and European markets.

The yield for the year was rather low in the great wheat regions of America, perhaps especially so in the country tributary to Chicago; and the European crop was also under average. But the reason for wheat ruling higher in Chicago than elsewhere is not to be sought mainly in the crop returns of the year; although the spring wheat region of the Northwest, and the trans-Mississippi states generally, harvested an exceptionally small crop of low grade, as was also, to a less extent the case that year with the Ohio Valley group of states. An advance in wheat set in about the time the spring wheat was harvested, and during the month of September operators on the Chicago market achieved the most remarkable corner in wheat that has ever been recorded. The price then advanced from about go cents in early September until the last week of the month, when it jumped to $1.60, and even touched $2. With the advent of October, when the operations of the speculators had borne their fruit, it fell by one-third or more, and ruled at $1.16-$1.17 for the first week of the month. From that point it receded, irregularly, in spite of the efforts of the local operators, and the year closed at about 99 cents. Thence the course was irregularly downwards through the succeeding year, with a temporary advance to $1.0 in February. Since 1887, the general course has been upwards, culminating, apparently, in the comparatively high average price obtained for the crop of 1891. The

---

[29]A curious fact to be noted in 1884 -5 with respect to the course of wheat prices- and in 1888 -9 it occurs again, and more markedly - is the decline that took place in Chicago prices, relatively to prices in the New York market, immediately after they had been held up to an unwarranted figure for a time by speculation. Although the average for the year in 1884 was 83 cents, the price fell as low as 69Y/ cents in December, and closed at about 72 cents. It opened at 72Y/ cents in 1885, and only in the spring of that year did it again rise to the level of 83 cents, about which it fluctuated from that time on. This season of decline was out of harmony with the export market. The average Chicago price was lower in 1884, apparently in consequence of its having been too high in 1883 and early in 1884, than it was the following year; while the price in New York, and still more distinctly in Liverpool, was lower in 1885 than in 1884. The movement in 1888-9 is quite analogous.

factors which have determined the general course of wheat prices since 1882 have been large and strong, with few disturbing causes. The fact of greatest weight, and most characteristic of the period, has been the relatively large supply. A glance at Chart IV. will show that this increased supply was not due to an increased output in America. Since 1880 the American wheat acreage has been practically stationary, taking the country as a whole. American yields have also not been nearly up to the average of the preceding ten years. The harvest has varied from year to year during this decade in much the same way as ever, but the harvests, both of wheat and of other staple crops, have run at a distinctly lower average than during the seventies.

It is even safe to say that, while the run of crops in wheat, and to a great extent also in corn, was on the whole over a normal average during the seventies, it was below normal, perhaps in about an equal degree, during the decade 1881-90. There is a further contrast between the run of wheat crops for the two periods. The earlier ten years were distinctly more favorable for winter wheat than for spring; so much so that the unusually high average for those years was due entirely to the exceptional excellence of the crops in the winter wheat region. The spring wheat of the Northwest during the seventies was, if anything, slightly below the normal average, taking the period as a whole. During the eighties- 1881 to 1890- there was no such marked difference in the condition of the two classes of grain. Both varied from year to year, and the two did not vary with even pace, but on the average the seasons were no less favorable to the one than to the other. There were extreme local variations, such as the bad year of 1887 in Kansas and other states of the same group, and 1890 in some of the states beyond the Mississippi, as well as in the Ohio Valley; and, taken in conjunction with the unsatisfactory general run of staple crops and prices, the very moderate or deficient yield of wheat was an active factor in producing the severe depression in the West through the closing years of the eighties. But if regard is had to the wheat crop alone, it is to be taken that all the great wheat areas fared not unequally during this period[30].

The characteristic features of the situation as affecting the course of wheat prices since 1887 have been: (1) crops, both of wheat and of other grains, have, in general, not varied widely from the normal; (2) very efficient means and methods of production have been in use, as compared with ten years earlier (for this country, especially, this applies to the production of other staples than grain in nearly an equal degree); (3) the means of transportation and communication in use have also been of a much greater efficiency, especially as affecting other exporting countries

---

[30] A review of the European crops from 1880 to 1890 will show the period to have been of a fair average character, with wheat rather more satisfactory than other grains and slightly over the normal average. Europe therefore came distinctly nearer supplying its own bread during these years than during the preceding ten. At the same time a greater proportion of the European crop had become immediately avail- able in the general market.

than the United States, and a steady improvement in this respect has been in progress during the entire period; (4) hence has resulted the definitive inclusion of the crops of practically all wheat growing countries in the supply that goes immediately to affect the price of wheat in any particular market; (5) a further effect of these mechanical, technical improvements, acting in conjunction with the improved business methods now in use, has been a diminution of the stocks customarily kept on hand; (6) as a consequence of the facts enumerated, there has been, especially during the earlier years of the decade, a distinctly larger available supply, relatively to the demand, than was offered in earlier years; (7) there has been an absence, relatively, of sudden and radical industrial changes immediately affecting grain production; (8) a very considerable decline in the prices of staple commodities has taken place, with a consequent prevailing weak or depressed tone in the industrial situation generally. Certain minor factors have also affected the general course of wheat prices. Notable among these is the imposition and continued increase of heavy import duties by France, Germany, Italy and Spain.

To what extent this factor has influenced the prices obtained by the American producer it is impossible to say, even approximately. Yet there is no question but the effect has been to limit the demand and lower the price, although probably in a very slight degree. The slightly heavier scale of duties of the American tariff on staple commodities, since 1883, has probably acted in the same direction on grain prices in the primary markets, though the effect of the increase can not have been at all considerable. As already noted, there was no great radical change directly affecting the production of wheat during the years after 1881, except the change in prices. But while the change in price was so nearly the only great change of the period, that change was unprecedented in magnitude and character, and the resulting, or, perhaps some would prefer to say, the accompanying change in the movement of the wheat acreage in this country has been no less serious and unprecedented. The total acreage sown to wheat, which for a series of years previous to 1880 had habitually increased by a yearly addition of something like ten per cent., practically did not increase at all, in the aggregate, from that time until 1891.

This result was not reached by a general and uniform cessation in the extension of wheat growing over the entire area in which wheat is largely grown. The acreage under wheat increased, on the whole, considerably in the prairie states and on the Pacific slope, and decreased to approximately the same extent in the Eastern and Ohio Valley states; but, without exception, in each of the groups of states represented in Chart V. the acreage under wheat suffered a serious diminution in 1885, immediately following the great permanent fall in price. This was the year of smallest wheat acreage since 1879, and shows the effect of the steep and protracted decline in prices during the years immediately preceding; though the price is not answerable for the whole of the diminution of area. Something is due to the very bad winter of 1884-5, which perceptibly diminished the acreage of winter wheat by "winter-killing." In 1886 there was a partial recovery in wheat acreage at all points; but the rate of increase in the sections where increase has taken place has been less from that time until 1890 than it had been previously, while at the same time the decrease in acreage in the great winter wheat states has been less pronounced since that time than before (see Chart V.). The other great American grain crop-which might also be called the great meat crop-is corn. The alternative, though by no means the only alternative, offered the wheat farmer is the production of some form of animal product. And a comparison with the movement of the corn acreage for the same period will show, approximately, the relative attractiveness of wheat and other farming in the wheat growing states. It is to be taken, with some not inconsiderable qualification, that any conspic-uous increase or decrease in the corn acreage indicates a corresponding movement in stock farming, taking the word in its broader meaning. If the line for corn acreage were traced, it would show a very strong and remark-ably steady upward movement from 1871 to 1886. Since 1886 the corn acreage has fluctuated, rather than scored any distinct advance.

The increase in the total acreage under corn since 1880 has also been due, for the most part, to an increase in the states west of the Mississippi, although there has at the same time been some increase in the South. The corn acreage of the Ohio Valley states has been, on the whole, stationary or slightly declining since that year. For the other minor grain crops, the movement has not been notably dissimilar from that of corn. On the whole, therefore, wheat has lost since 1880, relatively to other crops, in all the great wheat growing sections; more distinctly so in the Ohio Valley group of states and the more southerly states west of the Mississippi than elsewhere ; and this relative loss took place, chiefly, during the years before 1886. The exact area sown to wheat in any given year is not to be accepted as an unfailing index of the relative attractiveness of wheat growing at the time, as compared with other crops. The weather and the condition of the soil at the time of sowing have something to do with the number of acres sown, and the extent to which wheat has been winter-killed, and the land resown to other crops, may perceptibly influence the breadth of the crop.

But taking one year with another, the breadth of the wheat area affords a pretty fair indication of the relative profitableness of wheat growing. In the great winter wheat states and in the states immediately west of the Missis-sippi, there was, during the eighties, a very distinct movement towards a diversification of crops, to the partial neglect of wheat. The greatest single factor which has acted to bring about this change has been the decline in wheat prices; but other factors have acted in the same direction, for the most part with a slow, cumulative effect, and it is very difficult to say how much of the aggregate effect is to be attributed to any one cause. Stock growing continued to divert farmers from wheat to corn, though appar-ently rather less extensively than during the later years of the seventies. The climate of the northwestern states bordering on the Mississippi has been less favorable to the growth of spring wheat for some years past than it was years ago. The chinch bug has also been much more troublesome in the older spring wheat region than used to be the case. But the most effi-cient factor making for a change has been the economic or industrial fac-tor proper. The older wheat states are virtually nearer to a market for other,

less easily transported, products now than they were; and the greater capital required, especially in permanent investments the plant necessary for a
system of mixed farming-is much more readily at the command of the
farmers now, either through their own accumulations or through easier
terms of borrowing. A simple juxtaposition of the lines traced by the prices
of wheat and of other staples, therefore, is by no means sufficient for a
comparison of the relative profitableness of wheat and other farming under the changed conditions of the last decade as compared with the seventies. The lines of the charts afford a sufficiently accurate indication of what
has taken place in the Chicago and New York markets; but the local markets, while in a general way running a course parallel with that of the general markets on which they depend, are not affected in the same degree for
each staple by the changes in the situation that go to make the variation in
price. As a whole, prices in the primary markets have tended to approach
nearer to those in the general markets-the former have tended to rise relatively to the latter, but not equally for all staples. In a general way, the improvements that have been going on in transportation and communication have had a relatively greater effect on the less transportable articles.
So that, wheat being practically the most easily transportable of our farm
products, these other products have been left in a relatively more favorable position by the aggregate of changes that have taken place than the
course of prices in the general market alone would indicate[31]

The outcome of the movement has been that, as regards the older states,
wheat growing has been relatively (and probably, as counted in money,
absolutely) less profitable since 1882 than during the preceding ten years,
even apart from the distinctly less favorable run of seasons during the later
than the earlier period. Wheat has recovered some of its lost ground during the last two years. With respect to the newer wheat lands of the West
the case is not altogether similar. The legitimate effect of the course of
prices, as of other factors of a general character, on wheat growing, both in
the Northwest and South- west during the later eighties, was obscured by
the occurrence of several abnormally bad seasons. Also, the new lands
over which wheat growing has been extending in the West since 1881 offer
the most easily tilled, and, for a series of years at the start, the most fertile
of all American soils. The cost of production of wheat, apart from its delivery to the general market, is there- fore less on these new lands than on
any large area that has been under wheat before; and wheat growing has

---

[31] "Farm prices," as given in the annual reports of the Statistician of the United
States Department of Agriculture, go to corroborate this view. Lines traced by farm
prices (prices in the primary markets as reported by correspondents of the Department) might be given, showing that, while in the general markets the course of prices has apparently, on the whole, favored wheat relatively to other staples, in the
local markets the reverse is true. Indeed, a somewhat detailed comparison, of which
there is space here for nothing beyond the most general statement of results, shows
that so far as these Department "farm prices" are an adequate indication of the
course of the local markets, wheat during the eighties suffered a very distinct depreciation relatively to other staple farm products.

been extending, and profitably, too, in an average season, while selling at prices that would not have been remunerative for wheat grown elsewhere as a main crop.

To sum up: The indications afforded by the course of prices are that since the completion of the great decline in prices of farm products, 1884-5, wheat growing in the older wheat states has held a less favorable position, relatively to other farming, than it did during the seventies. All accounts converge to the support of that view. But it is doubtful whether, in the great winter wheat states of the Ohio Valley group, a relatively large acreage of wheat in a system of mixed farming has not continued to be more profitable throughout the whole period than a system which should tend to discard wheat growing as a staple crop; while it is to be taken as practically beyond doubt that with the changes of the last two or three years wheat growing in those states is again normally a profitable investment. The spring wheat states bordering on the Mississippi on the west are a case by themselves. From local causes, wheat growing has not been, relatively, a profitable branch of farming there the last few years. Of the newer wheat lands of the West it is to be said that wheat growing, with an average run of seasons, is undoubtedly profitable; rather, it is almost the only crop that can be profitably grown there by the farmers at present settled on those lands and under the present circumstances.

Chapter 6
The Food Supply And The Price Of Wheat

In 1879, in an address before the London Statistical Society, Mr. G. Shaw-Lefevre, said. If I were to venture a prediction on so difficult and obscure a question, I would incline to the opinion that wheat has during the past year reached its lowest point.

This forecast was made a couple of years before the beginning of the great protracted decline in the prices of all agricultural produce that set in in the early years of the eighties. The forces which brought on the decline were already at work, and had been at work for some years before Mr. Shaw-Lefevre made his prediction; but the causes which seem very obvious after the fact may be quite obscure before it, and the causes that make for a permanent decline in agricultural produce are commonly more uncertain of prevision than those that make for a permanent rise. The former are apt to be of the nature of innovations, whose scope and efficacy can not well be foretold, while the latter are as apt to be simply the cumulative action of factors with whose scope and method we are already familiar.

Recognising, then, the chance of an unforeseen decline, and recognising, also, that there is more than one known factor already at work to bring about a decline in agricultural products in the near future, the purpose of this paper is to attempt an estimate of the possible maximum advance in the price of wheat (as a representative product of agriculture) supposing the factors that make for a decline to remain in abeyance for the next ten years.

The great permanent fall in prices that took place during the first half of the last decade has served as an object lesson to enforce the truth that there is a close dependence of price on supply. The fact of this dependence has been made much of both by those who hope for an advance in prices of farm produce, and by those who deprecate the approach of a scarcity of bread. The assumption has been freely made that the date at which the land available for tillage shall have been definitively occupied is near at hand, and that when that day arrives a great and "sudden" advance in agricultural prices is to be looked for, with its consequences, of great gains for the farmer - for the American farmer perhaps, in an especial degree - and of distress for all peoples who get their supply of food largely from other countries. This sweeping generalisation merits some scrutiny.

It is unquestionably true that the price of wheat depends on the supply, but it is no less true that, other things being the same, the annual average supply of wheat depends, in the long run, on its price. The control exercised by the supply over the price is direct and transient. That exercised by the price over the annual average supply is of slower action, but it is also more permanent. We have therefore not said the last word in saying that when the demand shall have outgrown the present annual supply, the price of wheat will advance. The converse is also true when the price of wheat begins to advance appreciably beyond what will barely remunerate the growers of wheat to-day, the supply will presently increase. The date of the definitive occupation of the tillable area yet available will no doubt mark an advance in the price of wheat, other things remaining un-changed; but the date of a definitive advance in price will no less surely mark an increase in the output from the acreage already under cultivation in the older wheat-growing sections. When this event comes to pass the farmers in the older sections will find it to their advantage to give their land such additional attention as will increase the yield per acre from the land already in cultivation, and so to some extent cover the shortage to which the rise in price is due and break the force of the advance. At the same time recourse will he had in an increasing degree to lands which are scarcely profitable for tillage at the prices which have been ruling for some years past.

The increased demand that is expected to advance the price of wheat will come as a result of an increase of the population of bread-eating countries. An increased demand for wheat accordingly implies an increase of approximately the same proportions in the demand for other food products; therefore any considerable increase of the acreage sown to wheat will be practicable only as a feature in the general increase of the acreage of arable land. The increased supply of wheat, as of other food products, will therefore have to be obtained, in part, by an increased yield per acre from the acreage already in cultivation.

While we have by no means reached - or nearly reached - the limit of the possible extension of the wheat area in America, it is probably true that we are fast approaching the point beyond which there is no considerable ad-ditional amount of wheat lands equally fertile and otherwise equally avail-able with the last ten or twenty million acres already brought under culti-vation. It can hardly be said that the spread of cultivation in America dur-ing the past ten or twelve years has been to less fertile or less available lands; but for the next ten or twelve years, barring unforeseen develop-ments, any considerable further spread of the area of cultivation can not take place without recourse to less available lands. The practical working of the law of diminishing returns will therefore assume an importance for our farming which it has not had for some time past. This practical work-ing of the law will appear in the relation between the price and the yield per acre.

The yield per acre and the prices of farm produce vary considerably as between the different sections of the country, and, so far as concerns the older sections, they vary together, with some regularity; but the difference in prices between different localities is too slight and the difference in oth-er respects is too great to afford satisfactory figures from which to infer what is the effect, on the yield, of a given local advantage in price. The di-vergence in price is not pronounced nor easily ascertainable, as between states which are in other respects available for our comparison. Evidently no value can attach to a comparison of the newer, spring-wheat states with the older, winter-wheat states. But it may be remarked that Vermont, Massachusetts and Connecticut show a higher yield than any of the Ohio

Valley states. It will be more to the purpose, because the divergence both in price and in yield is great enough to afford tangible evidence of the efficacy of the forces at work, to compare the price and yield per acre in Great Britain with the price in Chicago and the yield per acre in the winter-wheat states lying about Chicago. The yield per acre of wheat in Great Britain is very considerably greater than in the states about Chicago. The immediate cause of its being so is the higher price obtained for wheat, and for other farm produce, by the British farmers; and the degree of effectiveness of the inducement offered them in the way of higher prices ought to help us to forecast the probable efficacy of an appeal of the same kind to the industry of their American competitors.

The winter-wheat states centering about Chicago and the great lakes - Ohio, Indiana, Illinois, Wisconsin and Michigan - may, in some respects, not unfairly be compared with Great Britain. They are like that country in being a country of mixed farming, and, as regards wheat production, mainly a winter-wheat country. Their farm lands have also been under cultivation for such a length of time as in large measure to obviate the complications which the "virgin soil" would introduce into any comparison of the newer states of the west with the countries of Europe. In some respects these states do not afford a close parallel to the farming lands of Great Britain. The climate is not the same, and the faults of the climate are not of the same kind. In the states mentioned there is more danger from drought than from wet seasons; in the United Kingdom it is all the other way. A bad season in England is sure to be a year of deficient heat, or excessive moisture, or both. Further, the soil of these states does not closely resemble the British soil in point of adaptation to wheat culture. These states do, however, afford as nearly fair a comparison with British soil and climate as any part of America that is a sufficiently representative wheat-growing region, and at every point where the comparison seems to be vitiated by inherent differences the difference is in favor of the states, as a superior country for wheat-growing and for mixed farming. The American soil is more fertile and more easily tilled; the climate of the states is better adapted for wheat-growing; the American farmers are probably not at all inferior to the British in intelligence or enterprise. So far as the inherent difference in natural advantages may lead us astray in drawing any inferences from a comparison of this group of states with Great Britain, the error would be in the direction of too low an estimate of the wheat-growing capacity of the states under the stimulus of a higher price. And as the object of the inquiry is to estimate the probable minimum effect on supply of a given permanent advance in price, rather than the maximum capacity of the states under such a stimulus, this is not a danger that need be specially guarded against.

An objection of greater weight may be found in the difference between British and American prices of staples, other than agricultural produce. The higher general level of prices of what the American farmer has to buy places him at a disadvantage, as compared with the British farmer, in precisely the same way as the lower price he gets for what he has to sell. The hindering effect of the higher price of staples must accordingly be allowed for in calculating the effect which a given rise in the price of farm products will have in the way of increasing the intensity of culture.

This higher range of prices does not comprise all articles of consumption used by the farmer. Lumber, and forest products generally, are lower here than in England. Farm implements of most kinds are rather cheaper; leather goods are scarcely higher; many of the staple food products are cheaper. But after all has been said, it is not to be questioned that the American farmer has to pay a somewhat higher average range of prices for what he buys (outside of agricultural products) than his British competitor. The American tariff to the extent to which it is protective, increases the price of the articles on which it is laid, and among these articles are many important items of the farmer's necessary consumption.

It is difficult to say, even approximately, how much of a handicap this added cost is to American farming. It assuredly does not amount to more than 20 per cent of the value of our farm products at Chicago prices; probably the actual additional cost to the farmers is considerably less than 20 per cent of the value of their products. Against this higher cost of necessaries in America may be offset the lower margin of cultivation in Great Britain, - using the term in the sense of a resort to poorer soils. The natural fertility of the poorest soils in cultivation in Great Britain in the system of mixed farming of which wheat culture is an integral part, is greatly lower than that of the poorest class of soils cultivated in the states named. This implies a correspondingly greater average cost of production of the products of British farming[32] and it affects also the cost of many of the necessaries of life to the British farmer.

The advantage is as definitely on the side of the states with respect to the margin of cultivation, as it is on the side of Great Britain with respect to the range of general prices. Here, again, it is impossible to say how great the advantage of the one over the other may be, but it is not unlikely that the disadvantage of the British farmer in this respect may completely offset the disadvantage which the American farmer has in the matter of higher general prices.

It may be thought that the fact that the agricultural depression in Great Britain during the whole of the period chosen for comparison (1884-92) has been severer than in America, would vitiate any British data for comparison with our own in any case where the point at issue turns on the question of a remunerative price. This difficulty is not a very serious one in any case, and does not affect the question in hand at all. What is required for the validity of the argument is: (1) that the inducements to wheat culture in Great Britain, relatively to other tillage, should not be greater than in the states; and (2) that the least fertile lands cultivated in the British

---

[32] This statement does not imply that rent is an element in the cost of production. What is claimed is that Great Britain, as a whole, because of its lower margin of cultivation, gets the products of its soil at a greater average expenditure than do the states, and that a given increment in the price will induce a less increment in yield at this lower margin than at the higher margin of cultivation existing in the states.

system of farming should not be intrinsically superior to the lands similarly at the margin of cultivation in the states. It needs no argument to establish that both these conditions are fully met and will continue to hold for an indefinite time to come.[33] .

If the considerations adduced are admitted to be valid, to the extent that wheat growing in a system of mixed farming in the states named lies under no other or greater disadvantage as compared with wheat growing in Great Britain than that indicated by the difference in the price of a given grade of wheat between Chicago and Liverpool, then we have the premises from which to deduce approximately what will be the maximum possible advance in price required to induce a given increase in the average yield per acre of wheat in the states. And this will afford some indication of what will be the maximum possible advance in price resulting from a given increase in the consumption of wheat.

The prices selected for comparison are average prices of American No. 2 Red Winter Wheat in Liverpool and in Chicago, since 1884. While this grade of wheat is not grown in England, the quotations for this grade are quite as significant for wheat prices in England as any quotations obtainable. The Gazette averages, which are usually quoted, are for British wheat, without respect to quality and the average quality of the grain from which the quotations are made up will accordingly vary from year to year, with the character of the harvest. Gazette averages are useless for any exact comparison. The reason for not making up the averages for a comparison of prices from a series of years reaching back of 1884 is obvious. Wheat culture had not, until that time, adjusted itself to the changed conditions of the market that supervened about 1880-82. The years immediately preceding 1884-85 were years of great changes in the price and acreage of wheat. By 1884 the decline was completed, and the price of wheat has moved on a lower level since that time than before. About the same time the decline in acreage in the states selected had also practically ceased[34] though a slight tendency to a further narrowing of the acreage has been perceptible since that time, at least until 1890.The average yield per acre of

---

[33] The depression in British farming, so far as it is not due to bad harvests, is due to the decline in prices; and this decline has affected grain production rather more strongly than other tillage. Its most pronounced economic result has been a readjustment of rents on lowered basis. Apart from adverse seasons, the British farmers' chief real grievance is too high rents. Prices have fallen some 30 percent, or more; money rents, except in isolated cases, have not been lowered to correspond. In addition to this, the farmers have suffered from a depreciation of the capital they have had invested in farming; which is also a considerable item.

[34] The extraordinary decline in wheat acreage in the Ohio valley group of states in 1885 was due quite as much to an unfavorable season as to a voluntary narrowing of the area. The acreage regained in 1886 more than half of what had been lost in 1885. The definitive effect on acreage of the decline in price that ended in 1884, was not had until the following year. In studying the movement of acreage under the influence of the new level of prices then established, the new period is to be considered as having begun with 1885.

wheat for the eight years since 1885 4[35] in the states selected has been about 13 3/4 bushels[36] .

This average includes the extraordinary harvest of 1891 (17 1/2 bushels per acre) But even counting 1891, this average is probably slightly short of the normal average yield for these states, the seasons during the latter half of the eighties having been, on the whole, rather unfavorable for winter wheat. The average yield of the same states for the years 1877-83, when the seasons were, on the whole, very favorable, was 14 3/4 bushels. The lower average yield during later years seems to be due, in a slight degree, to a partial displacement of wheat by other crops on some of the more fertile and better tilled soils; or perhaps more exactly, to a relative neglect of wheat-growing by some of the more capable and better equipped farmers; but the great cause of this discrepancy lies, no doubt, in the character of the seasons. When due weight is allowed to all these factors, we shall be very near the truth in assuming 14 bushels per acre to be the present normal average yield of wheat in these states.

For Great Britain the officially assumed normal average yield of wheat is 28.80 bushels per acre. The actual annual average for the eight years since 1885 is 29.57 bushels. It is difficult to say whether the officially assumed normal average is nearer the true normal than the recorded actual average. The London Economist, as well as some other authorities, claims the true normal average to exceed 29 bushels. The seasons during the eighties have been, on the whole, rather more favorable for wheat than the average of a long series of years. If this were the sole modifying circumstance the official normal average would have to be accepted as very near the true normal. But this circumstance does not account for the whole of the discrepancy between the average yield of today and that of some years ago. It

---

[35] The average yield for the years 1885-92 has been taken, as, for the present purpose, answering to the price during the years 1884-91. The yield for the year 1884 was the same as the average for 1885-92.

[36] The average annual yield has been:

Year	In the States; Bushels (Winchester)	In Great Britain; Bushels (Imperial)
1885	11.19	31.31
1886	14.41	26.89
1887	13.38	32.07
1888	12.02	28.05
1889	14.91	29.89
1890	11.74	30.74
1891	17.49	31.26
1892	14.40	26.38
Average	13.78	29.57

has been pointed out that the average has also probably been raised by the dropping of some of the inferior soils out of wheat cultivation. At the same time, improvements in agriculture seem also to have affected the average yield in the same direction. It will be safe to take 29 bushels per acre as the actual normal average yield of wheat in Great Britain.

The average yield in Great Britain exceeds the yield in the states by about 107 per cent. (15 bushels). The annual average price of American No. 2 Red Winter Wheat in Liverpool, for the years 1884-91, exceeds the average price of the same grade in Chicago by a trifle over 20 per cent. (18.095 cents per Winchester bushel).7[37] .It ought to be a safe inference that a gradual advance in the price of wheat in the Chicago market to the present level of the price in Liverpool (accompanied, as in the normal course of things it would be, by a corresponding advance in the prices of other farm produce) would result in such an advance in the intensity of culture in the states lying about Chicago as to increase the average yield of wheat, during the early stages of the advance, in the same proportion as the British yield is higher on account of the higher British price. That is to say, a sufficiently gradual and permanent moderate advance, of a given per cent., in price, in the Chicago market, should result in an increase in the yield per acre of wheat in these states, of at least five times as many per cent. Twenty per cent (18 cents per bushel) advantage in price in Liverpool carries with it 107 per cent. (15 bushels) advantage in the yield per acre in Great Britain. A gradual advance of 5 per cent. (4.36 cents per bushel) in the annual average price in Chicago ought to bring an increase of more than 20 per cent. (2.8 bushels) in the yield per acre of wheat in the states lying about Chicago, supposing the conditions of production otherwise to remain unchanged.

The aggregate annual production of the five states named, for the eight years 1885-92, has averaged slightly over 140 million bushels. If the price of wheat in Chicago were to advance permanently to 95.84 cents per bushel (10 per cent) we should have to expect the total annual production

[37] Annual average price of No. 2 Red Winter Wheat, in cents per bushel.

Year	Chicago	Liverpool
1885	89.3	107.2
1886	88.3	103.1
1887	77.6	99.6
1888	77.2	98.7
1889	92.5	107.4
1890	85.2	102.8
1891	89.5	105.3
1892	97.3	117.7
Average	87.13	105.225

of these states to rise to not much less than 210 million bushels (50 per cent.).Assuming that the advance in price would have an equivalent effect on the output in the other wheat regions (and the chances would seem to be that the effect would be relatively at least as great in the remoter wheat fields, since the per cent. advance in price in the remoter local markets would be appreciably greater, and any inability to increase the yield on the newer wheat lands would be fully offset by an extension of the area), and considering also that such an advance in price would induce some increase in acreage in all the wheat producing country, an ordinary average price of 96 cents in the Chicago markets might be expected to bring out an aggregate annual product of not less than 800 million bushels.

Conversely, No. 2 Red Winter Wheat cannot advance permanently to 96 cents in Chicago until there is a customary demand for about 800 million bushels of American wheat at the increased price. A ten per cent advance in price presumes something near a fifty per cent increase in the demand.

The increase in the demand for wheat will coincide approximately with the increase of the bread-eating population. Judging of the future by the past, it will be a liberal estimate to say that the bread-eating population of the countries which draw on the supplies of the general market to which America contributes, may be expected to increase by ten per cent in ten years. It has perhaps reached that rate of growth during the last decade, and it would be extravagant to expect that rate to be exceeded during the next decade.

The price which it would be necessary to offer for wheat in order to meet this increased demand by an increased production is more a matter of surmise than the probable rate of growth of population. If we could answer this question, we should know approximately what prices our farmers may look for in payment for their produce during the opening years of the twentieth century. There is reason to believe that, barring unforeseen innovations, at the point in the growth of the demand for food at which there will be an effective demand for one-and-one-half times as much American wheat as at present, the price will have to be advanced by not more than nine cents above the present ordinary average price in Chicago. In the meantime, a less increase in the demand could be met at a less advance in price. An increase of ten per cent. (200,000,000 bushels) in the world's consumption of wheat would mean, if the demand were distributed as it is at present, an increase of about 50 million bushels in the portion ordinarily required of America. This additional demand could be met, without increase of acreage, by an addition of about 1 1/4 bushels to the present average yield per acre of wheat; and this additional 1 1/4 bushels would be forthcoming without its being necessary to advance the price in the local markets by as much as two cents per bushel above the average of the last eight or nine years.

But the additional demand will not fall pro rata on the countries which now supply the world with wheat; and the like is true to almost the same extent of the supply of other agricultural products. America now, of late years, supplies rather less than one-fourth of the total wheat product. She will certainly be called on to contribute more than one-fourth of the additional 200 bushels that will be required before the end of another ten years, unless some unforeseen contingency should come in to change the complexion of things.

An advance in price would have some effect on the intensity of culture in all agricultural countries, but the effect would probably be very slight in such regions as the wheat lands of Russia and India, especially the latter. In these countries, as well as in large portions of Western Europe, notably in France, agriculture is in the hands of a population that does not respond readily to promptings from without. Whatever addition may be made to the wheat supply furnished by those countries - apart from additions due to improved facilities for transportation - will be made slowly, and will at best be inconsiderable for some time to come. The new demand will fall first and most heavily on the American, Australian and South American wheat lands, and on such portions of Europe as Great Britain, Austria, parts of Germany, &c., together with some contributions due to an increase of acreage in Russia.

This fact, that the intensity of culture of a considerable portion of the present wheat-producing area of the world will be but partially and feebly affected by a moderate advance in the price, will necessitate a higher production on the part of that portion which will more readily respond to the call. It results in a virtual narrowing of the area from which the additional supply can be obtained, so as to include little else than the newer wheat-growing countries, with portions of Western Europe. These regions will therefore be called on to furnish more than their pro rata contingent to the increase, and this greater rate of production in these countries will be obtained only at the cost of a greater advance in price.

Of these more manageable countries, not all would respond to the demand with equal alacrity. It is, for example, easier for America to add one-tenth to her average yield of 12 1/4 bushels than it is for England to add one-tenth to her yield of 29 bushels[38] .

This fact goes in the same direction and adds further to the necessity of a higher price in the American market than would have been required if America were called on to furnish her pro rata increase only.

America has of late contributed something less than one-quarter of the world's annual wheat supply. If the facts above recited are allowed the extreme weight implied in looking to this country for one-half instead of one-fourth of the additional 200 million bushels that will be required by the end of another ten years, then it will be necessary to increase the yield of wheat in America, not by one-tenth, as was assumed above, but by one-fifth; that is, from 12 1/3 bushels to 14.8 bushels per acre for the whole

---

[38] It must not be supposed that England, or any part of Europe, is near the limit of productivity. The London Economist of September 13, 1890, says: High authorities have estimated that we might double the produce of the soil in the United Kingdom even under our existing system of farming. As it is, there are farmers who grow nearly double the average of grain crops for the kingdom as a whole, and many who produce twice the average weight of roots and potatoes."

country, or from 14 bushels to 16.8 bushels per acre for the five states named. To maintain such an increase in the American yield of wheat would require an advance of less than 4 1/2 per cent. (3.8 cents per bushel) in the price of wheat in Chicago.

But as some increase in acreage is sure to result from any advance in price, allowance must be made for the increased supply to be obtained by this means. How great the effect on the acreage will be, it is impossible to say. On the other hand, it is pretty certainly true that any advance in price will not have as great an effect in increasing the yield in the newer states, especially in the spring-wheat country, as in the group of states with which we set out. The chief increase in product in the newer states will, for some time to come, be got by increasing the acreage. It may be accepted without much risk that this increase in acreage will fully make up for the slighter increase in the yield per acre, so that the conclusion already arrived at need not be modified on that account.

If, therefore, these premises are accepted as sound and adequate, there is small chance that the normal increase in the demand for bread will permanently raise the average price of No. 2 wheat above 91 cents in the Chicago market within the next ten years.

This estimate proceeds on the supposition that no considerable advance is taking place or will take place the next few years in the methods of farming or in any of the industries that have to do directly or indirectly with the food supply. This of course is an extreme position. If, as is quite probable, improved industrial knowledge and processes should appreciably lessen the cost of production of grain in the newer wheat countries, this estimate would probably prove too high. And if, as is still more probable, the prices of staple articles of consumption in America should decline, relatively to those of farm produce, the chance of any advance in wheat or in farm products generally, would be still further narrowed. If, for example, American import duties on staples should be lowered within the next ten years sufficiently to diminish the cost of the farmer's necessary articles of consumption by 20 per cent and such a result is possible), the chance of any permanent advance in wheat for the present would disappear. Even apart from any lowering of the cost of articles of necessary consumption, it is fully within the possibilities of the situation that no permanent advance in farm products need take place at all for a generation or more. Better methods and a more intimate knowledge of the natural processes concerned in farming are probably capable, as competent authorities insist, of so adding to the efficiency of our farming as not to admit of prices going higher than they are.

Agriculture is fast assuming the character of an "industry," in the modern sense, and the development of the next few decades may not improbably show us, in farming as in other occupations, a continual improvement in methods and a steady decline in cost of production, even in the face of a considerably increased demand.

Chapter 7
The Later Railway Combinations

The open concentration of railway control in the union of the New York Central, Lake Shore and Boston and Albany in the east, the Union Pacific, and Southern Pacific, and the Northern Pacific, Great Northern and Burlington in the west, and the less apparent but not less effective centralization by common ownership of independent systems, is making a radical change in transportation conditions which a few years ago would have not passed with the slight attention it is now receiving.

The consolidation movement in other industries contains elements of strikingly novel interest, which for the time being have so absorbed attention as to leave the railway combinations comparatively little notice. It is, however, as true now as it ever has been, that railway control and management is of fundamental and paramount importance to our industrial and commercial interests. Present prosperity with its higher prices and wider margin of profits may cause shippers to pay increased freight charges with little grumbling, but will the rates be lowered when less favorable conditions and lower prices compel the shipper to consider expenses more carefully than he is now doing?

In the past competition for a declining volume of traffic has compelled rival railway managers to lower rates during periods of depression, sometimes with disastrous results to the roads. These lower rates forced improvements and economies which enabled the roads to make a profit, even at the reduced rates, and the trend of rates has been steadily downward during the past three decades. Increased price of materials and higher wages are given as the excuse for the advance in rates, which has been made during the past two years. But the surplus of net earnings and the ability to pay dividends on stock which represents no investment of capital, indicates that power which restriction of competition gave, rather than the necessity of meeting higher expenses, led to the advance in rates. It is true that the increase in railway rates has been less than the addition to the price of tin plate, steel rails and other monopolized products, but this merely indicates more moderation in the use of the power which railway combination confers.

The community of interests may be directly charged with the orgy of speculation through which we have just passed. The better dividends which the advance in rates made possible naturally tended to increase the price of stocks. The purchase of securities for the purpose of securing unity of action tended in the same direction, and the speculation as to the outcome of these great combinations tended to stimulate the powerful gaming instinct which is so widespread and needs little to rouse it to activity.

If rates had been maintained at a level which would give only normal returns on the capital actually invested in railways, and if the heavy capitalists had not been buying for control, does any one imagine that stocks which represent no investment would have sold at par or above?

In 1870, 1880 and 1886 conditions somewhat similar to those of the past two years led to railway building on an extensive scale. Competitors sought to share the profits which were being realized or which seemed to be in sight. Combination now seems able to prevent the waste which paralleling and undue extension then caused and a share of the profits has been sought by purchasing, at high prices, the securities of existing roads.

In the years following the panics of 1873 and 1893, when low prices, lack of employment and other conditions accompanying periods of depression caused serious agitation against the railways, the antimonopoly feeling was materially mitigated by the fact that competition between rival lines had so reduced rates as to involve many roads in bankruptcy. It was evident that monopoly was by no means complete, that rates were as low as any reasonable man could ask and the appeals of demagogues were rejected by intelligent and reasonable voters.

The optimist of course hopes that the dark years of depression will not recur. The ardent advocate of combinations also maintains that the powerful men in control of our railways and other industries will be able to prevent panics and depression. But let us consider for a moment the probable action of the managers of our combined railway system in case a period of depression should occur. Assuming a reasonably complete union of interests, rates will probably not be lowered except, perhaps, on the products of the industrial combinations which the railway capitalists also control. This may be expected to aggravate the feeling against monopolies, and the populistic hostility will not be tempted by lower rates and by the financial difficulties of the railways unless this danger is avoided - unless the increased power which combination gives is used with the greatest wisdom and rarest moderation, unless those in control of the railways, and the great industrial combinations are gifted with the keenest insight, so that they find their own interest in using their enormous power under a full sense of the responsibility that it involves, they will raise a storm of discontent and antagonism which will end in transferring their power to political leaders who will probably use it more arbitrarily and certainly less intelligently.

Chapter 8

On the General Principles
of a Policy of Reconstruction

There are certain cardinal points of orientation that will guide any endeavor to reach a lasting settlement on the return of peace. In the main these are points of common sense, and as such they will doubtless already be present in the mind of all thoughtful persons who interest themselves in these matters. But it can do no harm to put down in set form certain of the elementary propositions that will so give the point of departure and will define the limitations of such measures of reconstruction as may reasonably be expected to go into effect.

It is assumed as a major premise that the controlling purpose of any prospective settlement will be the keeping of the peace at large; that the demands of the peace are paramount, whatever other matters of convenience or expediency may be brought in as subsidiaries. As a counterfoil of this premise there immediately follows the further proposition that there can be no return to the 'status quo ante'. The Great War was engendered by that scheme of life that has ruled human relations among civilized peoples in recent times; and a re-establishment of the scheme of relations among these peoples now may confidently be counted on to lead to the same disastrous issue.

Therefore the question presents itself: What can be done, by taking thought, to avoid a return to that fateful complication in the conduct of human affairs that has now come to be known as the 'status quo ante?' What manner of change in existing arrangements could be counted on to make sure that civilized mankind will not again run over the same sinister course to the same disastrous outcome in the near future? How far and in what respect will men be content to forsake their accustomed scheme of use and wont and law, as it has stood during these years out of which the Great War has arisen? Some substantial change is imperative, if the peace is to be kept; and, I apprehend, all thoughtful persons are now ready to agree that the peace must be kept, at all costs, and that any plan of reconstruction which does not promise peace and security will not be worth considering. It is imperative to change the scheme of use and wont, of law and order, as it runs between men and between nations, so far as regards those rights and relations out of which dissension habitually arises and about which men go to war. Now, it is an easy generalization, or rather it is a time-worn commonplace, that all such disputes as rise to the dignity of warfare in our time turn always about National Ambition or Business Enterprise, one or the other, or more commonly both together. Within the confines of modern civilization religious wars, e. g., wars undertaken avowedly for pillage, are out of date and are considered to be beneath the dignity of civilized statesmen. What one hears of is the national integrity, national destiny, national honor, or perhaps national opportunity, national expansion, national aggrandizement. These various objects of national ambition have at least the appearance of differing widely from one another; and it would doubtless appear that they are not all equally threatening to a state of peace and security at large. Indeed, many a kindly and thoughtful follower of the gospel of peace and good-will has committed himself to the view that the national integrity, or the national honor, e. g. is to be rated foremost among the things that are to be safeguarded in any eventual peace compact. Probably none but a relatively few among the law-abiding citizens would hesitate to choose war with the national honor intact, rather than peace without it. On the other hand, relatively few would choose to further national aggrandizement at the cost of war.

Yet, however much these different objects of national ambition may differ among themselves they have this much in common, that they are matters of political aspiration, and that they afford grievances to be redressed by recourse to arms. It is between nations, and on the ground of national claims and interests, that war is carried on; at least such is the case in the formal sense that it is as a nation only that any people figures as a recognized belligerent under the currently accepted rules of etiquette governing affairs of this kind. It will probably be admitted without argument that whenever a given community divests itself of its national character - as, e. g. Hawaii in 1898 such a people ceases to be admissible as a qualified belligerent, under the rules of international courtesy; and it will likewise be admitted that whenever any given community makes its way into free recognition as a belligerent, such recognition amounts to a recognition of the belligerent's national character. Of course these formalities are of the nature of diplomatic punctilio, and they do not gravely touch the substance of things; but then, the national integrity, the national honor, etc., also are always matters of formality and diplomatic punctilio, in great part; it will perhaps be admitted that they are of this nature in the main.

Such are the formalities of diplomatic and belligerent etiquette. But it does not follow that because a people can enter into the holy state of belligerency only as a nation and only on due observance of the national proprieties, that therefore such a people will necessarily be engaged in warlike enterprise only as a nation, and only on motives of national ambition. The present case of the United States may be taken to show the difference. This country entered on this enterprise only after a punctilious compliance with all the national courtesies in such cases made and provided, and on due allegation of specific national grievance to be redressed. But it has been an open secret from beforehand, and it has been made abundantly plain by the American administration since then, that the substantial motive of this enterprise has no color of national ambition. The national grievances alleged in the formal declaration were grave enough, no doubt; the record of them comprises an inordinate destruction of life and property and a remarkable series of crimes and atrocities; and yet it can fairly be said that the redressing of these national grievances is not of the essence of the contract which the country has undertaken.

The abiding purpose of America in the war is to bring about a settled state of peace and security. If all this is accomplished, then any national establishment may come to have little more than a decorative use; as a political agency it will be in a fair way to become obsolete through disuse What would be needed to put things in train for such an outcome would be that the pacific peoples pool their political issues; somewhat after the fashion in which they are now beginning to learn that it is expedient to pool their issues and their forces in the conduct of the war. It will probably not be questioned that this pooling of forces and issues for the conduct of the war is likely to go much farther than it has done hitherto, in case the war continues for an appreciable length of time; and the suggestion is ready to hand that the international pool so entered into under pressure of the war had best be designed on such lines that it may also eventually serve to keep the peace.

This would mean a further pooling of national issues in those respects in which national issues are apt to bring on dissension; which means issues of national ambition and issues of business enterprise under national auspices. But national ambition, in the way of territorial aggrandizement or warlike dominion, is a dead issue in America - it has been weighed and found wanting; so that, in effect, all that still remains in question is the issue between national business enterprise and free trade. Now, in the new era, and for the sake of peace and international good-will, will the American citizens be content to forego preferential advantages at the nation's cost - for such of their compatriots as are interested in tariff-protected industries, or are engaged in the foreign trade, or derive an income from investments and concessions in foreign parts? It is to be admitted that this is still a matter of grave doubt. And it may be an over-sanguine hope, but there should at least be something of a chance that the nation may yet, under pressure of sore apprehension, bring itself also to pool these issues of business traffic along with the rest of what goes to nourish political intrigue. At any rate, in that direction lies the best assurance of peace and security at large. And if America gives a lead in the direction of such a disclaimer of national discrimination, the lead so given should reasonably be expected to go far to persuade the other pacific nations into a collusive disclaimer of the same kind.

The upshot of all this would be, of course, that the national establishment would in great part cease to function, whether as an engine of vacant political intrigue or as a handmaid of private commercial enterprise. If such an arrangement can be achieved, or in the degree in which such a result can be approached, the hazard of dissension will be removed from among those pacific nations whose international concerns so would come within the jurisdiction of that league of pacific peoples that is held in prospect by the wiser statesmen of our time. But all this covers only one half, perhaps the smaller and less precarious half, of the precarious situation that will face the American people on the return of peace - more particularly if the peace at large is once established on that stable footing to which all good men hopefully look forward. Let no man be deceived into believing that the removal of international friction will of itself bring in an era of tranquility at home. So soon as all apprehension of national danger is at an end, and preoccupation with international strategy has ceased to divert men's attention, the table will be cleared for a single-minded deliberation on the state of the country at home. And there is already visible such a cleavage of interests, sentiment and ambitions as may reasonably be taken to argue for a stormy reckoning ahead.

Considered as a going concern, collectively engaged in the traffic of human living, the American commonwealth is perhaps not ready to go into the hands of a receiver; perhaps a liquidation had best be avoided, although the widely apprehended need of a deliberate reconstruction might be taken to argue that in the mind of many thoughtful persons something like a liquidation is felt to be nearly due. There is, at the best, a widespread apprehension that the affairs of this going concern are in something of a precarious case. The case may not be so grave; but the derangement of conditions caused by the war, as well as the degree in which the public attention now centers on public questions, mark the present as the appointed time to take stock and adopt any necessary change in the domestic policy.

In assuming or accepting the assumption that there is need of some reconstruction, it is assumed that the system of use and wont under which the community now lives and does its work is not altogether suited to current circumstances. It is more or less out of date. This also carries the further assumption that the evil to be remedied is of a systematic character and that merely palliative measures will no longer serve. This involves the proposition that some realignment of the working parts is necessary even at the cost of deranging any vested rights and interests that may stand in the way. Indeed, any degree of closer attention to the problem and purpose involved m proposed reconstruction will bring out the fact that the prime object is to reach such a revision of vested rights and economic relations as will result in a more tolerable scheme of life and work. That is what reconstruction means it is a revision of vested rights, for the common good. What is to be avoided at all costs is the 'status quo ante.

An illustrative case may serve to show what is intended by the phrase "vested rights," in the more comprehensive sense. In modern industry, as conducted by the methods of big business, it is one of the vested rights of the owner or employer freely to engage workmen on any terms on which they can be got, and to discharge them at discretion. It is another of his vested rights freely to employ as many or as few men as may suit his purpose, which is a quest of profits, and to work his own industrial plant more or less nearly up to its capacity, or not at all, as may suit his own purpose, in his quest of profits. On the other hand, among the vested rights of the workmen, or at least claimed as such, is their right to a job; so also an alleged right to discriminate as to what other men are to be associated with them on the job; also a right to quit work when they choose, i.e., to strike at discretion.

But taken in the large and seen from the point of view of the interest of the community, these vested rights and interests of the two parties in controversy will figure up to something that may be called a right to exercise an unlimited sabotage, in order to gain a private end, regardless of the community's urgent need of having the work go on without interruption and at full capacity. The slowing down or stoppage of the industrial process at any point or on any plea by those who control the equipment or the personnel of industry works mischief to the community by that much, and falls short of that service which the community has a right to expect.

In such a case, it is evident, the vested interests so working at cross purposes are thereby cheating the community of the full benefit of the modern state of the industrial arts; and it is plain that such a case of interests working at cross purposes is a fit subject of revision; such revision as will bring the industrial process to the highest practicable efficiency and reduce the sum of ill-will among the persons engaged to the lowest practicable dimensions. It should also be plain that the revision must be made primarily with a view to set up a condition of things that shall bring as much as may be of usefulness and content, and with only a secondary regard to the present vested interests of any one of the persons concerned.

This case of conflict between employer and employees, between the owner of plant and the owner of workmanlike skill and power, may serve to show what is here intended by incompatible or mismatched vested interests. It is not here intended to find fault with either party to such a conflict. It is unreservedly assumed that they are all honorable men and all within their rights, as these rights have been allowed to stand hitherto. It is because the existing arrangement, quite legitimately and dispassionately, works out in a running campaign of sabotage, that the whole matter is to come up for a revision and realignment in which vested interests are to be set aside, under a higher necessity than the received specifications of use and wont and law. It is not that the conduct of the persons concerned is to be adjudged immoral, illegitimate or improper; it is only that it, and the kind and degree of discretion which it involves, have in the course of time become insufferable, and are to be disallowed on the ground of urgent expediency. It is also no part of the present argument to indicate what ought, as a matter of expediency, to be done toward the elimination of "labor troubles." That will require knowledge, wisdom, patience and charity of a higher order.

The points and passages in the conduct of industrial affairs at which vested interests work at cross purposes among themselves or at cross purposes with the common good, are many and various, and it could serve no purpose to attempt an enumeration of them here. There are few lines of industry or trade where nothing of the sort occurs. The inefficiency of current railway enterprise, e. g. f as seen from the point of view of mal usefulness, has forced itself on the attention of the Administration under pressure of the war situation; so has the privately owned production and distribution of coal and the handling and distribution of food products. Shipping is coming under the same charge of costly incompetency, and the oil, steel, copper, and timber supply are only less obviously getting into the same general category of public utilities legitimately mishandled for private gain.

But to enumerate instances of such cross purposes between vested interests and the common good would scarcely be fruitful of anything but irritation. It may be more to the purpose to indicate what are the characteristics of the modern industries by virtue of which their business-like management comes to work at cross purposes with the needs of the community or of given classes in the community, and then to look for something like a systematic remedial treatment which might hopefully be turned to account - in case some person or persons endowed with insight and convictions were also charged with power to act.

It is believed that this working at cross purposes commonly and in a way necessarily, though not always, will rise to disquieting proportions when and in so far as the industrial process concerned has taken on such a character of routine, automatic articulation, or mechanical correlation, as to admit of its being controlled from a distance by such means of accountancy as are at the disposal of a modern business office. In many, perhaps in most cases this will imply an industrial plant of some appreciable size, with a correspondingly large force of employees; but much the same" outcome may also be had where that is not the case, as, e. g., an enterprise in automatic vending machines, a "news company," so-called, or a baggage-transfer concern of the larger sort.

The mischief which such a situation gives rise to may be either or both of two distinguishable kinds: disagreement and ill-will between employers and employees, and mischievous waste, expense and disservice imposed on the concern's customers. Not unusually the large and formidable concerns classed as big business will be found censurable on both counts. Again it is necessary to recall that this is not intended as implying that such management is blameworthy, but only that a businesslike management under such circumstances and within its prescriptive rights results in the untoward consequences here spoken of.

If this account of the state of things out of which mischief of this character is wont to arise is substantially correct, the description of the circumstances carries its own suggestion as to what should be a promising line of remedial measures. The mischief appears to arise out of, or in concomitance with, the disjunction of ownership and discretion from the personal direction of the work; and it appears to take on an added degree of mischance as soon as the discretionary control vested in ownership comes to be exercised by an employer who has no personal contact with the employees, and who has only a pecuniary acquaintance with the industrial processes employed or with the persons whose needs these processes are presumed to serve - that is to say, as soon as the man or staff in control pass into the class of supernumeraries, in respect to the mechanical work to be done, and retain only a pecuniary interest and habitually exercise only a pecuniary control.

Under these circumstances this central or superior control can evidently as well be exercised by some person who has no pecuniary interest in the enterprise, and who is therefore free to manage the industry with a view to its fullest usefulness and to the least practicable generation of ill-will on the side of the employees. Roughly speaking, any industrial process which can, and in so far as it can, be sufficiently well managed from a more or less remote office by methods of accountancy and for financial ends, can also, by the same token, be managed by a disinterested administrative officer without other than formal recourse to accountancy and without other than a secondary view to pecuniary results.

All of which patently goes to sum up the needed remedial measures, under two heads: (1) Disallowance of anything like free discretionary control or management on grounds of ownership alone, whether at first hand or delegated, whenever the responsible owner of the concern does not at the same time also personally oversee and physically direct the work in which hi- property is engaged, and in so far as he is not habitually engaged in the work in fellowship with his employees; (2) to take over and administer as a public utility any going concern that is in control of industrial or commercial work which has reached such a state of routine, mechanical systematization, or automatic articulation as to be habitually managed from an office by methods of accountancy.

Needless to say that when set out in this bald fashion, such a proposed line of remedial measures will appear to be shockingly subversive of law and order - iniquitous, impracticable, perhaps socialistic. And it is needless to argue its merits as it stands; particularly not to argue its merits within the equities of the existing law and order. Yet it may be as well to recall that any plan of reconstruction which shall hope to be of any slightest use for its main purpose must begin by violating one or another of the equities of the existing law and order. A reconstruction means a revision of the present working system, the present system of vested interests, and of the scheme of equities within which that system is now working at cross purposes with the common good. It is a question of how and how far a disallowance of these existing vested interests is to be carried out. And the two propositions set out above are, therefore, intended to mark the direction which such a remedial disallowance of prescriptive rights will obviously take; not the limit to which such a move will necessarily go. They are intended to indicate the method, not the degree, of correction that appears to be expedient.

There is no socialistic iconoclasm in it all, either covert or overt; nor need any slightest animus of moral esteem or disesteem be injected into the argument at any point. It is a simple matter of material expediency, in which one of the prime factors to be considered is the growing prospect of an inordinate popular distrust. And the point of it all is that the present system of managing the country's larger industrial concerns by business methods in behalf of vested interests is proving itself bankrupt under the strain of the war situation; so much so that it is already more than doubtful if the community at large will hereafter be content to leave its larger material interests at the mercy of those business motives, business methods, and business men whose management is now shown to work such waste and confusion as can not be tolerated at a critical time. The system of vested rights and interests is up for revision, reconstruction, realignment, with a view to the material good and the continued tranquillity of the community at large; and there is therefore a call for a workable scope and method of reconstructing the existing scheme of law and order on such lines as will insure popular content. In this bearing, the meaning of "reconstruction" is that America is to be made safe for the common man in his own apprehension as well as in substantial fact. Current events in Russia, for instance, attest that it is a grave mistake to let a growing disparity between vested rights and the current conditions of life overpass the limit of tolerance.

PHILOSOPHY

Chapter 1
Kant's Critique of Judgment

The place of the Critique of Judgment in Kant's system of philosophy is that of a mean between the two Critiques of the Pure and of the Practical Reason. A feeling of e lack of coherence between the other two critiques prompted him to the elaboration of this one, and the Doctrine of Method at the close of the work is mainly a sketch of the way in which he conceived that the results of this Critique were to be made useful in the system of philosophy to which he regarded all his critical work as preliminary. The outcome of the Critique of Practical Reason is the notion of freedom in the person; the outcome of the Critique of Pure Reason is the notion of strict determinism, according to natural law, in the world. It will hardly do to say that the two are contradictory, for they are so thoroughly disparate that, taken by themselves only and placed in juxtaposition, they do not even contradict each other. It is well known that it was on account of this disparity of the two notions that Kant was able to hold to the reality of personal freedom at the same time that he held to the doctrine of unavoidable determination according to natural law. But while he found the disparity of the two indispensable in order to the reality of freedom, he also found that, in order to free activity, a mediation between the two was likewise indispensable.

The idea of freedom of moral action contains the requirement that the concepts of morality are to be actualised in the sphere of rational law. Without the possibility of realising the concepts of morality in the realm of nature-without ability to affect events in the course of nature-morality would be only a fiction. The free person must be able to exert a causality on things, or else his freedom would be only an absurdity; but, even if it be granted that the person can and does come into the course of events as an efficient cause, that is not enough. Thus far the conclusions of the Critique of Practical Reason reach, but Kant was not satisfied with that. The action of the person must be capable of falling in with the line of activity of the causes among which it comes; otherwise it will act blindly and to no purpose. The agent must know what will be the effect of this or that action, if his activity is not to be nugatory, or worse than nugatory. And, in order to such a knowledge of the results of a contemplated action, the knowledge furnished by simple experience is not sufficient. Simple experience, whether we accept Kant's doctrine concerning the knowledge given by experience, as he has developed it in the Critique of Pure Reason, or not, cannot forecast the future.

Experience can, at the best, give what is or what has been, but cannot say what is to be. It gives data only, and data never go into the future unaided and of their own accord. Data do not tell what the effect of action will be, except as we are able to judge the future by the help of the data given. judgment must come in, if experience is to be of any use, and morality anything more than a dream. The power of judgment, or of reasoning, must mediate between theoretical knowledge and moral action; and the kind of judgment that is required is inductive reasoning. All this is simple enough. It is so simple and is so obvious that it is difficult to see it until it has been pointed out, and after it has been pointed out it seems to have been unnecessary to speak of it. Though Kant, in giving his reasons for undertaking the Critique of Judgment, speaks mainly of the indispensableness of this power of inductive reasoning for the purposes of morality, it is evident that it is no less indispensable in every other part of practical life. Today any attempt, in any science, which does not furnish us an induction, is counted good for nothing, and it is with this power of inductive reasoning that the most important part of the Critique of Judgment has to do.

In Kant's trichotomous scheme of the faculties and capacities of the intellect, the Power of judgment lies in the middle, between the Understanding and the Reason, just as the faculty of pleasure and pain lies between the faculties of cognition and of desire, and affords a connection and mediation between the two. The Understanding has to do with cognition, and is a priori legislative for empirical knowledge; the pure Reason has to do with desire, and is a priori legislative for action; by analogy we should be able to say, at least provisionally, that the Power of judgment has to do with the capacity of pleasure and pain, and legislates a priori concerning the adequate or subservient, the commensurate, appropriate, or adapted (das Zweckmässige).The Power of judgment is, in general, the power of thinking the particular under the universal. "If the universal (the rule, the principle, the law) is given, then the judgment which subsumes the particular under it is determinative. [Deductive reasoning.] But if only the particular is given, for which the judgment is to find a universal, then the judgment is only reflective. [Inductive reasoning.] (Kr. d. Urtheilskraft, ed. K. Kehrbach, 1878; Einl., IV.) Inasmuch as this Critique is a critique of the pure Power of judgment only-i.e., of the Power of judgment in so far as none of the principles of its action are borrowed from elsewhere-it has to do only with the reflective judgment; for, in order that the judgment be determinative, the universal which is to serve it as a rule in the work of subsumption must be given, and so must be present as a premise, and will condition the action of the judgment working under it. The determinative judgment is simply the activity of the intellect in general in applying the laws given by Understanding and Reason, and, as such, its action has been analysed in the two critiques which treat of those faculties. The determinative judgment, subsuming particular data under general laws which are also data, is nothing but the activity of the Understanding in combining simple experience into a synthetic whole, under those laws of the Understanding which are a necessary condition of experience. Therefore the discussion of the determinative judgment belongs in the critique of the theoretical Reason. The reflective judgment passes beyond the simple data of experience and seeks a universal which is not given in empirical cognition; therefore it must proceed according to a principle not given to it from without. It has a power of self-direction, and therefore calls for a critique of its own.

This is the starting-point of the Critique of Judgment, and, if this had been borne in mind, it might have saved many of Kant's critics a good deal of mistaken criticism. As a rule, the criticisms offered on his doctrine of Teleology have gone to work as though his starting-point had been from the developed principle of Final Cause, and as though he had proceeded from that principle to the notion of adaptation, and thence to that of aesthetic appropriateness, which is precisely reversing the truth. They have taken up the Critique wrong end foremost, and it is no wonder that they have found fault with it. Kant's doctrine of Final Cause is arrived at from a consideration of the way in which the reflective judgment works; the nature of the reflective judgment is not deduced from a preconceived notion about finality.

The office of the reflective judgment is to find unity in multiplicity, or to give unity to multiplicity. Its action is not only synthetic, but it is to make a synthesis which shall reach beyond, and include more than what is given in simple experience. The problem of this Critique, as of the other two, is: How are synthetic judgments a priori possible? But, while the faculties under consideration in the other two Critiques have to do with laws unavoidably given and unavoidably applied to given data, the reflective judgment has to find the laws to be applied to given data. The reflective judgment is the faculty of search. It is the faculty of adding to our knowledge something which is not and cannot be given in experience. It is to reduce the manifold of nature, the various concepts we have of the things in the world, to a synthetic totality. It has to bring the facts given in experience under laws and principles, and to bring empirical concepts under higher concepts. Whatever is ascertained, and so becomes an item of knowledge, becomes therewith a point of departure for the reflective judgment. The reflective judgment is continually reaching over beyond the known, and grasping at that which cannot come within experience. Its object is a synthesis, a systematisation of whatever is known; and, in order to the attainment of a system, its procedure must be governed by some principle.

As the result aimed at lies beyond experience, the principle according to which it is to proceed cannot be given by experience. The principle is not taken from outside the power of judgment, for, if such were the case, the judgment working under that principle would be determinative and not reflective; therefore the principle according to which the reflective judgment proceeds must originate with the reflective judgment itself; or, in other words, it must be an a priori principle of the intellect, and must hold its place as a principle only in relation to the reflective judgment. It cannot be the same principle, in the same form, as any of the principles governing the other faculties.

The nature of this principle is to be found from a consideration of the work it is to do. The reflective judgment is to generalise, to reduce our knowledge to a system under more general laws than any given by experience. Its office is to systematise, and to systematise is but another expression for reducing things to intelligent orders; that is, to think things as though they had been made according to the laws of an understanding, to think them as though made by an intelligent cause. But to think things in a system as though they were made by an intelligent cause is not the same as to think that they are made by such a cause. So much is not required by the principle. All that is required is that the things be thought as falling under a system of law according to which they adapt themselves to the laws of our understanding - that they are such in the manner of their being as they would be if they were made with a view to the exigencies of our capacity of knowing. The principle of the reflective judgment is, therefore, primarily the requirement of adaptation on the part of the object to the laws of the activity of our faculties of knowledge, or, briefly, adaptation to our faculties.

Now, whenever the intellect finds the objects of its knowledge to be such as to admit of the unhampered activity of the faculties employed about them, there results a gratification such as is always felt on the attainment of an end striven for. The more nearly the concept of the object known approaches to what such a concept might have been if it had been constructed simply under the guidance of the laws of the mind's own activity and without being in any way hindered or modified by external reality - that is, the more nearly the activity of the mind in thinking a given thought coincides with what would be the mind's activity if that activity were guided by its own intrinsic laws alone and were not influenced or hampered by the environment - the more fully will the requirements of the mind's activity be realised, and the more intense will be the gratification felt in contemplating the object of thought which so employs the mind. A feeling of gratification, or the contrary, accordingly, goes along with the activity of the reflective judgment as a sanction and a test of its normality.

What this feeling of gratification testifies to is, that the play of the faculties of the intellect is free, or but little hampered by the empirical element in its knowledge. It therefore indicates that the objects contemplated are, in the form in which they are present in thought, adapted to the faculties. This adaptation of knowledge to our faculties may take place in two different ways, or rather it may take place at two different stages in the elaboration of the material gained by experience. A simple datum may be given to the apprehension such as to conform to the normal action of our faculty of knowledge, and, by its so conforming, it shows adaptation to the faculties that are employed about it. In such a case, the concept which is contemplated and found adapted is not thereby an item of knowledge which goes to make up our conception of the world system, or to make a part of any systematic or organised whole. As a datum of the apprehension, it is considered singly by itself only in relation to the apprehending subject, no thought being given to its making or not making an integral part of our knowledge of reality. In so far as concerns the adaptation conceived to belong to the concept, it is no matter whether any external reality corresponds to the concept or not; and, therefore, it makes no difference, as to the adaptation, whether the concept is derived from experience or is a pure figment.

The adaptation belonging to such a concept, which is only a datum of the apprehension, is, therefore, subjective only. It is only a question of the conformation or non-conformation of a simple concept (Vorstellung) to the norms of the apprehension. The question is, how far the concept given is suited to the normal activity of the faculty of cognition; whatever may be the objective validity of the concept, that does not enter into consideration at all. This being the case, the only way to judge of the adaptation of such a concept is to take cognisance of the way in which the faculties act on occasion of it, and the test can only be whether the faculties act unhampered and satisfactorily; and the only indication of the normal activity of the faculties, again, is the resulting feeling of gratification or dissatisfaction. If the concept, simply as such, pleases, it is normal or adapted; if it displeases, it is not. The object corresponding to such a concept. which pleases in its simple apprehension, is said to be beautiful, and the reflective judgment, in so far as it proceeds on the simple adaptation of the data of apprehension to the faculties of cognition, is aesthetic judgment. It is of a purely subjective character, and its action is not based on logical, but wholly on pathological grounds. The decision of the aesthetic judgment is made on the ground of the feeling called forth by the apprehension of the concept, and the feeling is, therefore, in this case, the only authority that has a voice in the matter.

From these considerations it follows that there can be no objective principle of aesthetic judgment. The principle which governs taste must accordingly exert its authority, not through the means of logical argument and proof, but by an appeal to the nature of men in respect to reflective judgment in general. "The principle of taste is the subjective principle of the judgment in general" (Kr. d. U., p. 148). The universal validity which a judgment in a matter of taste bespeaks can, therefore, rest only on the assumption of an essential similarity of all men in respect to the feeling involved in such a judgment.

On the other hand, the data of cognition may also be contemplated, with reference to their adaptation, at the stage at which they are no longer simple data of apprehension, but constitute a part of our knowledge of reality. That is, they (the concepts) may be considered as making a part of our knowledge of nature, and, consequently, as entering into a system in which they must stand in relation to other data. Their adaptation will consequently here be found, if at all, in the logical relations of concepts-items of empirical knowledge or laws of nature - to one another, and the conformity of these relations to the normal activity of the faculties; not in the immediate adaptation of particular items or data of experience to be taken up by the faculties, as was the case in the aesthetic judgment. And since the faculties, in dealing with the relations of concepts as making up our knowledge of reality, have to do with the relations of real objects as known to us, the relations of the concepts, in which the adaptation is supposed to lie, are here conceived to be real relations of objects; the adaptation of these concepts, as standing in logical relations to one another, to the normal activity of the mind, therefore comes to be looked on as a quality of the objects contemplated. The objects are conceived to stand in such relations of dependence and interaction as correspond to the logical relations of the concepts we have of them.

Now, as a matter of fact, the connection or relation of our concepts which will be found adapted to our faculties, and which answers the requirements of their normal action, is one according to which they make a systematic, connected whole. The relations of objects which shall correspond in the world of reality to this logical relation of our concepts are such relations of interaction and interdependence as will bind the particular things in the world of reality together into a whole, in which the existence of one thing is dependent on that of another, and in which no one thing can exist without mutually conditioning and being conditioned by every other. That is, the adaptation found, or sought to be found, in concepts when contemplated in their logical aspect, is conceived to be an adaptation of things to one another in such a way that each is at the same time the means and the end of the existence of every other. Such a conception of the world of reality, in which things are united into an organised whole, can proceed only on the assumption that the particular things which go to make up the organic whole are subject to laws of a character similar to that of the logical laws according to which our mind subsumes the particular under the general, and holds together all the material gained by our cognition in a systematic totality of knowledge; which is the same as saying that in such a conception is contained the idea that the world is made according to laws similar to the laws of our understanding, and therefore that it is made by an intelligent cause, and made with intention and purpose. To put the same thing in another way:

To conceive the world in the way required by the reflective judgment is to conceive it as being made so as to harmonise with the laws of our understanding; that is, in being made, it is adapted to our faculties, and therefore made by a cause working according to laws like those of our understanding, and with a view to the exigencies of our understanding in comprehending the world. The cause producing the world must therefore be conceived to have worked it out according to a preconceived notion of what it was to be, and the realization of the form in which the world so created actually exists, accordingly, has its ground in an idea conceived by the cause which created it. The idea of what the world was to be precedes and conditions the world as it actually comes into existence-which is precisely what we mean when we say that the world was created by final cause. All this argument for a final cause in the world rests on the action of the reflective judgment, and its validity therefore extends only so far as the principle of the reflective judgment reaches. That principle is the requirement of adaptation, on the part of our knowledge, to the normal action of our faculties of knowing; it is therefore of subjective validity only, and can say nothing as to the nature of external reality. The finality which is attributed to external reality, on the ground of the adaptation found by the reflective judgment, is simply and only an imputed finality, and the imputation of it to reality is based on the same ground of feeling as every other act of the reflective judgment. Our imputation of finality to the things of the world, and our teleological arguments for an intelligent cause of the world, proceed on subjective grounds entirely, and give no knowledge of objective fact, and furnish no proof that is available for establishing even a probability in favor of what is claimed.

What is proved by the tenacity with which we cling to our teleological conception of the world is, that the constitution of our intellect demands this conception - that our faculties, in their normal action, must arrive at this before they can find any halting-place. The mind is not satisfied with its knowledge of a thing, or of any event or fact, until it is able to say, not only how the thing is, or how it came about, but also why it is as it is, and what was the purpose of its coming to pass. At least it must be able to assert, before it will rest from its search, that the thing or event has a purpose; the proposition may be put into this general form, and we may be obliged, oftentimes, to leave the matter in this state of generality; but we cannot believe, concerning anything, that there is no reason why it is, or why it is as it is. It is, of course, possible to give our attention to any item of knowledge - to employ ourselves about any object or any process or law in nature - without bringing in the notion of purpose; but our knowledge of it cannot be regarded as complete until we have asked the question why it is.

But though this question of teleology is of extreme importance, yet a knowledge of the teleological end of a given thing, or the purpose of an action or event as considered from the standpoint of the economy of the universe, is not absolutely necessary in order to human life, nor even in order to a high degree of development in moral life. In truth, a knowledge of ultimate particular ends and purposes is of no use whatever in the affairs of everyday life; and, therefore, the principle of teleology, as being the principle of conscious purpose in the world, is not indispensable in order to such knowledge of things as is required by the exigencies of life. The knowledge we need and use can be got, and got in sufficient completeness for all purposes of utility, without any appeal to, or any aid from, the developed principle of finality; and, if the exercise of the reflective judgment, in its logical application, consisted in the decision of teleological questions alone, its value would be small enough. Such, however, is not the case.

The principle of the logical use of the reflective judgment was found to be the general principle of adaptation; and since, in its logical use, the judgment has to do with reality, the principle which shall govern the reflective judgment here will be that of objective adaptation; that is, adaptation which is conceived to belong to things objectively. The motive which leads to the application of this principle to our knowledge of things was found to be a feeling of dissatisfaction with our knowledge so long as it consists only in a chaotic manifold of concepts. We are dissatisfied with a conception of reality which makes it only a congeries of things, without connection, system, or order, beyond juxtaposition in space and succession and duration in time. Yet such a congeries is all that unaided experience can give; and the determinative (deductive) judgment can do little to bring further order into this chaos. It is true, we have the general law of cause and effect given, and it looks as though we ought to be able to establish some system by the aid of it, when experience gives us the data to which the law applies; but further thought will show that we should be as helpless with that law as without it if no further principle came in to guide us in the application of it. We should have the law which says:

Every change has a cause and an effect"; and all that the data of experience would enable us to say further would be that this law in general applies to these data. The abstract law and the data, simply under the action of the determinative judgment, could never get so far as to afford us ground for asserting that a given effect has a given cause; still less that a given cause will produce a given effect. The truth of this is shown by the nature of our knowledge of particular causes. We can never designate, with that certainty which belongs to every deliverance of the deductive judgment, what is the cause of any given effect.

We may have no doubt as to what is the cause of a given effect; but still, if it should turn out that the effect under consideration has some other cause than the one we counted on, we should not, therefore, conclude that the world is out of joint. It is possible that we may be mistaken in our opinion as to particular cases of cause and effect - even the most certain of them - which would not be the case if we arrived at our knowledge of them by simple deductive reasoning from data of experience and an a priori law. There is always an element of probability, however slight, in our knowledge of particular causes; but simple experience - cognition - never has anything to say about probability; it only says what is, and leaves no room for doubt or probability.

In order to find what is the cause of a given effect, and, still more, what will be the effect of a given cause, we need a guiding principle beyond anything that experience gives. We have to go beyond what is given us, and so we need a principle of search. That is what is afforded by this principle of adaptation. The mind is unsatisfied with things until it can see how they belong together. The principle of adaptation says that the particular things do belong together, and sets the mind hunting to find out how. The principle of adaptation says that, in order to the normal action of the faculties, things must be conceived as adapted to one another so as to form a systematic totality - that things must be conceived to be so co-ordinated in their action as to make up an organized whole - and the mind goes to make its knowledge of reality conform to its own normal activity; or, in other words, to find what particular cases of interaction under the law of cause and effect will stand the test of the principle of adaptation. What the principle of adaptation does for us is, therefore, in the first place, that it makes us guess, and that it guides our guessing. If it were not that we are dissatisfied with our knowledge so long as it remains in the shape of a mere manifold, we should never seek to get beyond a congeries of things in time and space; and, if it were not that the principle of adaptation shows us what we are to seek further, we should never find anything further in our knowledge.

But the principle of adaptation cannot give us any new data, nor can it tell us anything new about the data we have. All it can do is to guide us in guessing about the given data, and then leave it to experience to credit or discredit our guesses. That is, it is a regulative, not a constitutive principle

of knowledge, according to the distinction which Kant makes in his classification of a priori principles of the mind. Now, as has already been pointed out, the direction in which this principle will lead us is that of generalisation, since no such principle is needed in order to deductive reasoning.
In order to analyse the content of our empirical knowledge, there is no
guessing necessary; all that is then required is that we take a more complete inventory of what we already know. The guessing, under the principle of adaptation, is in the direction of a higher systematisation of what we
know.

The principle suggests that, in order to conform to the norms of our faculties, things should fall into a system under laws of such or such a character; that they should stand in such or such relations of interaction and co-
ordination; and that the laws which are given a priori as applying to things
should apply to them in such or such a way; and so it leads to an hypothesis as to the nature of particular things and the laws of their connection.
The principle guides us to an hypothesis, but it has nothing to say as to the
validity of the hypothesis in the world of reality. It proceeds on the basis of
a feeling, and so it can decide whether the hypothesis suits the mind, but
not at all whether it applies to reality. Experience alone can say whether
the hypothesis fits the things it is intended for; or, rather, it can say whether it appears to fit them, since, inasmuch as an hypothesis never can become an object of experience in the same sense as things are objects of
experience, it can also not have that empirical certainty which belongs to
our knowledge of individual things. The testimony of experience as to the
validity of the hypothesis can only be of a cumulative character, and all it
can do is to give it a greater or less degree of probability. It is of the nature
of circumstantial evidence.

The principle of adaptation, in its logical use, is accordingly the principle
of inductive reasoning. The need felt by the mind of bringing order and
systematic coherence into the knowledge it acquires, and therefore of
conceiving the things about which it is engaged as adapted to one another,
affords, at the same time, the motive and the guiding principle for induction. The unrest felt on account of the inharmonious and forced activity of
the faculties, when engaged about a mere manifold or a discordant mis-
cellany, drives the mind to seek a concord for its own activities, and, consequently, a reconciliation of the conflicting elements of its knowledge.
The reason for the unrest felt in contemplating external things simply as
individual and unconnected things lies in the fact that the mind is adapted
to conceive the subject-matter of its knowledge in the form of a connected
whole. If the mind had not an inherent capacity for thinking things as
connected into a totality, or at least as being connected in a systematic
way and under definite laws, it could not feel the lack of totality in contemplating things under the mere form of juxtaposition in time and space.
It would not be dissatisfied with things as mere data if it knew of nothing
better; and it would not seek for anything different if the conception of
things, as a mere congeries, satisfied the requirements of its normal activity.

But the requirement of totality, of adaptation of part to part, being present, the mind has no alternative but to reflect and reflect on the material given it, and make the most it can out of it in the way of a systematic whole; and the requirement of adaptation points out the direction which its search must take. One consequence of this is that the search is never ended, as, from the nature of the case, the requirement can never be fulfilled. As soon as a result is obtained by the process of induction, that result becomes, for the purposes of the question in hand, a fact of empirical knowledge, and therefore acquires the character, not of a completed whole, but of an isolated and disconnected datum. As fast as one step of induction is completed it becomes a means to another step, which must inevitably follow it.

According to what has just been said, the motive and guiding principle of inductive reasoning, and, with it, of the teleological judgment, is the requirement of adaptation or totality in our knowledge. When we find this requirement answered, in greater or less degree, the consequence is more or less of a feeling of gratification, just as there is always a feeling of gratification on the successful completion of an undertaking, or the attainment of a desired end. This feeling of gratification may therefore be regarded as a sanction to the principle of the reflective judgment, and, in the last resort, it is this feeling of gratification alone which can decide whether the principle has been applied successfully in any given case.

Therefore, so far as concerns the distinctive characteristics of the reflective judgment - and, therefore, of inductive reasoning - it proceeds on subjective ground entirely. Its motive is subjective, and, though the evidence by which it seeks to establish the results aimed at is of empirical origin, yet the criterion, to which the result must conform in order to answer the purposes for which it is sought to be established, is subjective.

The consequence of this subjectivity of the principle of induction is that the results it arrives at are only more or less probable. Yet, singular as it might seem, hardly any part of our knowledge except that got by induction is of any immediate use for practical purposes. For by induction alone can we reduce things to system and connection, and so bring particular things and events under definite laws of interaction; therefore by induction alone can we get such knowledge as will enable us to forecast the future; and knowledge which shall help us to forecast the future - to tell what will take place under given circumstances and as the result of given actions - is the only knowledge which can serve as a guide in practical life, whether moral or otherwise.

SOCIAL APPLICATIONS
OF EVOLUTIONARY REASONING

Chapter 1

The Evolution
of the Scientific Point of View

A discussion of the scientific point of view which avowedly proceeds from this point of view itself has necessarily the appearance of an argument in a circle; and such in great part is the character of what here follows. It is in large part an attempt to explain the scientific point of view in terms of itself, but not altogether. This inquiry does not presume to deal with the origin or the legitimation of the postulates of science, but only with the growth of the habitual use of these postulates, and the manner of using them. The point of inquiry is the changes which have taken place in the secondary postulates involved in the scientific point of view - in great part a question of the progressive redistribution of emphasis among the preconceptions under whose guidance successive generations of scientists have gone to their work.

The sciences which are in any peculiar sense modern take as an (unavowed) postulate the fact of consecutive change. Their inquiry always centers upon some manner of process. This notion of process about which the researches of modern science cluster, is a notion of a sequence, or complex, of consecutive change in which the nexus of the sequence, that by virtue of which the change inquired into is consecutive, is the relation of cause and effect. The consecution, moreover, runs in terms of persistence of quantity or of force. In so far as the science is of a modern complexion, in so far as it is not of the nature of taxonomy simply, the inquiry converges upon a matter of process; and it comes to rest, provisionally, when it has disposed of its facts in terms of process. But modern scientific inquiry in any case comes to rest only provisionally; because its prime postulate is that of consecutive change, and consecutive change can, of course, not come to rest except provisionally. By its own nature the inquiry cannot reach a final term in any direction. So it is something of a homiletical commonplace to say that the outcome of any serious research can only be to make two questions grow where one question grew before. Such is necessarily the case because the postulate of the scientist is that things change consecutively. It is an unproven and unprovable postulate - that is to say, it is a metaphysical preconception - but it gives the outcome that every goal of research is necessarily a point of departure; every term is transitional[39].

---

[39] It is by no means unusual for modern scientists to deny the truth of this characterization, so far as regards this alleged recourse to the concept of causation. They deny that such a concept - of efficiency, activity, and the like - enters, or can legitimately enter, into their work, whether as an instrument of research or as a means or

guide to theoretical formulation. They even deny the substantial continuity of the sequence of changes that excite their scientific attention. This attitude seems particularly to commend itself to those who by preference attend to the mathematical formulations of theory and who are chiefly occupied with proving up and working out details of the system of theory which have previously been left unsettled or uncovered. The concept of causation is recognized to be a metaphysical postulate, a matter of imputation, not of observation; whereas it is claimed that scientific inquiry neither does nor can legitimately, nor, indeed, currently, make use of a postulate more metaphysical than the concept of an idle concomitance of variation, such as is adequately expressed in terms of mathematical function. The contention seems sound, to the extent that the materials - essentially statistical materials - with which scientific inquiry is occupied are of this non-committal character, and that the mathematical formulations of theory include no further element than that of idle variation. Such is necessarily the case because causation is a fact of imputation, not of observation, and so cannot be included among the data; and because nothing further than non-committal variation can be expressed in mathematical terms. A bare notation of quantity can convey nothing further. If it were the intention to claim only that the conclusions of the scientists are, or should be, as a matter of conservative caution, overtly stated in terms of function alone, then the contention might well be allowed. Causal sequence, efficiency or continuity is, of course, a matter of metaphysical imputation. It is not a fact of observation, and cannot be asserted of the facts of observation except as a trait imputed to them. It is so imputed, by scientists and others, as a matter of logical necessity, as a basis of a systematic knowledge of the facts of observation. Beyond this, in their exercise of scientific initiative, as well as in the norms which guide the systematisation of scientific results, the contention will not be made good - at least not for the current phase of scientific knowledge. The claim, indeed, carries its own refutation. In making such a claim, both in rejecting the imputation of metaphysical postulates and in defending their position against their critics, the arguments put forward by the scientists run in causal terms. For the polemical purposes, where their antagonists are to be scientifically confuted, the defenders of the non-committal postulate of concomitance find that postulate inadequate. They are not content, in this precarious conjuncture, simply to attest a relation of idle quantitative concomitance (mathematical function) between the allegations of their critics, on the one hand. and their own controversial exposition of these matters on the other hand. They argue that they do not "make use of" such a postulate as "efficiency," whereas they claim to "make use of" the concept of function. But "make use of " is not a notion of functional variation but of causal efficiency in a somewhat gross and highly anthropomorphic form. The relation between their own thinking and the "principles" which they "apply" or the experiments and calculations which they "institute" in their "search" for facts, is not held to be of this non-committal kind. It will not be claimed that the shrewd insight and the bold initiative of a man eminent in the empirical sciences bear no more efficient or con sequential a relation than that of mathematical function to the ingenious experiments by which he tests his hypotheses and extends the secure bounds of human knowledge. Least of all is the masterly experimentalist himself in a position to deny that his intelligence counts for something more efficient than idle concomitance in such a case. The connection between his premises, hypotheses, and experiments, on the one hand, and his theoretical results, on the other hand, is not felt to be of the nature of mathematical function. Consistently adhered to, the principle of "function" or concomitant variation precludes recourse to experiment, hypotheses or inquiry - indeed, it precludes "recourse" to anything whatever. Its notation does not comprise anything so anthropomorphic. The case is

A hundred years ago, or even fifty years ago, scientific men were not in the habit of looking at the matter in this way. At least it did not then seem a matter of course, lying in the nature of things, that scientific inquiry could not reach a final term in any direction. To-day it is a matter of course, and will be so avowed without argument. Stated in the broadest terms, this is the substantial outcome of that nineteenth-century movement in science with which the name of Darwin is associated as a catch-word.

This use of Darwin's name does not imply that this epoch of science is mainly Darwin's work. What merit may belong to Darwin, specifically, in these premises, is a question which need not detain the argument. He may, by way of creative initiative, have had more or less to do with shaping the course of things scientific. Or, if you choose, his voice may even be taken as only one of the noises which the wheels of civilisation make when they go round. But by scientifically colloquial usage we have come to speak of pre-Darwinian and post-Darwinian science, and to appreciate that there is a significant difference in the point of view between the scientific era which preceded and that which followed the epoch to which his name belongs.

Before that epoch the animus of a science was, on the whole, the animus of taxonomy; the consistent end of scientific inquiry was definition and classification, - as it still continues to be in such fields of science as have not been affected by the modern notion of consecutive change. The scientists of that era looked to a final term, a consummation of the changes

---

illustrated by the latter-day history of theoretical physics. Of the sciences which affect a non-committal attitude in respect of the concept of efficiency and which claim to get along with the notion of mathematical function alone, physics is the most outspoken and the one in which the claim has the best prima facie validity. At the same time, latter-day physicists, for a hundred years or more, have been much occupied with explaining how phenomena which to all appearance involve action at a distance do not involve action at a distance at all. The greater theoretical achievements of physics during the past century lie within the sweep of this (metaphysical) principle that action at a distance does not take place, that apparent action at a distance must be explained by effective contact, through a continuum, or by a material transference. But this principle is nothing better than an unreasoning repugnance on the part of the physicists to admitting action at a distance. The requirement of a continuum involves a gross form of the concept of efficient causation. The "functional" concept, concomitant variation, requires no contact and no continuum. Concomitance at a distance is quite as simple and convincing a notion as concomitance within contact or by the intervention of a continuum, if not more so. What stands in the way of its acceptance is the irrepressible anthropomorphism of the physicists. And yet the great achievements of physics are due to the initiative of men animated with this anthropomorphic repugnance to the notion of concomitant variation at a distance. All the generalisations on undulatory motion and translation belong here. The latter-day researches in light, electrical transmission, the theory of ions, together with what is known of the obscure and late-found radiations and emanations, are to be credited to the same metaphysical preconception, which is never absent in any "scientific" inquiry in the field of physical science. It is only the "occult" and "Christian" "Sciences" that can dispense with this metaphysical postulate and take recourse to "absent treatment."

which provoked their inquiry, as well as to a first beginning of the matters with which their researches were concerned. The questions of science were directed to the problem, essentially classificatory, of how things had been in the presumed primordial stable equilibrium out of which they, putatively, bad come, and bow they should be in the definitive state of settlement into which things were to fall as the outcome of the play of forces which intervened between this primordial and the definitive stable equilibrium. To the pre-Darwinian taxonomists the center of interest and attention, to which all scientific inquiry must legitimately converge, was the body of natural laws governing phenomena under the rule of causation. These natural laws were of the nature of rules of the game of causation. They formulated the immutable relations in which things "naturally" stood to one another before causal disturbance took place between them, the orderly unfolding of the complement of causes involved in the transition over this interval of transient activity, and the settled relations that would supervene when the disturbance bad passed and the transition from cause to effect had been consummated, - the emphasis falling on the consummation.

The characteristic feature by which post-Darwinian science is contrasted with what went before is a new distribution of emphasis, whereby the process of causation, the interval of instability and transition between initial cause and definitive effect, has come to take the first place in the inquiry; instead of that consummation in which causal effect was once presumed to come to rest. This change of the point of view was, of course, not abrupt or catastrophic. But it has latterly gone so far that modern science is becoming substantially a theory of the process of consecutive change, which is taken as a sequence of cumulative change, realized to be self-continuing or self-propagating and to have no final term. Questions of a primordial beginning and a definitive outcome have fallen into abeyance within the modern sciences, and such questions are in a fair way to lose all claim to consideration at the hands of the scientists. Modern science is ceasing to occupy itself with the natural laws - the codified rules of the game of causation - and is concerning itself wholly with what has taken place and what is taking place.

Rightly seen from this ultra-modern point of view, this modern science and this point of view which it affects are, of course, a feature of the current cultural situation, - of the process of life as it runs along under our eyes. So also, when seen from this scientific point of view, it is a matter of course that any marked cultural era will have its own characteristic attitude and animus toward matters of knowledge, will bring under inquiry such questions of knowledge as lie within its peculiar range of interest, and will seek answers to these questions only in terms that are consonant with the habits of thought current at the time. That is to say, science and the scientific point of view will vary characteristically in response to those variations in the prevalent habits of thought which constitute the sequence of cultural development; the current science and the current scientific point of view, the knowledge sought and the manner of seeking it,

are a product of the cultural growth. Perhaps it would all be better characterised as a by-product of the cultured growth.

This question of a scientific point of view, of a particular attitude and animus in matters of knowledge, is a question of the formation of habits of
thought; and habits of thought are an outcome of habits of life. A scientific
point of view is a consensus of habits of thought current in the community, and the scientist is constrained] to believe that this consensus is formed
in response to a more or less consistent discipline of habituation to which
the community is subjected, and that the consensus can extend only so far
and maintain its force only so long as the discipline of habituation exercised by the circumstances of life enforces it and backs it up. The scheme
of life, within which lies the scheme of knowledge, is a consensus of habits
in the individuals which make up the community. The individual subjected to habituation is each a single individual agent, and whatever affects
him in any one line of activity, therefore, necessarily affects him in some
degree in all his various activities. The cultural scheme of any community
is a complex of the habits of life and of thought prevalent among the
members of the community. It makes up a more or less congruous and
balanced whole, and carries within it a more or less consistent habitual
attitude toward matters of knowledge - more or less consistent according
as the community's cultural scheme is more or less congruous throughout
the body of the population; and this in its turn is in the main a question of
how nearly uniform or consonant are the circumstances of experience and
tradition to which the several classes and members of the community are
subject.

So, then, the change which has come over the scientific point of view between pre-Darwinian and post-Darwinian times is to be explained, at least
in great

part, by the changing circumstances of life, and therefore of habituation,
among the people of Christendom during the life-history of modern science. But the growth of a scientific point of view begins farther back than
modern Christendom, and a record of its growth would be a record of the
growth of human culture. Modern science demands a genetic account of
the phenomena with which it deals, and a genetic inquiry into the scientific point of view necessarily will have to make up its account with the
earlier phases of cultural growth. A life-history of human culture is a large
topic, not to be attempted here even in the sketchiest outline. The most
that can be attempted is a hasty review of certain scattered questions and
salient points in this life-history.

In what manner and with what effect the idle curiosity of mankind first
began to tame the facts thrown in its way, far back in the night of time, and
to break them in under a scheme of habitual interpretation, what may
have been the earliest norms of systematic knowledge, such as would
serve the curiosity of the earliest generations of men in a way analogous to
the service rendered the curiosity of later generations by scientific inquiry
- all that is, of course, a matter of long-range conjecture, more or less wild,
which cannot be gone into here. But among such peoples of the lower cultures as have been consistently observed, norms of knowledge and

schemes for its systematization are always found. These norms and systems of knowledge are naive and crude, perhaps, but there is fair ground for presuming that out of the like norms and systems in the remoter ages of our own antecedents have grown up the systems of knowledge cultivated by the peoples of history and by their representatives now living.

It is not unusual to say that the primitive systems of knowledge are constructed on animistic lines; that animistic sequence is the rule to which the facts are broken in. This seems to be true, if "animism" be construed in a sufficiently naive and inchoate sense. But this is not the whole case. In their higher generalisations, in what Powell calls their "sophiology," it appears that the primitive peoples are guided by animistic norms; they make up their cosmological schemes, and the like, in terms of personal or quasi-personal activity, and the whole is thrown into something of a dramatic form. Through the early cosmological lore runs a dramatic consistency which imputes something in the way of initiative and propensity to the phenomena that are to be accounted for. But this dramatisation of the facts, the accounting for phenomena in terms of spiritual or quasi-spiritual initiative, is by no means the whole case of primitive men's systematic knowledge of facts. Their theories are not all of the nature of dramatic legend, myth, or animistic life-history, although the broader and more picturesque generalisations may take that form. There always runs along by the side of these dramaturgic life-histories, and underlying them, an obscure system of generalisations in terms of matter-of-fact. The system of matter-of-fact generalisations, or theories, is obscurer than the dramatic generalisations only in the sense that it is left in the background as being less picturesque and of less vital interest, not in the sense of being less familiar, less adequately apprehended, or less secure.

The peoples of the lower cultures "know" that the broad scheme of things is to be explained in terms of creation, perhaps of procreation, gestation, birth, growth, life and initiative; and these matters engross the attention and stimulate speculation. But they know equally well the matter of fact that water will run down hill, that two stones are heavier than one of them, that an edge-tool will cut softer substances, that two things may be tied together with a string, that a pointed stick may be stuck in the ground, and the like. There is no range of knowledge that is held more securely by any people than such matters of fact; and these are generalisations from experience; they are theoretical knowledge, and they are a matter of course. They underlie the dramatical generalisations of the broad scheme of things, and are so employed in the speculations of the myth-makers and the learned.

It may be that the exceptional efficiency of a given edge-tool, e.g., will be accounted for on animistic or quasi-personal grounds, - grounds of magical efficacy; but it is the exceptional behavior of such a tool that calls for explanation on the higher ground of animistic potency, not its work-day performance of common work. So also if an edge-tool should fail to do what is expected of it as a matter of course, its failure may require an explanation in other terms than matter-of-fact. But all that only serves to bring into evidence the fact that a scheme of generalisations in terms of matter-of-fact is securely held and is made use of as a sufficient and ulti-mate explanation of the more familiar phenomena of experience. These commonplace matter-of-fact generalisations are not questioned and do not clash with the higher scheme of things.

All this may seem like taking pains about trivialities. But the data with which any scientific inquiry has to do are trivialities in some other bearing than that one in which they are of account. In all succeeding phases of culture, developmentally subsequent to the primitive phase supposed above, there is found a similar or analogous division of knowledge be-tween a higher range of theoretical explanations of phenomena, an ornate scheme of things, on the one hand, and such an obscure range of matter-of-fact generalisations as is here spoken of, on the other hand. And the evolution of the scientific point of view is a matter of the shifting fortunes which have in the course of cultural growth overtaken the one and the other of these two divergent methods of apprehending and systematising the facts of experience.

The historians of human culture have, no doubt justly, commonly dealt with the mutations that have occurred on the higher levels of intellectual enterprise, in the more ambitious, more picturesque, and less secure of these two contrasted ranges of theoretical knowledge; while the lower range of generalisations, which has to do with work-day experience, has in great part been passed over with scant ceremony as lying outside the cur-rent of ideas, and as belonging rather among the things which engage the attention than among the modes, expedients and creations of this atten-tion itself. There is good reason for this relative neglect of the work-day matters of fact. It is on the higher levels of speculative generalisation that the impressive mutations in the development of thought have taken place, and that the shifting of points of view and the clashing of convictions have drawn men into controversy and analysis of their ideas and have given rise to schools of thought. The matter-of-fact generalisations have met with relatively few adventures and have afforded little scope for intellectual initiative and profoundly picturesque speculation. On the higher levels speculation is freer, the creative spirit has some scope, because its excur-sions are not so immediately and harshly checked by material facts.

In these speculative ranges of knowledge it is possible to form and to maintain habits of thought which shall be consistent with themselves and with the habit of mind and run of tradition prevalent in the community at the time, though not thereby consistent with the material actualities of life in the community. Yet this range of speculative generalisation, which makes up the higher learning of the barbarian culture, is also controlled, checked, and guided by the community's habits of life; it, too, is an inte-gral part of the scheme of life and is an outcome of the habituation en-forced by experience. But it does not rest immediately on men's dealings with the refractory phenomena of brute creation, nor is it guided, undis-guised and directly, by the habitual material (industrial) occupations. The fabric of institutions intervenes between the material exigencies of life and the speculative scheme of things.

The higher theoretical knowledge, that body of tenets which rises to the dignity of a philosophical or scientific system, in the early culture, is a complex of habits of thought which reflect the habits of life embodied in the institutional structure of society -, while the lower, matter-of-fact generalisations of work-day efficiency - the trivial matters of course - reflect the workmanlike habits of life enforced by the commonplace material exigencies under which men live. The distinction is analogous, and indeed, closely related, to the distinction between "intangible" and "tangible" assets. And the institutions are more flexible, they involve or admit a larger margin of error, or of tolerance, than the material exigencies. The latter are systematised into what economists have called "the state of the industrial arts," which enforce a somewhat rigorous standardisation of whatever knowledge falls within their scope; whereas the institutional scheme is a matter of law and custom, politics and religion, taste and morals, on all of which matters men have opinions and convictions, and on which all men "have a right to their own opinions." The scheme of institutions is also not necessarily uniform throughout the several classes of society; and the same institution (as, e.g., slavery, ownership, or royalty) does not impinge with the same effect on all parties touched by it. The discipline of any institution of servitude, e.g., is not the same for the master as for the serf, etc. if there is a considerable institutional discrepancy between an tipper and a lower class in tile community, leading to divergent line of habitual interest or discipline; if by force of the cultural scheme the institutions of society are chiefly in the keeping of one class, whose attention is then largely engrossed with the maintenance of the scheme of law and order; while the workmanlike activities are chiefly in the hands of another class, in whose apprehension the maintenance of law and order is at the best a wearisome tribulation, there is likely to be a similarly considerable divergence or discrepancy between the speculative knowledge, cultivated primarily by the tipper class, and the work-day knowledge which is primarily in the keeping of the lower class.

Such, in particular, will be the case if the community is organised on a coercive plan, with well-marked ruling and subject classes. The important and interesting institutions in such a case, those institutions which fill a large angle in men's vision and carry a great force of authenticity, are the institutions of coercive control, differential authority and subjection, personal dignity and consequence; and the speculative generalisations, the institutions of the realm of knowledge, are created in the image of these social institutions of status and personal force, and fall into a scheme drawn after the plan of the code of honor. The work-day generalisations, which emerge from the state of the industrial arts, concomitantly fall into a deeper obscurity, answering to the depth of indignity to which workmanlike efficiency sinks under such a cultural scheme; and they can touch and check the current speculative knowledge only remotely and incidentally. Under such a bifurcate scheme of culture, with its concomitant two-cleft systematisation of knowledge, "reality" is likely to be widely dissociated from fact - that is to say, the realities and verities which are accepted as authentic and convincing on the plane of speculative generalisation; while science has no show - that is to say, science in that modern sense of the term which implies a close contact, if not a coincidence, of reality with fact.

Whereas, if the institutional fabric, the community's scheme of life, changes in such a manner as to throw the work-day experience into the foreground of attention and to center the habitual interest of the people on the immediate material relations of men to the brute actualities, then the interval between the speculative realm of knowledge, on the one hand, and the work-day generalisations of fact, on the other hand, is likely to lessen, and the two ranges of knowledge are likely to converge more or less effectually upon a common ground. When the growth of culture falls into such lines, these two methods and norms of theoretical formulation may presently come to further and fortify one another, and something in the way of science has at least a chance to arise.

On this view there is a degree of interdependence between the cultural situation and the state of theoretical inquiry. To illustrate this interdependence, or the concomitance between the cultural scheme and the character of theoretical speculation, it may be in place to call to mind certain concomitant variations of a general character which occur in the lower cultures between the scheme of life and the scheme of knowledge. In this tentative and fragmentary presentation of evidence there is nothing novel to be brought forward; still less is there anything to be offered which carries the weight of authority. On the lower levels of culture, even more decidedly than on the higher, the speculative systematisation of knowledge is prone to take the form of theology (mythology) and cosmology. This theological and cosmological lore serves the savage and barbaric peoples as a theoretical account of the scheme of things, and its characteristic traits vary in response to the variations of the institutional scheme under which the community lives. In a prevailingly peaceable agricultural community, such, e.g., as the more peaceable Pueblo Indians or the more settled Indians of the Middle West, there is little coercive authority, few and slight class distinctions involving superiority and inferiority; property rights are few, slight and unstable; relationship is likely to be counted in the female line. In such a culture the cosmological lore is likely to offer explanations of the scheme of things in terms of generation or germination and growth.

Creation by fiat is not obtrusively or characteristically present. The laws of nature bear the character of an habitual behavior of things, rather than that of an authoritative code of ordinances imposed by an overruling providence. The theology is likely to be polytheistic in an extreme degree and in an extremely loose sense of the term, embodying relatively little of the suzerainty of God. The relation of the deities to mankind is likely to be that of consanguinity, and as if to emphasise the peaceable, non-coercive character of the divine order of things, the deities are, in the main, very apt to be females. The matters of interest dealt with in the cosmological theories are chiefly matters of the livelihood of the people, the growth and care of the crops, and the promotion of industrial ways and means.

With these phenomena of the peaceable culture may be contrasted the order of things found among a predatory pastoral people - and pastoral peoples tend strongly to take on a predatory cultural scheme. Such a people will adopt male deities, in the main, and will impute to them a coercive, imperious, arbitrary animus and a degree of princely dignity. They will also tend strongly to a monotheistic, patriarchal scheme of divine government; to explain things in terms of creative fiat; and to a belief in the control of the natural universe by rules imposed by divine ordinance. The matters of prime consequence in this theology are matters of the servile relation of man to God, rather than the details of the quest of a livelihood. The emphasis falls on the glory of God rather than on the good of man. The Hebrew scriptures, particularly the Jahvistic elements, show such a scheme of pastoral cultural and predatory theoretical generalisations.

The learning cultivated on the lower levels of culture might be gone into at some length if space and time permitted, but even what has been said may serve to show, in the most general way, what are the characteristic marks of this savage and barbarian lore. A similarly summary characterisation of a cultural situation nearer home will bear more directly on the immediate topic of inquiry. The learning of mediaeval Christendom shows such a concomitance between the scheme of knowledge and the scheme of institutions, somewhat analogous to the barbaric Hebrew situation. The mediaeval scheme of institutions was of a

coercive, authoritative character, essentially a scheme of graded mastery and graded servitude.. in which a code of honor and a bill of differential dignity held the most important place. The theology of that time was of a like character. It was a monotheistic, or rather a monarchical system, and of a despotic complexion. The cosmological scheme was drawn in terms of fiat: and the natural. philosophy was occupied, in the main and in its most solemn endeavors, with the corollaries to be subsumed under the divine fiat. When the philosophical speculation dealt with facts it aimed to interpret them into systematic consistency with the glory of God and the divine purpose.

The "realities" of the scholastic lore were spiritual, quasi-personal, intangible, and fell into a scale of differential dignity and prepotency. Matter-of-fact knowledge and work-day information were not then fit topics of dignified inquiry. The interval, or discrepancy, between reality and actuality was fairly wide. Throughout that era, of course, work-day knowledge also continually increased in volume and consistency; technological proficiency was gaining; the effective control of natural processes was growing larger and more secure; showing that matter-of-fact theories drawn from experience were being extended and were made increasing use of. Put all this went on in the field of industry; the matter-of-fact theories were accepted as substantial and ultimate only for the purposes of industry, only as technological maxims, and were beneath the dignity of science.

With the transition to modern times industry comes into the foreground in the west-European scheme of life, and the institutions of European civilisation fall into a more intimate relation with the exigencies of industry and technology. The technological range of habituation progressively counts for more in the cultural complex, and the discrepancy between the technological discipline and the discipline of law and order under the institutions then in force grows progressively less. The institutions of law and order take on a more impersonal, less coercive character. Differential dignity and invidious discriminations between classes gradually lose force.

The industry which so comes into the foreground and so affects the scheme of institutions is peculiar in that its most obvious and characteristic trait is the workmanlike initiative and efficiency of the individual handicraftsman and the individual enterprise of the petty trader. The technology which embodies the theoretical substance of this industry is a technology of workmanship, in which the salient factors are personal skill, force and diligence. Such a technology, running as it does in great part on personal initiative, capacity, and application, approaches nearer to the commonplace features of the institutional fabric than many another technological system might; and its disciplinary effects in some considerable measure blend with those of the institutional discipline. The two lines of habituation, in the great era of handicraft and petty trade, even came to coalesce and fortify one another; as in the Organisation of the craft gilds and of the industrial towns. Industrial life and usage came to intrude creatively into the cultural scheme on the one hand and into the scheme of authentic knowledge on the other hand. So the body of matter-of-fact knowledge, in modern times, is more and more drawn into the compass of theoretical inquiry; and theoretical inquiry takes on more and more of the animus and method of technological generalisation. But the matter-of-fact elements so drawn in are construed in terms of workmanlike initiative and efficiency, as required by the technological preconceptions of the era of handicraft.

In this way, it may be conceived modern science comes into the field under the cloak of technology and gradually encroaches on the domain of authentic theory previously held by other, higher, nobler, more profound, more spiritual, more intangible conceptions and systems of knowledge. In this early phase of modern science its central norm and universal solvent is the concept of workmanlike initiative and efficiency. This is the new organon. Whatever is to be explained must be reduced to this notation and explained in these terms; otherwise the inquiry does not come to rest. But when the requirements of this notation in terms of workmanship have been duly fulfilled the inquiry does come to rest. By the early decades of the nineteenth century, with a passable degree of thoroughness, other grounds of validity and other interpretations of phenomena, other vouchers for truth and reality, bad been eliminated from the quest of authentic knowledge and from the terms in which theoretical results were conceived or expressed.

The new organon had made good its pretensions. In this movement to establish the hegemony of workmanlike efficiency - under the style and title of the "law of causation," or of "efficient cause" - in the realm of knowledge, the English-speaking communities took the lead after the earlier scientific onset of the south-European communities had gone up in the smoke of war, politics and religion during the great era of state-making. The ground of this British lead in science is apparently the same as that of the British lead in technology which came to a head in the Industrial Revolution; and these two associated episodes of European civilisation are apparently both traceable to the relatively peaceable run of life, and so of habituation, in the English-speaking communities, as contrasted with the communities of the continent.[40]

Along with the habits of thought peculiar to the technology of handicraft, modern science also took over and assimilated much of the institutional preconceptions of the era of handicraft and petty trade. The "natural laws," with the formulation of which this early modern science is occupied, are the rules governing natural "uniformities of sequence"; and they punctiliously formulate the due procedure of any given cause creatively working out the achievement of a given effect, very much as the craft rules sagaciously specified the due routine for turning out a staple article of merchantable goods. But these "natural laws" of science are also felt to have something of that integrity and prescriptive moral force that belongs to the principles of the system of "natural rights" which the era of handicraft has contributed to the institutional scheme of later times. The natural laws were not only held to be true to fact but they were also felt to be right and good.

They were looked upon is intrinsically meritorious and beneficent, and were held to carry a sanction of their own. This habit of uncritically imputing merit and equity to the "natural laws" of science continued in force

---

[40] A broad exception may perhaps be taken at this point, to the effect that this sketch of the growth of the scientific animus overlooks the science of the Ancients. The scientific achievements of classical antiquity are a less obscure topic to-day than ever before during modern times, and the more there is known of them the larger is the credit given them. But it is to be noted that, (a) the relatively large and free growth of scientific inquiry in classical antiquity is to be found in the relatively peaceable and industrial Greek communities (with an industrial culture of unknown pre-Hellenic antiquity), and (b) that the sciences best and chiefly cultivated were those which rest on a mathematical basis, if not mathematical sciences in the simpler sense of the term. Now, mathematics occupies a singular place among the sciences, in that it is, in its pure form, a logical discipline simply; its subject matter being the logic of quantity, and its researches being of the nature of an analysis of the intellect's modes of dealing with matters of quantity. Its generalisations are generalisations of logical procedure, which are tested and verified by immediate self-observation. Such a science is in a peculiar degree, but only in a peculiar degree, independent of the detail-discipline of daily life, whether technological or institutional, and, given the propensity - the intellectual enterprise, or "idle curiosity" - to go into speculation in such a field, the results can scarcely vary in a manner to make the variants inconsistent among themselves; nor need the state of institutions or the state of the industrial arts seriously color or distort such analytical work in such a field. Mathematics is peculiarly independent of cultural circumstances, since it deals analytically with mankind's native gifts of logic, not with the ephemeral traits acquired by habituation.

through much of the nineteenth century; very much as the habitual acceptance of the principles of "natural rights" has held on by force of tradition long after the exigencies of experience out of which these "rights"
sprang ceased to shape men's habits of life[41] .This traditional attitude of
submissive approval toward the "natural laws" of science has not Yet been
wholly lost, even among the scientists of the passing generation, many of
whom have uncritically invested these "laws" with a prescriptive rectitude
and excellence; but so far, at least, has this animus progressed toward disuse that it is now chiefly a matter for expatiation in the pulpit, the accred-
ited vent for the exudation of effete matter from the cultural organism.

The traditions of the handicraft technology lasted over as a commonplace habit of thought in science long after that technology bad ceased to
be the decisive element in the industrial situation: while a new technology,
with its inculcation of new habits of thought, new preconceptions, gradually made its way among the remnants of the old, altering them, blending
with them, and little by little superseding them. The new technological
departure, which made its first great epoch in the so-called industrial
revolution, in the technological ascendancy of the machine-process,
brought a new and characteristic discipline into the cultural situation. The
beginnings of the machine-era lie far back, no doubt; but it is only of late,
during the past century at the most, that the machine-process can be said
to have come into the dominant place in the technological scheme; and it
is only later still that its discipline has, even in great part, remodeled the
current preconceptions as to the substantial nature of what goes on in the
current of phenomena whose changes excite the scientific curiosity. It is
only relatively very lately, whether in technological work or in scientific
inquiry, that men have fallen into the habit of thinking in terms of process
rather than in terms of the workmanlike efficiency of a given cause working to a given effect.

These machine-made preconceptions of modern science, being habits
of thought induced by the machine technology in industry and in daily
life, have of course first and most consistently affected the character of
those sciences whose subject matter lies nearest to the technological field
of the machine-process; and in these material sciences the shifting to the
machine -made point of view has been relatively very consistent, giving a
highly impersonal interpretation of phenomena in terms of consecutive
change, and leaving little of the ancient preconceptions of differential re-

---

[41] "Natural laws," which are held to be not only correct formulations of the sequence of cause and effect in a given situation but also meritoriously right and equitable rules governing the run of events, necessarily impute to the facts and events
in question a tendency to a good and equitable, if not beneficent, consummation.,
since it is necessarily the consummation, the effect considered as an accomplished
outcome, that is to be adjudged good and equitable, if anything. Hence these "natural laws," as traditionally conceived, are laws governing the accomplishment of an
end - that is to say, laws as to bow a sequence of cause and effect comes to rest in a
final term.

ality or creative causation. In such a science as physics or chemistry, e.g., we are threatened with the disappearance or dissipation of all stable and efficient substances; their place being supplied, or their phenomena being theoretically explained, by appeal to unremitting processes of inconceivably high-pitched consecutive change.

In the sciences which lie farther afield from the technological domain, and which, therefore, in point of habituation, are remoter from the center of disturbance, the effect of the machine discipline may even yet be scarcely appreciable. In such lore as ethics, e.g., or political theory, or even economics, much of the norms of the regime of handicraft still stands over; and very much of the institutional preconceptions of natural rights, associated with the regime of handicraft in point of genesis, growth and content, is not only still intact in this field of inquiry, but it can scarcely even be claimed that there is ground for serious apprehension of its prospective obsolescence. Indeed, something even more ancient than handicraft and natural rights may be found surviving in good vigor in this "moral" field of inquiry, where tests of authenticity and reality are still sought and found by those who cultivate these lines of inquiry that lie beyond the immediate sweep of the machine's discipline. Even the evolutionary process of cumulative causation as conceived by the adepts of these sciences is infused with a preternatural, beneficent trend; so that "evolution" is conceived to mean amelioration or "improvement." The metaphysics of the machine technology has not yet wholly, perhaps not mainly, superseded the metaphysics of the code of honor in those lines of inquiry that have to do with human initiative and aspiration. Whether such a shifting of the point of view in these sciences shall ever be effected is still an open question. Here there still are spiritual verities which transcend the sweep of consecutive change. That is to say, there are still current habits of thought which definitively predispose their bearers to bring their inquiries to rest on grounds of differential reality and invidious merit.

Chapter 2

The Place of Science
in Modern Civilisation

It is commonly held that modern Christendom is superior to any and all
other systems of civilized life. Other ages and other cultural regions are by
contrast spoken of as lower, or more archaic, or less mature. The claim is
that the modern culture is superior on the whole, not that it is the best or
highest in all respects and at every point. It has, in fact, not an all-around
superiority, but a superiority within a closely limited range of intellectual
activities, while outside this range many other civilizations surpass that of
the modern occidental peoples. But the peculiar excellence of the modern
culture is of such a nature as to give it a decisive practical advantage over
all other cultural schemes that have gone before or that have come into
competition with it. It has proved itself fit to survive in a struggle for existence as against those civilizations which differ from it in respect of its distinctive traits.

Modern civilization is peculiarly matter-of-fact. It contains many elements that are not of this character, but these other elements do not belong exclusively or characteristically to it. The modern civilized peoples
are in a peculiar degree capable of an impersonal, dispassionate insight
into the material facts with which mankind has to deal. The apex of cultural growth is at this point. Compared with this trait the rest of what is
comprised in the cultural scheme is adventitious, or at the best it is a by-
product of this hard-headed apprehension of facts. This quality may be a
matter of habit or of racial endowment, or it may be an outcome of both;
but whatever be the explanation of its prevalence, the immediate consequence is much the same for the growth of civilization. A civilization
which is dominated by this matter-of-fact insight must prevail against any
cultural scheme that lacks this element. This characteristic of western civilization comes to a head in modern science, and it finds its highest material expression in the technology of the machine industry. In these things
modern culture is creative and self-sufficient; and these being given, the
rest of what may seem characteristic in western civilization follows by easy
consequence. The cultural structure clusters about this body of matter-of-
fact knowledge as its substantial core. Whatever is not consonant with
these opaque creations of science is an intrusive feature in the modern
scheme, borrowed or standing over from the barbarian past.

Other ages and other peoples excel in other things and are known by
other virtues. In creative art, as well as in critical taste, the faltering talent
of Christendom can at the best follow the lead of the ancient Greeks and
the Japanese. In deft workmanship the handicraftsmen of the middle Ori-
ent, as well as of the Far East, stand on a level securely above the highest
European achievement, old or new. In myth-making, folklore, and occult

symbolism many of the lower barbarians have achieved things beyond what the latter-day priests and poets know how to propose. In metaphysical insight and dialectical versatility many orientals, as well as the Schoolmen of the Middle Ages, easily surpass the highest reaches of the New Thought and the Higher Criticism. In a shrewd sense of the religious verities, as well as in an unsparing faith in devout observances, the people of India or Thibet, or even the mediaeval Christians, are past-masters in comparison even with the select of the faith of modern times. In political finesse, as well as in unreasoning, brute loyalty, more than one of the ancient peoples give evidence of a capacity to which no modern civilized nation may aspire. In warlike malevolence and abandon, the hosts of Islam, the Sioux Indian. and the "heathen of the northern sea" have set the mark above the reach of the most strenuous civilized warlord.

To modern civilized men, especially in their intervals of sober reflection, all these things that distinguish the barbarian civilization seem of dubious value and are required to show cause why they should not be slighted. It is not so with the knowledge of facts. The making of states and dynasties, the founding of families, the prosecution of feuds, the propagation of creeds and the creation of sects, the accumulation of fortunes, the consumption of superfluities - these have all in their time been felt to justify themselves as an end of endeavor; but in the eyes of modern civilized men all these things seem futile in comparison with the achievements of science. They dwindle in men's esteem as time passes, while the achievements of science are held higher as time passes. This is the one secure holding-ground of latterday conviction, that "the increase and diffusion of knowledge among men" is indefeasibly right and good.

When seen in such perspective as will clear it of the trivial perplexities of workday life, this proposition is not questioned within the horizon of the western culture, and no other cultural ideal holds a similar unquestioned place in the convictions of civilized mankind.

On any large question which is to be disposed of for good and all the final appeal is by common consent taken to the scientist. The solution offered in the name of science is decisive so long as it is not set aside by a still more searching scientific inquiry. This state of things may not be altogether fortunate, but such is the fact. There are other, older grounds of finality that may conceivably be better, nobler, worthier, more profound, more beautiful. It might conceivably be preferable, as a matter of cultural ideals, to leave the last word with the lawyer, the duelist, the priest, the moralist, or the college of heraldry. In past times people have been content to leave their weightiest questions to the decision of some one or other of these tribunals, and, it cannot be denied, with very happy results in those respects that were then looked to with the greatest solicitude. But whatever the common-sense of earlier generations may have held in this respect, modern common-sense holds that the scientist's answer is the only ultimately true one. In the last resort enlightened common-sense sticks by the opaque truth and refuses to go behind the returns given by the tangible facts.

Quasi lignum vitae in paradiso Dei, et quasi lucerna fulgoris in domo Domini, such is the place of science in modern civilization. This latter-day faith in matter-of-fact knowledge may be well grounded or it may not. It has come about that men assign it this high place, perhaps idolatrously, perhaps to the detriment of the best and most intimate interests of the race, There is room for much more than a vague doubt that this cult of science is not altogether a wholesome growth - that the unmitigated quest of knowledge, of this matter-of-fact kind, makes for race-deterioration and discomfort on the whole, both in its immediate effects upon the spiritual life of mankind, and in the material consequences that follow from a great advance in matter-of-fact knowledge.

But we are not here concerned with the merits of the case. The question here is: How has this cult of science arisen? What are its cultural antecedents? How far is it in consonance with hereditary human nature? and, What is the nature of its hold on the convictions of civilized men?

In dealing with pedagogical problems and the theory of education, current psychology is nearly at one in saying that all learning is of a ,"pragmatic" character; that knowledge is inchoate action inchoately directed to an end; that all knowledge is , functional;" that it is of the nature of use. This, of course, is only a corollary under the main postulate of the latter-day psychologists, whose catchword is that the Idea is essentially active. There is no need of quarreling with this "pragmatic" school of psychologists. Their aphorism may not contain the whole truth, perhaps, but at least it goes nearer to the heart of the epistemological problem than any earlier formulation. It may confidently be said to do so because, for one thing, its argument meets the requirements of modern science. It is such a concept as matter of-fact science can make effective use of; it is drawn in terms which are, in the last analysis, of an impersonal, not to say tropismatic, character; such as is demanded by science, with its insistence on opaque cause and effect. While knowledge is construed in teleological terms, in terms of personal interest and attention, this teleological aptitude is itself reducible to a product of unteleological natural selection. The teleological bent of intelligence is a hereditary trait settled upon the race by the selective action of forces that look to no end. The foundations of pragmatic intelligence arc not pragmatic, nor even personal or sensible.

This impersonal character of intelligence is, of course, most evident on the lower levels of life. If we follow Mr. Loeb, e. g., in his inquiries into the psychology of that life that lies below the threshold of intelligence, what we meet with is an aimless but unwavering motor response to stimulus[42] .The response is of the nature of motor impulse, and in so far it is "pragmatic," if that term may fairly be applied to so rudimentary a phase of sensibility. The responding organism may be called an "agent" in so far. It is only by a figure of speech that these terms are made to apply to tropis-

---

[42] Jacques Loeb, Heliotropismus der Thiere and Comparative Psychology and Physiology of the Brain.

matic reactions. Higher in the scale of sensibility and nervous complication instincts work to a somewhat similar outcome. On the human plane, intelligence (the selective effect of inhibitive complication) may throw the response into the form of a reasoned line of conduct looking to an outcome that shall be expedient for the agent.

This is naive pragmatism of the developed kind. There is no longer a question but that the responding organism is an "agent," and that his intelligent response to stimulus is of a teleological character. But that is not all. The inhibitive nervous complication may also detach another chain of response to the given stimulus, which does not spend itself in a line of motor conduct and does not fall into a system of uses. Pragmatically speaking, this outlying chain of response is unintended and irrelevant. Except in urgent cases, such an idle response seems commonly to be present as a subsidiary phenomenon. If credence is given to the view that intelligence is, in its elements, of the nature of an inhibitive selection, it sterns necessary to assume some such chain of idle and irrelevant response to account for the further course of the elements eliminated in giving the motor response the character of a reasoned line of conduct. So that associated with the pragmatic attention there is found more or less of an irrelevant attention, or idle curiosity. This is more particularly the case where a higher range of intelligence is present. This idle curiosity is, perhaps, closely related to the aptitude for play, observed both in man and in the lower animals[43]. The aptitude for play, as well as the functioning of idle curiosity, seems peculiarly lively in the young, whose aptitude for sustained pragmatism is at the same time relatively vague and unreliable.

This idle curiosity formulates its response to stimulus, not in terms of an expedient line of conduct, nor even necessarily in a chain of motor activity, in terms of sequence of activities going on in the observed phenomena. The "interpretation" of the facts under the guidance of this idle curiosity may take the form of anthropomorphic or animistic explanations of the "conduct" of the objects observed. The interpretation of the facts takes a dramatic form. The facts are conceived in an animistic way, and a pragmatic animus is imputed to them. Their behavior is construed as a reasoned procedure and their part looking to the advantage of these animistically conceived objects, or looking to the achievement of some end which these objects are conceived to have at heart for reasons of their own.

Among the savage and lower barbarian peoples there is commonly current a large body of knowledge organized in this way into myths and legends, which need have no pragmatic value for the learner of them and no intended bearing on his conduct of practical affairs, They may come to

---

[43] Cf. Gross, Spiele der Thiere, chap. 3 (esp. pp. 65-76), and chap. 5; The Play of Man, Part III, sec. 3; Spencer, Principles of Psychology, secs. 533-35.

have a practical value imputed to them as a ground of superstitious observances, but they may also not[44] .

All students of the lower cultures are aware of the dramatic character of the myths current among these peoples, and they are also aware that, particularly among the peaceable communities, the great body of mythical lore is of an idle kind, as having very little intended bearing on the practical conduct of those who believe in these myth-dramas. The myths on the one hand, and the workday knowledge of uses, materials, appliances, and expedients on the other hand, may be nearly independent of one another. Such is the case in an especial degree among those peoples who are prevailingly of a peaceable habit of life, among whom the myths have not in any great measure been canonized into precedents of divine malevolence.

The lower barbarian's knowledge of the phenomena of nature, in so far as they are made the subject of deliberate speculation and are organized into a consistent body, is of the nature of life-histories. This body of knowledge is in the main organized under the guidance of an idle curiosity. In so far as it is systematized under the canons of curiosity rather than of expediency, the test of truth applied throughout this body of barbarian knowledge is the test of dramatic consistency. In addition to their dramatic cosmology and folk legends, it is needless to say, these peoples have also a considerable body of worldly wisdom in a more or less systematic form. In this the test of validity is usefulness[45] .

The pragmatic knowledge of the early days differs scarcely at all in character from that of the maturest phases of culture. Its highest achievements in the direction of systematic formulation consist of didactic exhortations to thrift, prudence, equanimity, and shrewd management - a body of maxims of expedient conduct. In this field there is scarcely a degree of advance from Confucius to Samuel Smiles. Under the guidance of the idle curiosity, on the other hand, there has been a continued advance toward a more and more comprehensive system of knowledge. With the advance in intelli-

---

[44] The myths and legendary lore of the Eskimo, the Pueblo Indians, and some tribes of the northwest coast afford good instances of such idle creations. Cf. various Reports of the Bureau of American Ethnology; also, e. g., Tylor, Primitive Culture, esp. the chapters on "Mythology" and "Animism."

[45] "Pragmatic" is here used in a more restricted sense than the distinctively pragmatic school of modern psychologists would commonly assign the term. "Pragmatic", "teleological" and the like terms have been extended to cover imputation of purpose as well as conversion to use. It is not intended to criticise this ambiguous use of terms, nor to correct it; but the terms are here used only in the latter sense, which alone belongs to them by force of early usage and etymology. "Pragmatic" knowledge, therefore, is such as is designed to serve an expedient end for the knower, and is here contrasted with the imputation of expedient conduct to the facts observed. The reason for preserving this distinction is simply the present need of a simple term by which to mark the distinction between worldly wisdom and idle learning.

gence and experience there come closer observation and more detailed analysis of facts[46] .

The dramatization of the sequence of phenomena may then fall into somewhat less personal, less anthropomorphic formulations of the processes observed; but at no stage of its growth - at least at no stage hitherto reached - does the output of this work of the idle curiosity lose its dramatic character. Comprehensive generalizations are made and cosmologies are built up, but always in dramatic form. General principles of explanation are settled on, which in the earlier days of theoretical speculation seem invariably to run back to the broad vital principle of generation. Procreation, birth, growth, and decay constitute the cycle of postulates within which the dramatized processes of natural phenomena run their course. Creation is procreation in these archaic theoretical systems, and causation is gestation and birth. The archaic cosmological schemes of Greece, India, Japan, China, Polynesia, and America, all run to the same general effect on this head[47] .

Throughout this biological speculation there is present, obscurely in the background, the tacit recognition of a material causation, such as conditions the vulgar operations of workday life from hour to hour. But this causal relation between vulgar work and product is vaguely taken for granted and not made a principle for comprehensive generalizations. It is overlooked as a trivial matter of course. The higher generalizations take their color from the broader features of the current scheme of life. The habits of thought that rule in the working-out of a system of knowledge are such as are fostered by the more impressive affairs of life, by the institutional structure under which the community lives. So long as the ruling institutions are those of blood-relationship, descent, and clannish discrimination, so long the canons of knowledge are of the same complexion.

When presently a transformation is made in the scheme of culture from peaceable life with sporadic predation to a settled scheme of predaceous life, involving mastery and servitude, gradations of privilege and honor, coercion and personal dependence, then the scheme of knowledge undergoes an analogous change. The predacious, or higher barbarian, culture is, for the present purpose, peculiar in that it is ruled by an accentuated pragmatism. The institutions of this cultural phase are conventionalized relations of force and fraud. The questions of life are questions of expedient conduct as carried on under the current relations of mastery and subservience. The habitual distinctions are distinctions of personal force, advantage, precedence, and authority. A shrewd adaptation to this System of graded dignity and servitude becomes a matter of life and death, and men learn to think in these terms as ultimate and definitive. The System of knowledge, even in so far as its motives are of a dispassionate or idle kind,

---

[46] Cf. Ward, Pure Sociology, esp. pp. 437-48.
[47] Cf., e. g., Tylor, Primitive Culture, chap. 8.

falls into the like terms, because such are the habits of thought and the standards of discrimination enforced by daily life[48] .

The theoretical work of such a cultural era, as, for instance, the Middle Ages, still takes the general shape of dramatization, but the postulates of the dramaturgic theories and the tests of theoretic validity are no longer the same as before the scheme of graded servitude came to occupy the field. The canons which guide the work of the idle curiosity are no longer those of generation, blood-relationship, and homely life, but rather those of graded dignity, authenticity, and dependence. The higher generalizations take on a new complexion, it may be without formally discarding the older articles of belief. The cosmologies of these higher barbarians are cast in terms of a feudalistic hierarchy of agents and elements, and the causal nexus between phenomena is conceived animistically after the manner of sympathetic magic. The laws that are sought to be discovered in the natural universe are sought in terms of authoritative enactment. The relation in which the deity, or deities, are conceived to stand to facts is no longer the relation of progenitor, so much as that of suzerainty. Natural laws are corollaries under the arbitrary rules of status imposed on the natural universe by an all-powerful Providence with a view to the maintenance of his own prestige. The science that grows in such a spiritual environment is of the class represented by alchemy and astrology, in which the imputed degree of nobility and prepotency of the objects and the symbolic force of their names are looked to for an explanation of what takes place.

The theoretical output of the Schoolmen has necessarily an accentuated pragmatic complexion, since the whole cultural scheme under which they lived and worked was of a strenuously pragmatic character. The current concepts of things were then drawn in terms of expediency, personal force, exploit, prescriptive authority, and the like, and this range of concepts was by force of habit employed in the correlation of facts for purposes of knowledge even where no immediate practical use of the knowledge so gained was had in view. At the same time a very large proportion of the scholastic researches and speculations aimed directly at rules of expedient conduct, whether it took the form of a philosophy of life under temporal law and custom, or of a scheme of salvation under the decrees of an autocratic Providence. A naive apprehension of the dictum that all knowledge is pragmatic would find more satisfactory corroboration in the intellectual output of scholasticism than in any system of knowledge of an older or a later date.

With the advent of modern times a change comes over the nature of the inquiries and formulations worked out under the guidance of the idle curiosity - which from this epoch is often spoken of as the scientific spirit. The change in question is closely correlated with an analogous change in institutions and habits of life, particularly with the changes which the modern era brings in industry and in the economic organization of socie-

---

[48] Cf. James, *Psychology*, chap. 9, esp. sec. 5.

ty. It is doubtful whether the characteristic intellectual interests and teachings of the new era can properly be spoken of as less "pragmatic," as that term is sometimes understood, than those of the scholastic times; but they are of another kind, being conditioned by a different cultural and industrial situation[49].

In the life of the new era conceptions of authentic rank and differential dignity have grown weaker in practical affairs, and notions of preferential reality and authentic tradition similarly count for less in the new science. The forces at work in the external world are conceived in a less animistic manner, although anthropomorphism still prevails, at least to the degree required in order to give a dramatic interpretation of the sequence of phenomena.

The changes in the cultural situation which seem to have had the most serious consequences for the methods and animus of scientific inquiry are those changes that took place in the field of industry. Industry in early modern times is a fact of relatively greater preponderance, more of a tone-giving factor, than it was under the regime of feudal status. It is the characteristic trait of the modern culture, very much as exploit and fealty were the characteristic cultural traits of the earlier times. This early-modern industry is, in an obvious and convincing degree, a matter of workmanship. The same has not been true in the same degree either before or since. The workman, more or less skilled and with more or less specialized efficiency, was the central figure in the cultural situation of the time; and so the concepts of the scientists carne to be drawn in the image of the workman. The dramatizations of the sequence of external phenomena worked out under the impulse of the idle curiosity were then conceived in terms of workmanship. Workmanship gradually supplanted differential dignity as the authoritative canon of scientific truth, even on the higher levels of speculation and research.

This, of course, amounts to saying in other words that the law of cause and effect was given the first place, as contrasted with dialectical consistency and authentic tradition. But this early-modern law of cause and effect - the law of efficient causes - is of an anthropomorphic kind. "Like causes produce like effects," in much the same sense as the skilled workman's product is like the workman; "nothing is found in the effect that was not contained in the cause," in much the same manner.

These dicta are, of course, older than modern science, but it is only in the early days of modern science that they come to rule the field with an unquestioned sway and to push the higher grounds of dialectical validity to one side. They invade even the highest and most recondite fields of

---

[49] As currently employed, the term "pragmatic" is made to cover both conduct looking to the agent's preferential advantage, expedient conduct, and workmanship directed to the production of things that may or may not be of advantage to the agent. If the term be taken in the latter meaning, the culture of modern times is no less "pragmatic" than that of the Middle Ages. It is here intended to be used in the former sense.

speculation, so that at the approach to the transition from the early-modern to the late-modern period, in the eighteenth century they determine the outcome even in the counsels of the theologians. The deity, from having been in mediaeval times primarily a suzerain concerned with the maintenance of his own prestige, becomes primarily a creator engaged in the workmanlike occupation of making things useful for man. His relation to man and the natural universe is no longer primarily that of a progenitor, as it is in the lower barbarian culture, but rather that of a talented mechanic.

The "natural laws" which the scientists of that era make so much of are no longer decrees of a preternatural legislative authority, but rather details of the workshop specifications handed down by the master-craftsman for the guidance of handicraftsmen working out his designs. In the eighteenth-century science these natural laws are laws specifying the sequence of cause and effect, and will bear characterization as a dramatic interpretation of the activity of the causes at work, and these causes are conceived in a quasi-personal manner. In later modern times the formulations of causal sequence grow more impersonal and more objective, more matter-of-fact; but the imputation of activity to the observed objects never ceases, and even in the latest and maturest formulations of scientific research the dramatic tone is not wholly lost. The causes at work are conceived in a highly impersonal way, but hitherto no science (except ostensibly mathematics) has been content to do its theoretical work in terms of inert magnitude alone. Activity continues to be imputed to the phenomena with which science deals; and activity is, of course, not a fact of observation, but is imputed to the phenomena by the observer[50].

This is, also of course, denied by those who insist on a purely mathematical formulation of scientific theories, but the denial is maintained only at the cost of consistency. Those eminent authorities who speak for a colorless mathematical formulation invariably and necessarily fall back on the (essentially metaphysical) preconception of causation as soon as they go into the actual work of scientific inquiry[51].

Since the machine technology has made great advances, during the nineteenth century, and has become a cultural force of wide-reaching consequence, the formulations of science have made another move in the direction of impersonal matter-of-fact. The machine process has displaced the workman as the archetype in whose image causation is conceived by the scientific investigators. The dramatic interpretation of natural phenomena has thereby become less anthropomorphic; it no longer constructs the life-history of a cause working to produce a given effect -

---

[50] Epistemologically speaking, activity is imputed to phenomena for the purpose of organizing them into a dramatically consistent system.

[51] Cf., e. g., Karl Pearson, Grammar of Science, and compare his ideal of inert magnitudes as set forth in his exposition with his actual work as shown in chaps. 9, 10, and 12, and more particularly in his discussions of "Mother Right" and related topics in The Chances of Death.

after the manner of a skilled workman producing a piece of wrought goods - but it constructs the life-history of a process in which the distinction between cause and effect need scarcely be observed in an itemized and specific way, but in which the run of causation unfolds itself in an unbroken sequence of cumulative change. By contrast with the pragmatic formulations of worldly wisdom these latter-day theories of the scientists appear highly opaque, impersonal, and matter-of-fact; but taken by themselves they must be admitted still to show the constraint of the dramatic prepossessions that once guided the savage myth-makers.

In so far as touches the aims and the animus of scientific inquiry, as seen from the point of view of the scientist, it is a wholly fortuitous and insubstantial coincidence that much of the knowledge gained under machine-made canons of research can be turned to practical account. Much of this knowledge is useful, or may be made so, by applying it to the control of the processes in which natural forces are engaged. This employment of scientific knowledge for useful ends in technology, in the broad sense in which the term includes, besides the machine industry proper, such branches of practice as engineering, agriculture, medicine, sanitation, and economic reforms. The reason why scientific theories can be turned to account for these practical ends is not that these ends are included in the scope of scientific inquiry. These useful purposes lie outside the scientist's interest. It is not that he aims, or can aim, at technological improvements. His inquiry is as "idle" as that of the Pueblo myth-maker. But the canons of validity under whose guidance he works are those imposed by the modern technology, through habituation to its requirements; and therefore his results are available for the technological purpose. His canons of validity are made for him by the cultural situation; they are habits of thought imposed on him by the scheme of life current in the community in which he lives; and under modern conditions this scheme of life is largely machine-made. In the modern culture, industry, industrial processes, and industrial products have progressively gained upon humanity, until these creations of man's ingenuity have latterly come to take the dominant place in the cultural scheme; and it is not too much to say that they have become the chief force in shaping men's daily life, and therefore the chief factor in shaping men's habits of thought.

Hence men have learned to think in the terms in which the technological processes act. This is particularly true of those men who by virtue of a peculiarly strong susceptibility in this direction become addicted to that habit of matter-of-fact inquiry that constitutes scientific research.

Modern technology makes use of the same range of concepts, thinks in the same terms, and applies the same tests of validity as modern science. In both, the terms of standardization, validity, and finality are always terms of impersonal sequence, not terms of human nature or of preternatural agencies. Hence the easy co-partnership between the two. Science and technology play into one another's hands. The processes of nature with which science deals and which technology turns to account, the sequence of changes in the external world, animate and inanimate, run in terms of brute causation, as do the theories of science.

These processes take no thought of human expediency or inexpediency. To make use of them they must be taken as they are, opaque and unsympathetic. Technology, therefore, has come to proceed on an interpretation of these phenomena in mechanical terms, not in terms of imputed personality nor even of workmanship. Modern science, deriving its concepts from the same source, carries on its inquiries and states its conclusions in terms of the same objective character as those employed by the mechanical engineer.

So it has come about, through the progressive change of the ruling habits; of thought in the community that the theories of science have progressively diverged from the formulations of pragmatism, ever since the modern era set in. From an organization of knowledge on the basis of imputed personal or animistic propensity the theory has changed its base to an imputation of brute activity only, and this latter is conceived in an increasingly matter-of-fact manner; until, latterly, the pragmatic range of knowledge and the scientific are more widely out of touch than ever, differing not only in aim, but in matter as well. In both domains knowledge runs in terms of activity, but it is on the one hand knowledge of what had best be done, and on the other hand knowledge of what takes place; on the one hand knowledge of ways and means, on the other hand knowledge without any ulterior purpose. The latter range of knowledge may serve the ends of the former, but the converse does not hold true.

These two divergent ranges of inquiry are to be found together in all phases of human culture. What distinguishes the present phase is that the discrepancy between the two is now wider than ever before. The present is nowise distinguished above other cultural eras by any exceptional urgency or acumen in the search for pragmatic expedients. Neither is it safe to assert that the present excels all other civilizations in the volume or the workmanship of that body of knowledge that is to be credited to the idle curiosity. What distinguishes the present in these premises is (1) that the primacy in the cultural scheme has passed from pragmatism to a disinterested inquiry whose motive is idle curiosity, and (2) that in the domain of the latter the making of myths and legends in terms of imputed personality, as well as the construction of dialectical systems in terms of differential reality, has yielded the first place to the making of theories in terms of matter-of-fact sequence[52] .

Pragmatism creates nothing but maxims of expedient conduct. Science creates nothing but theories[53]. It knows nothing of policy or utility, of better or worse. None of all that is comprised in what is today accounted scientific knowledge. Wisdom and proficiency of the pragmatic sort does not contribute to the advance of a knowledge of fact. It has only an incidental bearing on scientific research, and its bearing is chiefly that of inhibition and misdirection. Wherever canons of expediency are intruded into or are

---

[52] Cf. James, Psychology, Vol. II, chap. 28, pp. 633-71, esp. p. 640 note,

[53] Cf. Ward, Principles of Psychology, pp. 439-43.

attempted to be incorporated in the inquiry, the consequence is an unhappy one for science, however happy it may be for some other purpose
extraneous to science.

The mental attitude of worldly wisdom is at cross-purposes with the disinterested scientific spirit, and the pursuit of it induces an intellectual bias
that is incompatible with scientific insight. Its intellectual output is a body
of shrewd rules of conduct, in great part designed to take advantage of
human infirmity. Its habitual terms of standardization and validity are
terms of human nature, of human preference, prejudice, aspiration, endeavor, and disability, and the habit of mind that goes with it is such as is
consonant with these terms. No doubt, the all-pervading pragmatic animus of the older and non-European civilizations has had more than anything else to do with their relatively slight and slow advance in scientific
knowledge. In the modern scheme of knowledge it holds true, in a similar
manner and with analogous effect, that training in divinity, in law, and in
the related branches of diplomacy, business tactics, military affairs, and
political theory, is alien to the skeptical scientific spirit and subversive of
it.

The modern scheme of culture comprises a large body of worldly wisdom, as well as of science. This pragmatic lore stands over against science
with something of a jealous reserve. The pragmatists value themselves
somewhat on being useful as well as being efficient for good and evil. They
feel the inherent antagonism between themselves and the scientists, and
look with some doubt on the latter as being merely decorative triflers, although they sometimes borrow the prestige of the name of science - as is
only good and well, since it is of the essence of worldly wisdom to borrow
anything that can be turned to account. The reasoning in these fields turns
about questions of personal advantage of one kind or another, and the
merits of the claims canvassed in these discussions are decided on
grounds of authenticity.

Personal claims make up the subject of the inquiry, and these claims are
construed and decided in terms of precedent and choice, use and wont,
prescriptive authority, and the like. The higher reaches of generalization in
these pragmatic inquiries are of the nature of deductions from authentic
tradition, and the training in this class of reasoning gives discrimination in
respect of authenticity and expediency. The resulting habit of mind is a
bias for substituting dialectical distinctions and decisions *de jure* in the
place of explanations *de facto*. The so-called "sciences" associated with
these pragmatic disciplines, such as jurisprudence, political science, and
the like, is a taxonomy of credenda. Of this character was the greater part
of the "science" cultivated by the Schoolmen, and large remnants of the
same kind of authentic convictions are, of course, still found among the
tenets of the scientists, particularly in the social sciences, and no small
solicitude is still given to their cultivation. Substantially the same value as
that of the temporal pragmatic inquiries belongs also, of course, to the
"science" of divinity. Here the questions to which an answer is sought, as
well as the aim and method of inquiry, are of the same pragmatic charac-

ter, although the argument runs on a higher plane of personality, and seeks a solution in terms of a remoter and more metaphysical expediency.

In the light of what has been said above, the questions recur: How far is the scientific quest of matter-of-fact knowledge consonant with the inherited intellectual aptitudes and propensities of the normal man? and, What foothold has science in the modern culture? The former is a question of the temperamental heritage of civilized mankind, and therefore it is in large part a question of the circumstances which have in the past selectively shaped the human nature of civilized mankind. Under the barbarian culture, as well as on the lower levels of what is currently called civilized life, the dominant note has been that of competitive expediency for the individual or the group, great or small, in an avowed struggle for the means of life. Such is still the ideal of the politician and business man, as well as of other classes whose habits of life lead them to cling to the inherited barbarian traditions.

The upper-barbarian and lower-civilized culture, as has already been indicated, is pragmatic, with a thoroughness that nearly bars out any non-pragmatic ideal of life or of knowledge. Where this tradition is strong there is but a precarious chance for any consistent effort to formulate knowledge in other terms than those drawn from the prevalent relations of personal mastery and subservience and the ideals of personal gain.

During the Dark and Middle Ages, for instance, it is true in the main that any movement of thought not controlled by considerations of expediency and conventions of status are to be found only in the obscure depths of vulgar life, among those neglected elements of the population that lived below the reach of the active class struggle. What there is surviving of this vulgar, non-pragmatic intellectual output takes the form of legends and folk-tales, often embroidered on the authentic documents of the Faith. These are less alien to the latest and highest culture of Christendom than are the dogmatic, dialectical, and chivalric productions that occupied the attention of the upper classes in mediaeval times. It may seem a curious paradox that the latest and most perfect flower of the western civilization is more nearly akin to the spiritual life of the serfs and villeins than it is to that of the grange or the abbey. The courtly life and the chivalric habits of thought of that past phase of culture have left as nearly no trace in the cultural scheme of later modern times as could well be. Even the romancers who ostensibly rehearse the phenomena of chivalry, unavoidably make their knights and ladies speak the language and the sentiments of the slums of that time, tempered with certain schematized modern reflections and speculations. The gallantries, the genteel inanities and devout imbecilities of mediaeval high-life would be insufferable even to the meanest and most romantic modern intelligence. So that in a later, less barbarian age the precarious remnants of folklore that have come down through that vulgar channel - half savage and more than half pagan - are treasured as containing the largest spiritual gains which the barbarian ages of Europe have to offer.

The sway of barbarian pragmatism has, everywhere in the western world, been relatively brief and relatively light; the only exceptions would be found in certain parts of the Mediterranean seaboard. But wherever the barbarian culture has been sufficiently long-lived and unmitigated to work out a thoroughly selective effect in the human material subjected to it, there the pragmatic animus may be expected to have become supreme and to inhibit all movement in the direction of scientific inquiry and eliminate all effective aptitude for other than worldly wisdom. What the selective consequences of such a protracted regime of pragmatism would be for the temper of the race may be seen in the human flotsam left by the great civilizations of antiquity, such as Egypt, India, and Persia. Science is not at home among these leavings of barbarism. In these instances of its long and unmitigated dominion the barbarian culture has selectively worked out a temperamental bias and a scheme of life from which objective, matter-of-fact knowledge is virtually excluded in favor of pragmatism, secular and religious. But for the greater part of the race, at least for the greater part of civilized mankind, the regime of the mature barbarian culture has been of relatively short duration, and has had a correspondingly superficial and transient selective effect.

It has not had force and time to eliminate certain elements of human nature handed down from an earlier phase of life, which are not in full consonance with the barbarian animus or with the demands of the pragmatic scheme of thought. The barbarian-pragmatic habit of mind, therefore, is not properly speaking a temperamental trait of the civilized peoples, except possibly within certain class limits (as, e. g., the German nobility). It is rather a tradition, and it does not constitute so tenacious a bias as to make head against the strongly materialistic drift of modern conditions and set aside that increasingly urgent resort to matter-of-fact conceptions that makes for the primacy of science. Civilized mankind does not in any great measure take back atavistically to the upper-barbarian habit of mind. Barbarism covers too small a segment of the life-history of the race to have given an enduring temperamental result. The unmitigated discipline of the higher barbarism in Europe fell on a relatively small proportion of the population, and in the course of time this select element of the population was crossed and blended with the blood of the lower elements whose life always continued to run in the ruts of savagery rather than in those of the high-strung, finished barbarian culture that gave rise to the chivalric scheme of life.

Of the several phases of human culture the most protracted, and the one which has counted for most in shaping the abiding traits of the race, is unquestionably that of savagery. With savagery, for the purpose in hand, is to be classed that lower, relatively peaceable barbarism that is not characterized by wide and sharp class discrepancies or by an unremitting endeavor of one individual or group to get the better of another. Even under the full-grown barbarian culture - as, for instance, during the Middle Ages - the habits of life and the spiritual interests of the great body of the population continue in large measure to bear the character of savagery. The savage phase of culture accounts for by far the greater portion of the life-history of mankind, particularly if the lower barbarism and the vulgar life of later barbarism be counted in with savagery, as in a measure they properly should. This is particularly true of those racial elements that have entered into the composition of the leading peoples of Christendom.

The savage culture is characterized by the relative absence of pragmatism from the higher generalizations of its knowledge and beliefs. As has been noted above, its theoretical creations are chiefly of the nature of mythology shading off into folklore. This genial spinning of apocryphal yarns is, at its best, an amiably inefficient formulation of experiences and observations in terms of something like a life-history of the phenomena observed. It has, on the one hand, little value, and little purpose, in the way of pragmatic expediency, and so it is not closely akin to the pragmatic-barbarian scheme of life; while, on the other hand, it is also ineffectual as a systematic knowledge of matter-of-fact. It is a quest of knowledge, perhaps of systematic knowledge, and it is carried on under the incentive of the idle curiosity. In this respect it falls in the same class with the civilized man's science; but it seeks knowledge not in terms of opaque matter-of-fact, but in terms of some sort of a spiritual life imputed to the facts. It is romantic and Hegelian rather than realistic and Darwinian. The logical necessities of its scheme of thought are necessities of spiritual consistency rather than of quantitative equivalence. It is like science in that it has no ulterior motive beyond the idle craving for a systematic correlation of data; but it is unlike science in that its standardization and correlation of data run in terms of the free play of imputed personal initiative rather than in terms of the constraint of objective cause and effect.

By force of the protracted selective discipline of this past phase of culture, the human nature of civilized mankind is still substantially the human nature of savage man. The ancient equipment of congenital aptitudes and propensities stands over substantially unchanged, though overlaid with barbarian traditions and conventionalities and readjusted by habituation to the exigencies of civilized life. In a measure, therefore, but by no means altogether, scientific inquiry is native to civilized man with his savage heritage, since scientific inquiry proceeds on the same general motive of idle curiosity as guided the savage myth-makers, though it makes use of concepts and standards in great measure alien to the myth-makers' habit of mind. The ancient human predilection for discovering a dramatic play of passion and intrigue in the phenomena of nature still asserts itself. In the most advanced communities, and even among the adepts of modern science, there comes up persistently the revulsion of the native savage against the inhumanly dispassionate sweep of the scientific quest, as well as against the inhumanly ruthless fabric of technological processes that have come out of this search for matter-of-fact knowledge. Very often the savage need of a spiritual interpretation (dramatization) of phenomena breaks through the crust of acquired materialistic habits of thought, to find such refuge as may be had in articles of faith seized on and held by sheer force of instinctive conviction. Science and its creations are more or less uncanny, more or less alien, to that fashion of craving for knowledge that by ancient inheritance animates mankind. Furtively or by an overt breach of consistency, men still seek comfort in marvelous articles of savage-born lore, which contradict the truths of that modern science whose dominion they dare not question, but whose findings at the same time go beyond the breaking point of their jungle-fed spiritual sensibilities.

The ancient ruts of savage thought and conviction are smooth and easy; but however sweet and indispensable the archaic ways of thinking may be to the civilized man's peace of mind, yet such is the binding force of matter-of-fact analysis and inference under modern conditions that the findings of science are not questioned on the whole. The name of science is after all a word to conjure with. So much so that the name and the mannerisms, at least, if nothing more of science, have invaded all fields of learning and have even overrun territory that belongs to the enemy. So there are "sciences" of theology, law, and medicine, as has already been noted above. And there are such things as Christian Science, and "scientific" astrology, palmistry, and the like. But within the field of learning proper there is a similar predilection for an air of scientific acumen and precision where science does not belong. So that even that large range of knowledge that has to do with general information rather than with theory - what is loosely termed scholarship - tends strongly to take on the name and forms of theoretical statement.

However decided the contrast between these branches of knowledge on the one hand, and science properly so called on the other hand, yet even the classical learning, and the humanities generally, fall in with this predilection more and more with each succeeding generation of students. The students of literature, for instance, are more and more prone to substitute critical analysis and linguistic speculation, as the end of their endeavors, in the place of that discipline of taste and that cultivated sense of literary form and literary feeling that must always remain the chief end of literary training, as distinct from philology and the social sciences. There is, of course, no intention to question the legitimacy of a science of philology or of the analytical study of literature as a fact in cultural history, but these things do not constitute training in literary taste, nor can they take the place of it. The effect of this straining after scientific formulations in a field alien to the scientific spirit is as curious as it is wasteful. Scientifically speaking, the quasi-scientific inquiries necessarily begin nowhere and end in the same place; while in point of cultural gain they commonly come to nothing better than spiritual abnegation. But these blindfold endeavors to conform to the canons of science serve to show how wide and unmitigated the sway of science is in the modern community.

Scholarship - that is to say an intimate and systematic familiarity with past cultural achievements - still holds its place in the scheme of learning, in spite of the unadvised efforts of the short-sighted to blend it with the work of science, for it affords play for the ancient genial propensities that ruled men's quest of knowledge before the coming of science or of the outspoken pragmatic barbarism. Its place may not be so large in proportion to the entire field of learning as it was before the scientific era got fully under way. But there is no intrinsic antagonism between science and scholarship, as there is between pragmatic training and scientific inquiry. Modern scholarship shares with modern science the quality of not being pragmatic in its aim. Like science it has no ulterior end. It may be difficult here and there to draw the line between science and scholarship, and it may even more be unnecessary to draw such a line; yet while the two ranges of discipline belong together in many ways, and while there are many points of contact and sympathy between the two; while the two together make up the modern scheme of learning; yet there is no need of confounding the one with the other, nor can the one do the work of the other. The scheme of learning has changed in such manner as to give science the more commanding place, but the scholar's domain has not thereby been invaded, nor has it suffered contraction at the hands of science, whatever may be said of the weak-kneed abnegation of some whose place, if they have one, is in the field of scholarship rather than of science.

All that has been said above has of course nothing to say as to the intrinsic merits of this quest of matter-of-fact knowledge. In point of fact, science gives its tone to modern culture. One may approve or one may deprecate the fact that this opaque, materialistic interpretation of things pervades modern thinking. That is a question of taste, about which there is no disputing. The prevalence of this matter-of-fact inquiry is a feature of modern culture, and the attitude which critics take toward this phenomenon is chiefly significant as indicating how far their own habit of mind coincides with the enlightened common-sense of civilized mankind. It shows in what degree they are abreast of the advance of culture. Those in whom the savage predilection or the barbarian tradition is stronger than their habituation to civilized life will find that this dominant factor of modern life is perverse, if not calamitous; those whose habits of thought have been fully shaped by the machine process and scientific inquiry are likely to find it good. The modern western culture, with its core of matter-of-fact knowledge, may be better or worse than some other cultural scheme, such as the classic Greek, the mediaeval Christian, the Hindu, or the Pueblo Indian. Seen in certain lights, tested by certain standards, it is doubtless better; by other standards, worse. But the fact remains that the current cultural scheme, in its maturest growth, is of that complexion; its characteristic force lies in this matter-of-fact insight; its highest discipline and its maturest aspirations are these. In point of fact, the sober common-sense of civilized mankind accepts no other end of endeavor as self-sufficient and ultimate. That such is the case seems to be due chiefly to the ubiquitous presence of the machine technology and its creations in the life of modern communities. And so long as the machine process continues to hold its dominant place as a disciplinary factor in modern culture, so long must the spiritual and intellectual life of this cultural era maintain the character which the machine process gives it.

But while the scientist's spirit and his achievements stir an unqualified admiration in modern men, and while his discoveries carry conviction as nothing else does, it does not follow that the manner of man which this quest of knowledge produces or requires comes near answering to the current ideal of manhood, or that his conclusions are felt to be as good and beautiful as they are true. The ideal man, and the ideal of human life, even in the apprehension of those who most rejoice in the advances of science, is neither the finking skeptic in the laboratory nor the animated slide-rule. The quest of science is relatively new. It is a cultural factor not comprised, in anything like its modern force, among those circumstances whose selective action in the far past has given to the race the human nature which it now has. The race reached the human plane with little of this searching knowledge of facts; and throughout the greater part of its life-history on the human plane it has been accustomed to make its higher generalizations and to formulate its larger principles of life in other terms than those of passionless matter-of-fact. This manner of knowledge has occupied an increasing share of men's attention in the past, since it bears in a decisive way upon the minor affairs of workday life; but it has never until now been put in the first place, as the dominant note of human culture. The normal man, such as his inheritance has made him, has therefore good cause to be restive under its dominion.

Chapter 3
The Mutation Theory and the Blond Race

The theories of racial development by mutation, associated with the name of Mendel, when they come to be freely applied to man, must greatly change the complexion of many currently debated questions of race - as to origins, migrations, dispersion, chronology, cultural derivation and sequence. In some respects the new theories should simplify current problems of ethnology, and they may even dispense with many analyses and speculations that have seemed of great moment in the past.

The main postulate of the Mendelian theories - the stability of type - has already done much service in anthropological science, being commonly assumed as a matter of course in arguments dealing with the derivation and dispersion of races and peoples. It is only by force of this assumption that ethnologists are able to identify any given racial stock over intervals of space or time, and so to trace the racial affinities of any given people. Question has been entertained from time to time as to the racial fixity of given physical traits - as, e.g., stature, the cephalic indices, or hair and eye color - but on the whole these and other standard marks of race are still accepted as secure grounds of identification[54].

Indeed, without some such assumption any ethnological inquiry must degenerate into mere wool-gathering .But along with this, essentially Mendelian, postulate of the stability of types, ethnologists have at the same time habitually accepted the incompatible Darwinian doctrine that racial types vary incontinently after a progressive fashion, arising through insensible cumulative variations and passing into new specific forms by the same method, under the Darwinian rule of the selective survival of slight and unstable (non-typical) variations. The effect of these two incongruous premises has been to leave discussions of race derivation somewhat at loose ends wherever the two postulates cross one another.

If it be assumed, or granted, that racial types are stable, it follows as a matter of course that these types or races have not arisen by the cumulative acquirement of unstable non-specific traits, but must have originated by mutation or by some analogous method, and this view must then find its way into anthropology as into the other biological sciences. When such a step is taken an extensive revision of questions of race will be unavoidable, and an appreciable divergence may then be looked for among speculations on the mutational affinities of the several races and cultures.

Among matters so awaiting revision are certain broad questions of derivation and ethnography touching the blond race or races of Europe. Much

---

[54] Cf., however, W. Ridgeway, "The Application of Zoological Laws to Man," Report, British Association for Advancement of Science (Dublin), 1908.

attention, and indeed much sentiment, has been spent on this general topic. The questions involved are many and diverse, and many of them have been subject of animated controversy, without definitive conclusions.

The mutation theories, of course, have immediately to do with the facts of biological derivation alone, but when the facts are reviewed in the light of these theories it will be found that questions of cultural origins and relationship are necessarily drawn into the inquiry. In particular, an inquiry into the derivation and distribution of the blond stock will so intimately involve questions of the Aryan speech and institutions as to be left incomplete without a somewhat detailed attention to this latter range of questions. So much so that an inquiry into the advent and early fortunes of the blond stock in Europe will fall, by convenience, under two distinct but closely related captions:

The Origin of the Blond Type, and The Derivation of the Aryan Culture. (a) It is held, on the one hand, that there is but a single blond race, type or stock (Keane, Lapouge, Sergi), and on the other hand that there are several such races or types, more or less distinct but presumably related (Deniker, Beddoe, and other, especially British, ethnologists). (b) There is no good body of evidence going to establish a great antiquity for the blond stock, and there are indications, though perhaps inconclusive, that the blond strain, including all the blond types, is of relatively late date - unless a Berber (Kabyle) blond race is to be accepted in a more unequivocal manner than hitherto. (c) Neither is there anything like convincing evidence that this blond strain has come from outside of Europe - except, again, for the equivocal Kabyle - or that any blond race has ever been widely or permanently distributed outside of its present European habitat. (d)

The blond race is not found unmixed. In point of pedigree all individuals showing the blond traits are hybrids, and the greater number of them show their mixed blood in their physical traits. (e) There is no community, large or small, made up exclusively of blonds, or nearly so, and there is no good evidence available that such an all-blond or virtually all-blond community ever has existed, either in historic or prehistoric times. The race appears never to have lived in isolation. (f) It occurs in several (perhaps hybrid) variants - unless these variants are to be taken (with Deniker) as several distinct races. (g) Counting the dolicho-blond as the original type of the race, its nearest apparent relative among the races of mankind is the Mediterranean (of Sergi), at least in point of physical traits. At the same time the blond race, or at least the dolicho-blond type, has never since neolithic times, so far as known, extensively and permanently lived in contact with the Mediterranean. (h) The various (national) ramifications of the blond stock - or rather the various racial mixtures into which an appreciable blond element enters - are all, and to all appearance have always been, of Aryan ("Indo-European," "Indo-Germanic") speech - with the equivocal exception of the Kabyle. (i) Yet far the greater number and variety (national and linguistic) of men who use the Aryan speech are not prevailingly blond, or even appreciably mixed with blond. (j) The blond race, or the peoples with an appreciable blond admixture, and particularly the communities in which the dolicho-blond element prevails, show little or none of the peculiarly Aryan institutions - understanding by that phrase not the known institutions of the ancient Germanic peoples, but that range of institutions said by competent philologists to be reflected in the primitive Aryan speech. (k) These considerations raise the presumption that the blond race was not originally of Aryan speech or of Aryan culture, and they also suggest (l) that the Mediterranean, the nearest apparent relative of the dolicho-blond, was likewise not originally Aryan.

Accepting the mutation theory, then, for the purpose in hand, and leaving any questions of Aryanism on one side for the present, a canvass of the situation so outlined may be offered in such bold, crude and summary terms as should be admissible in an analysis which aims to be tentative and provisional only. It may be conceived that the dolichocephalic blond originated as a mutant of the Mediterranean type (which it greatly resembles in its scheme of biometric measurements[55] probably some time after that race had effected a permanent lodgment on the continent of Europe. The Mediterranean stock may be held (Sergi and Keane) to have come into Europe from Africa,[56] whatever its remoter derivation may have been. It is, of course, not impossible that the mutation which gave rise to the dolicbo-blond may have occurred before the parent stock left Africa, or rather before it was shut out of Africa by the submergence of the land connection across Sicily, but the probabilities seem to be against such a view. The conditions would appear to have been less favorable to a mutation of this kind in the African habitat of the parent stock than in Europe, and less favorable in Europe during earlier quaternary time than toward the close of the glacial period.

The causes which give rise to a variation of type have always been sufficiently obscure, whether the origin of species be conceived after the Darwinian or the Mendelian fashion, and the mutation theories have hitherto afforded little light on that question. Yet the Mendelian postulate that the type is stable except for such a mutation as shall establish a new type raises at least the presumption that such a mutation will take place only under exceptional circumstances, that is to stay, under circumstances so substantially different from what the type is best adapted to as to subject it to some degree of physiological strain. It is to be presumed that no mutation will supervene so long as the conditions of life do not vary materially from what they have been during the previous uneventful life-history of the type. Such is the presumption apparently involved in the theory and such is also the suggestion afforded by the few experimental cases of observed mutation, as, e.g., those studied by De Vries.

A considerable climatic change, such as would seriously alter the conditions of life either directly or through its effect on the food supply, might be conceived to bring on a mutating state in the race; or the like effect

---

[55] Cf. Sergi, The Mediterranean Race, ch. xi, xiii.
[56] Sergi, Arii e Italici; Keane, Man Past and Present, ch. xii.

might be induced by a profound cultural change, particularly any such change in the industrial arts as would radically affect the material conditions of life. These considerations, mainly speculative it is true, suggest that the dolicho-blond mutant could presumably have emerged only at a time when the parent stock was exposed to notably novel conditions of life, such as would be presumed (with De Vries) to tend to throw the stock into a specifically unstable (mutating) state; at the same time these novel conditions of life must also have been specifically of such a nature-as to favor the survival and multiplication of this particular human type. The climatic tolerance of the dolicho-blond, e.g., is known to be exceptionally narrow. Now, it is not known, indeed there is no reason to presume, that the Mediterranean race was exposed to such variations of climate or of culture before it entered Europe as might be expected to induce a mutating state in the stock, and at the same time a mutant gifted with the peculiar climatic intolerance of the dolicho-blond would scarcely have survived tinder the conditions offered by northern Africa in late quaternary time. But the required conditions are had later on in Europe, after the Mediterranean was securely at home in that continent.

The whole episode may be conceived to have run off somewhat in the following manner. The Mediterranean race is held to have entered Europe in force during quaternary time, presumably after the quaternary period was well advanced, most likely during the last genial, interglacial period. This race then brought the neolithic culture, but without the domestic animals (or plants?) that are a characteristic feature of the later neolithic age, and it encountered at least the remnants of an older, palaeolithic population. This older European population was made up of several racial stocks, some of which still persist as obscure and minor elements in the later peoples of Europe. The (geologic) date to be assigned this intrusion of the Mediterranean race into Europe is of course not, and can perhaps never be, determined with any degree of nicety or confidence. But there is a probability that it coincides with the recession of the ice-sheet, following one or another of the severer periods of glaciations, that occurred before the submergence of the land connection between Europe and Africa, over Gibraltar, Sicily, and perhaps Crete. How late in quaternary time the final submergence of the Mediterranean basin occurred is still a matter of surmise; the intrusion of the Mediterranean race into Europe appears, on archaeological evidence, to have occurred in late quaternary time, and in the end this archaeological evidence may help to decide the geologic date of the severance of Europe from Africa.

The Mediterranean race seems to have spread easily over the habitable surface of Europe and shortly to have grown numerous and taken rank as the chief racial element in the neolithic population; which argues that no very considerable older population occupied the European continent at the time of the Mediterranean invasion; which in turn implies that the fairly large (Magdalenian) population of the close of the palaeolithic age was in great part destroyed or expelled by the climatic changes that coincided with or immediately preceded the advent of the Mediterranean race. The known characteristics of the Magdalenian culture indicate a technology, a situation and perhaps a race, somewhat closely paralleled by the Eskimo;[57] which argues that the climatic situation before which this Magdalenian race and culture gave way would have been that of a genial interglacial period rather than a period of glaciation.

During this genial (perhaps sub-tropical) inter-glacial period immediately preceding the last great glaciation the Magdalenian stock would presumably find Europe climatically untenable, judging by analogy with the Eskimo; whereas the Mediterranean stock should have found it an eminently favorable habitat, for this race has always succeeded best in a warm-temperate climate.

Both the extensive northward range of the early neolithic (Mediterranean) settlements and the total disappearance of the Magdalenian culture from the European continent point to a climatic situation in Europe more favorable to the former race and more unwholesome for the latter than the conditions known to have prevailed at any time since the last interglacial period, especially in the higher latitudes. The indications would seem to be that the whole of Europe, even the Baltic and Arctic seaboards, became climatically so fully impossible for the Magdalenian race during this interglacial period as to result in its extinction or definitive expulsion; for when, in recent times, climatically suitable conditions return, on the Arctic seaboard, the culture which takes the place that should have been occupied by the Magdalenian is the Finnic (Lapp) - a culture unrelated to the Magdalenian either in race or technology, although of much the same cultural level and dealing with a material environment of much the same character. And this genial interval that was fatal to the Magdalenian was, by just so much, favorable to the Mediterranean race.

But glacial conditions presently returned, though with less severity than the next preceding glacial period; and roughly coincident with the close of the genial interval in Europe the land connection with Africa was cut off by submergence, shutting off retreat to the south. How far communication with Asia may have been interrupted during the subsequent cold period, by the local glaciation of the Caucasus, Elburz and Armenian highlands, is for the present apparently not to be determined, although it is to be presumed that the outlet to the east would at least be seriously obstructed during the glaciation. There would then be left available for occupation, mainly by the Mediterranean race, central and southern Europe together with the islands, notably Sicily and Crete, left over as remnants of the earlier continuous land between Europe and Africa.

The southern extensions of the mainland, and more particularly the islands, would still afford a favorable place for the Mediterranean race and its cultural growth. So that the early phases of the great Cretan (Aegean) civilisation are presumably to be assigned to this period that is covered by the last advance of the ice in northern Europe. But the greater portion of

---

[57] Cf. W. J. Sollas, " Palaeolithic Races and their Modern Representatives," Science Progress, vol. iv, 1909-1910.

the land area so left accessible to the Mediterranean race, in central or even in southern Europe, would have been under glacial or subglacial climatic conditions. For this race, essentially native to a warm climate, this situation on the European mainland would be sufficiently novel and trying, particularly throughout that ice-fringed range of country where they would be exposed to such cold and damp as this race has never easily tolerated.

The situation so outlined would afford such a condition of physiological strain as might be conceived to throw the stock into a specifically unstable state and so bring on a phase of mutation. At the same time this situation, climatic and technological, would be notably favorable to the survival and propagation of a type gifted with all the peculiar capacities and limitations of the dolicho-blond; so that any mutant showing the traits characteristic of that type would then have had an eminently favorable chance of survival. Indeed, it is doubtful, in the present state of the available evidence, whether such a type of man could have survived in Europe from or over any period of quaternary time prior to the last period of glaciation. The last preceding interglacial period appears to have been of a sufficiently genial (perhaps sub-tropical) character throughout Europe to have definitively eliminated the Magdalenian race and culture, and a variation of climate in the genial sense sufficiently pronounced to make Europe absolutely untenable for the Magdalenian - presumed to be something of a counterpart to the Eskimo both in race and culture - should probably have reached the limit of tolerance for the dolicho-blond as well. The latter is doubtless not as intolerant of a genial – warm-temperate - climate as the former, but the dolicho-blond after all stands much nearer to the Eskimo in this matter of climatic tolerance than to either of the two chief European stocks with which it is associated. Apparently no racial stock with a climatic tolerance approximately like that of the Eskimo, the Magdalenian, or the current races of the Arctic seaboard, survived over the last interglacial period; and if the dolicho-blond is conceived to have lived through that period it would appear to have been by a precariously narrow margin. So that, on one ground and another, the mutation out of which the dolicho-blond has arisen is presumably to be assigned to the latest period of glaciation in Europe, and with -some probability to the time when the latest glaciation was at its maximum, and to the region where glacial and seaboard influences combined to give that racial type a differential advantage over all others.

This dolicho-blond mutation may, of course, have occurred only once, in a single individual, but it should seem more probable, in the light of De Vries' experiments, that the mutation will have been repeated in the same specific form in several individuals in the same general locality and in the same general period of time. Indeed, it would seem highly probably that several typically distinct mutations will have occurred, repeatedly, at roughly the same period and in the same region, giving rise to several new types, some of which, including the dolicho-blond, will have survived. Many, presumably the greater number, of these mutant types will have disappeared, selectively, being unfit to survive under those sub-glacial seaboard conditions that were eminently favorable to the dolicho-blond; while other mutants arising out of the same mutating period and adapted to climatic conditions of a more continental character, suitable to more of a continental habitat, less humid, at a higher altitude and with a wider seasonal variation of temperature, may have survived in the regions farther inland, particularly eastward of the selectively defined habitat of the dolicho-blond. These latter may have given rise to several blond races, such as are spoken for by Deniker[58] and certain British ethnologists.

The same period of mutation may well have given rise also to one or more brunet types, some of which may have survived. But if any new brunet type has come up within a period so recent as this implies, the fact has not been noted or surmised hitherto - unless the brunet races spoken for by Deniker are to be accepted as typically distinct and referred to such an origin. The evidence for the brunet stocks has not been canvassed with a question of this kind in view. These stocks have not been subject of such eager controversy as the dolicho-blond, and the attention given them has been correspondingly less. The case of the blond is unique in respect of the attention spent on questions of its derivation and prehistory, and it is also singular in respect of the facility with which it can be isolated for the purposes of such an inquiry. This large and persistent attention, from all sorts of ethnologists, has brought the evidence bearing on the dolicho-blond into such shape as to permit more confident generalizations regarding that race than any other.

In any case the number of mutant individuals, whether of one or of several specific types, will have been very few as compared with the numbers of the parent stock from which they diverged, even if they may have been somewhat numerous as counted absolutely, and the survivors whose offspring produced a permanent effect on the European peoples will have been fewer still. It results that these surviving mutants will not have been isolated from the parent stock, and so could not breed in isolation, but must forthwith be crossed on the parent stock and could therefore yield none but hybrid offspring. From the outset, therefore, the community or communities in which the blond mutants were propagated would be made up of a mixture of blond and brunet, with the brunet greatly preponderating.

It may be added that in all probability there were also present in this community from the start one or more minor brunet elements besides the predominant Mediterranean, and that at least shortly after the close of the glacial period the new brachycephalic brunet (Alpine) race comes into the case; so that the chances favor an early and persistent crossing of the dolicho-blond with more than one brunet type, and hence they favor complications and confusion of types from the start. It follows that, in point of pedigree, according to this view there neither is nor ever has been a pure-

---

[58] The Races of Mankind; and "Les six races composant la population de l' Europe," Journal Anth. Inst., 1906.

bred dolicho-blond individual since the putative original mutant with which the type came in. But tinder the Mendelian rule of hybrids it is none the less to be expected that, in the course of time and of climatically selective breeding, individuals (perhaps in appreciable numbers) will have come up from time to time showing the type characters unmixed and unweakened, and effectively pure-bred in point of heredity. Indeed, such individuals, effectively pure-bred or tending to the establishment of a pure line, will probably have emerged somewhat frequently under conditions favorable to the pure type. The selective action of the conditions of life in the habitat most favorable to the propagation of the dolicho-blond has worked in a rough and uncertain way toward the establishment, in parts of the Baltic and North Sea region, of communities made up prevailingly of blonds. Yet none of these communities most favorably placed for a selective breeding in the direction of a pure dolicho-blond population have gone far enough in that direction to allow it safely to be said that the composite population of any such given locality is more than half blond. Placed as it is in a community of nations made up of a hybrid mixture of several racial stocks there is probably no way at present of reaching a convincing demonstration of the typical originality of this dolicho-bland mutant, as contrasted with the other blond types with which it is associated in the European population; but certain general considerations go decidedly, perhaps decisively, to enforce such a view: (a) This type shows such a pervasive resemblance to a single one of the known older and more widely distributed types of man (the Mediterranean) as to suggest descent by mutation from this one rather than derivation by crossing of any two or more known types.

The like can not be said of the other blond types, all and several of which may plausibly be explained as hybrids of known types. They have the appearance of blends, or rather of biometrical compromises, between two or more existing varieties of man. Whereas it does not seem feasible to explain the dolicho-blond as such a blend or compromise between any known racial types. (b) The dolicho-bland occurs, in a way, centrally to the other blond types, giving them a suggestive look of being ramifications of the blond stock, by hybridization, into regions not wholly suited to the typical blond. The like can scarcely be said for any of the other European types or races. The most plausible exception would be Deniker's East-European or Oriental race, Beddce's Saxon, which stands in a somewhat analogous spacial relation to the other blond types. But this brachycephalic blond is not subject to the same sharp climatic limitations that hedge about the dolicho-blond; it occurs apparently with equally secure viability within the littoral home area of the dolicho-blond and in continental situations where conditions of altitude and genial climate would bar the latter from permanent settlement.

The ancient and conventionally accepted center of diffusion of blondness in Europe lies within the seaboard region bordering on the south Baltic, the North Sea and the narrow waters of the Scandinavian peninsulas. Probably, if this broad central area of diffusion were to be narrowed down to a particular spot, the consensus of opinion as to where the narrower area of characteristic blondness is to be looked for, would converge on the lands immediately about the narrow Scandinavian waters. This would seem to hold true for historic and for prehistoric times alike. This region is at the same time, by common consent, the peculiar home of the dolicho-blond, rather than of any other blond type. (c) The well known but little discussed climatic limitation of the blond race applies particularly to the dolicho-blond, and only in a pronouncedly slighter degree to the other blond types. The dolicho-blond is subject to a strict regional limitation, the other blond types to a much less definite and wider limitation of the same kind. Hence these others are distributed somewhat widely, over regions often remote and climatically different from the home area of the dolicho-blond, giving them the appearance of being dispersed outward from this home area as hybrid extensions of the central and typical blond stock. A further and equally characteristic feature of this selective localization of the dolicho-blond race is the fact that while this race does not succeed permanently outside the seaboard region of the south Baltic and North Sea, there is no similar selective bar against other races intruding into this region. Although the dolicho-blond perhaps succeeds better within its home area than any other competing stock or type, yet several other types of man succeed so well within the same region as to hold it, and apparently always to have held it, in joint tenancy with the dolicho-blond.

A close relationship, amounting to varietal identity, of the Kabyle with the dolicho-blond has been spoken for by Keane and by other ethnologists. But the very different climatic tolerance of the two races should put such an identity out of the question. The Kabyle lives and thrives best, where his permanent home area has always been, in a high and dry country, sufficiently remote from the sea to make it a continental rather than a littoral habitat. The dolicho-blond, according to all available evidence, can live in the long run only in a seaboard habitat, damp and cool, at a high latitude and low altitude. There is no known instance of this race having gone out from its home area on the northern seaboard into such a region as that inhabited by the Kabyle and having survived for an appreciable number of generations. That this type of man should have come from Mauritania, where it could apparently not live under the conditions known to have prevailed there in the recent or the remoter past, would seem to be a biologic impossibility. Hitherto, when the dolicho-blond has migrated into such or a similar habitat it has not adapted itself to the new climatic requirements but has presently disappeared off the face of the land. Indeed, the experiment has been tried in Mauritanian territory. If the Kabyle blond is to be correlated with those of Europe, it will in all probability have to be assigned an independent origin, to be derived from an earlier mutation of the same Mediterranean stock to which the dolicho-blond is to be traced.

Questions of race in Europe are greatly obscured by the prevalence of hybrid types having more or less fixity and being more or less distinctly localized. The existing European peoples are hybrid mixtures of two or more racial stocks. The further fact is sufficiently obvious, though it has received less critical attention than might be, that these several hybrid populations have in the course of time given rise to a number of distinct national and local types, differing characteristically from one another and having acquired a degree of permanence, such as to simulate racial characters and show well marked national and local traits in point of physiognomy and temperament. Presumably, these national and local types of physique and temperament are hybrid types that have been selectively bred into these characteristic forms in adaptation to the peculiar circumstances of environment and culture under which each particular local population is required to live, and that have been so fixed (provisionally) by selective breeding of the hybrid material subject to such locally uniform conditions -except so far as the local characters in question are of the nature of habits and are themselves therefore to be classed as an institutional element rather than as characteristics of race.

It is evident that under the Mendelian law of hybridization the range of favorable, or viable, variations in any hybrid population must be very large - much larger than the range of fluctuating (non-typical) variations obtainable under any circumstances in a pure-bred race. It also follows from these same laws of hybridization that by virtue of the mutual exclusiveness of allelomorphic characters or groups of characters it is possible selectively to obtain an effectually "pure line" of hybrids combining characters drawn from each of the two or more parent stocks engaged, and that such a composite pure line may selectively be brought to a provisional fixity[59] in any such hybrid population. And under conditions favorable to a type endowed with any given hybrid combination of characters so worked out the given hybrid type (composite pure line) may function in the racial mixture in which it is so placed very much as an actual racial type would behave under analogous circumstances; so that, e.g., under continued intercrossing such a hybrid population would tend cumulatively to breed true to this provisionally stable hybrid type, rather than to the actual racial type represented by any one of the parent stocks of which the hybrid population is ultimately made up, unless the local conditions should selectively favor one or another of these ultimate racial types.

Evidently, too, the number of such provisionally stable composite pure lines that may be drawn from any hybrid mixture of two or more parent stocks must be very considerable - indeed virtually unlimited; so that on this ground there should be room for any conceivable number of provisionally stable national or local types of physique and temperament, limited only by the number of characteristically distinguishable local environments or situations that might each selectively act to characterize and establish a locally characteristic composite pure line; each answering to the selective exigencies of the habitat and cultural environment in which it is placed, and each responding to these exigencies in much the same fashion as would an actual racial type - provided only that this provisionally stable composite pure line is not crossed on pure-bred individuals of ei-

---

[59] Illustrated by the various pure breeds or "races" of domestic animals.

ther of the parent stocks from which it is drawn, pure-bred in respect of the allelomorphic characters which give the hybrid type its typical traits.

When the hybrid type is so crossed back on one or other of its parent stocks it should be expected to break down; but in so slow-breeding a species as man, with so large a complement of unit characters (some 4000 it has been estimated), it will be difficult to decide empirically which of the two lines - the hybrid or the parent stock - proves itself in the offspring effectively to be a racial type; that is to say, which of the two (or more) proves to be an ultimately stable type arisen by a Mendelian mutation, and which is a provisionally stable composite pure line selectively derived from a cross. The inquiry at this point, therefore, will apparently have to content itself with arguments of probability drawn from the varying behavior of the existing hybrid types under diverse conditions of life.

Such general consideration of the behavior of the blond types of Europe, other than the dolicho-blond, and more particularly consideration of their viability under divergent climatic conditions, should apparently incline to the view that they are hybrid types, of the nature of provisionally stable composite pure lines.

So far, therefore, as the evidence has yet been canvassed, it seems probable on the whole that the dolicho-blond is the only survivor from among the several mutants that may have arisen out of this presumed mutating period; that the other existing blond types, as well as certain brunets, are derivatives of the hybrid offspring of the dolicho-blond crossed on the parent Mediterranean stock or on other brunet stocks with which the race has been in contact early or late; and that several of these hybrid lines have in the course of time selectively been established as provisionally stable types (composite pure lines), breakable only by a fresh cross with one or other of the parent types from which the hybrid line sprang, according to the Mendelian rule[60].

All these considerations may not be convincing, but they are at least suggestive to the effect that if originality is to be claimed for any one of the blond types or stocks it can best be claimed for the dolicho-blond, while the other blond types may better be accounted for as the outcome of the crossing of this stock on one or another of the brunet stocks of Europe.

---

[60] Mr. R. B. Bean's discussion of Deniker's "Six Races," e. g., goes far to show that such is probably the standing of the blond types, other than the dolicho-blond, among these six races of Europe; although such is not the conclusion to which Mr. Bean comes. Philippine Journal of Science, September, 1909.

Chapter 4
The Blond Race and the Aryan Culture

It has been argued in an earlier paper[61] that the blond type or types of man (presumably the dolichocephalic blond) arose by mutation from the Mediterranean stock during the last period of severe glaciation in Europe. This would place the emergence of this racial type roughly coincident with the beginning of the European neolithic; the evidence going presumptively to show that the neolithic technology came into Europe with the Mediterranean race, at or about the same time with that race, and that the mutation which gave rise to the dolicho-blond took place after the Mediterranean race was securely settled in Europe. Since this blond mutant made good its survival under the circumstances into which it so was thrown it should presumably be suited by native endowment to the industrial and climatic conditions that prevailed through the early phases of the neolithic age in Europe; that is to say, it would be a type of man selectively adapted to the technological situation characteristic of the early neolithic but lacking as yet the domestic animals (and crop-plants?) that presently give much of its character to that culture.

Beginning, then, with the period of the last severe glaciation, and starting with this technological equipment, those portions of the European population that contained an appreciable and increasing admixture of the blond may be conceived to have ranged across the breadth of Europe, particularly in the lowlands, in the belt of damp and cool country that fringed the ice, and to have followed the receding ice-sheet northward when the general climate of Europe began to take on its present character with the returning warmth and dryness. By force of the strict climatic limitation to which this type is subject, the blond element, and more particularly the dolicho-blond, will presently have disappeared by selective elimination from the population of those regions from which the ice-sheet and its fringe of cool and humid climate had receded. The cool and humid belt suited to the propagation of the blond mutant (and its blond hybrids) would shift northward and shorten down to the seaboard as the glacial conditions in which it had originated presently ceased. So that presently, when Europe finally lost its ice-sheet, the blond race and its characteristic hybrids would be found confined nearly within the bounds which have marked its permanent extension in historic times. These limits have, no doubt, fluctuated somewhat in response to secular variations of climate; but on the whole they appear to have, been singularly permanent and singularly rigid. Apparently after the dolicho-blond had come to occupy the restricted habitat which the stock has since continued to hold on the

---

[61] "The Mutation Theory and the Blond Race," in The Journal of Race Development, April, 1913.

northern seaboard of Europe, toward the close of what is known in Danish chronology as the "older stone age," the early stock of domestic animals appear to have been introduced into Europe from Asia; the like statement will hold more doubtfully for the older staple crop plants, with the reservation that their introduction appears to antedate that of the domestic animals. At least some such date seems indicated by their first ap pearance in Denmark late in the period of the "kitchen middens." Virtually all of these essential elements of their material civilisation appear to have come to the blond-hybrid communities settled on the narrow Scandinavian waters, as to the rest of Europe, from Turkestan. This holds true at least for the domestic animals as a whole, the possible exceptions among the early introductions being not of great importance. Some of the early crop plants may well have come from what is now Mesopotamian or Persian territory, and may conceivably have reached western Europe appreciably earlier, without affecting the present argument. If the European horse bad been domesticated in palaeolithic times, as appears at least extremely probable, that technological gain appears to have been lost before the close of the palaeolithic age; perhaps along with the extinction of the European horse.

These new elements of technological equipment, the crop plants and animals, greatly affected the character of the neolithic culture in Europe; visibly so as regards the region presumably occupied by the dolichoblond, - or the blond-hybrid peoples. On the material side of the community's life they would bring change direct and immediate, altering the whole scheme of ways and means and shifting the pursuit of a livelihood to new lines; and on the immaterial side their effect would be scarcely less important, in that the new ways and means and the new manner of life requisite and induced by their use would bring on certain new institutional features suitable to a system of mixed farming- Whatever may have been the manner of their introduction, whether they were transmitted peaceably by insensible diffusion from group to group or were carried in with a high band by a new intrusive population that overran the country and imposed its own cultural scheme upon the Europeans along with the new ways and means of life, - in any case these new cultural elements will have spread over the face of Europe somewhat gradually and will have reached the blond hybrid communities in their remote corner of the continent only after an appreciable lapse of time. Yet, it is to be noted, it is after all relatively early in neolithic times that certain of the domestic plants and animals first come into evidence in the Scandinavian region.

The crop plants appear to have come in earlier than the domestic animals, being perhaps brought in by the peoples of the Mediterranean race at their first occupation of Europe in late quaternary time. With tillage necessarily goes a sedentary manner of life. So that at their first introduction the domestic animals were intruded into a system of husbandry carried on by a population living in settled communities, and drawing their livelihood in great part from the tilled ground but also in part from the sea and from the game-bearing forests that covered much of the country at that time. It was into such a situation that the domestic animals were intruded on their first coming into Europe, - particularly into the seaboard region of north Europe.

On the open ranges of western and central Asia, from which these domestic animals came, and even in the hill country of that general region, the peoples that draw their livelihood from cattle and sheep are commonly of a nomadic habit of life, in the sense that the requirements of forage for their herds and flocks bold them to an unremitting round of seasonal migration. It results that, except in the broken hill country, these peoples habitually make use of movable habitations, live in camps rather than in settled, sedentary communities. Certain peculiar institutional arrangements also result from this nomadic manner of life associated with the care of flocks and herds on a large scale. But on their introduction into Europe the domestic animals appear on the whole not to have supplanted tillage and given rise to such a nomadic-pastoral scheme of life, exclusively given to cattle raising, but rather to have fallen into a system of mixed farming which combined tillage with a sedentary or quasi-sedentary grazing industry. Such particularly appears to have been the case in the seaboard region of the north, where there is no evidence of tillage having been displaced by a nomadic grazing industry. Indeed, the small-scale and broken topography of this European region has never admitted a large-scale cattle industry, such as has prevailed on the wide Asiatic ranges. An exception, at least partial and circumscribed, may perhaps be found in the large plains of the extreme Southeast and in the Danube valley; and it appears also that grazing, after the sedentary fashion, took precedence of tillage in prehistoric Ireland as well as here and there in the hilly countries of southern and central Europe.

Such an introduction of tillage and grazing would mean a revolutionary change in the technology of the European stone age, and a technological revolution of this kind will unavoidably bring on something of a radical change in the scheme of Institutions under which the community lives; primarily in the institutions governing the details of its economic life, but secondarily also in its domestic and civil relations. When such a change comes about through the intrusion of new material factors the presumption should be that the range of institutions already associated with these material factors in their earlier home will greatly influence the resulting new growth of institutions in the new situation, even if circumstances may not permit these alien institutions to be brought in and put Into effect with the scope and force which they may have had in the culture out of which they have come. Some assimilation is to be looked for even if circumstances will not permit the adoption of the full scheme of institutions, and the institutions originally associated with the intrusive technology will be found surviving with least loss or qualification in those portions of the invaded territory where the invaders have settled in force, and particularly where conditions have permitted them to retain something of their earlier manner of life.

The bringers of these new elements of culture, material and immaterial, had acquired what they brought with them on the open sheep and cattle ranges of the central Asiatic plains and uplands, - as is held to be the unequivocal testimony of the Aryan speech, and as is borne out by the latest explorations in that region. These later explorations indicate west-central Turkestan as the probable center of the domestication and diffusion of the animals, if not also of the crop plants, that have stocked Europe. Of what race these bearers of the new technology and culture may have been, and just what they brought into Europe, is all a matter of inference and surmise. It was once usual to infer, as a ready matter of course, that these immigrant pastoral nomads from the Asiatic uplands were "Aryans," "Indo-Europeans," "Indo-Germans," of a predominantly blond physique. But what has been said above as well as in the earlier paper referred to comes near excluding the possibility of these invaders being blonds, or more specifically the dolicho-blond. It is, of course, conceivable, with Keane (if his speculations on this head are to be taken seriously), that a fragment of the alleged blond race from Mauretania may have wandered off into Turkestan by way of the Levant, and so may there have acquired the habits of a pastoral life, together with the Aryan speech and institutions, and may then presently have carried these cultural factors into Europe and imposed them on the European population, blond and brunet. But such speculations, which once were allowable though idle, have latterly been put out of all question, at least for the present, by the recent Pumpelly explorations in Turkestan. It is, for climatic reasons, extremely improbable that any blond stock should have inhabited any region of the central-Asiatic plains or uplands long enough to acquire the pastoral habits of life and the concomitant Aryan speech and institutions, and it is fairly certain that the dolicho-blond could not have survived for that length of time under the requisite conditions of climate and topography.

It is similarly quite out of the question that the dolichoblond, arising as a mutant type late in quaternary time, should have created the Aryan speech and culture in Europe, since neither the archaeological evidence nor the known facts of climate and topography permit the hypothesis that a pastoral-nomadic culture of home growth has ever prevailed in Europe on a scale approaching that required for such a result. And there is but little more possibility that the bringers of the new (Aryan) culture should have been of the Mediterranean race; although the explorations referred to make it nearly certain that the communities which domesticated the pastoral animals (and perhaps the crop-plants) in Turkestan were of that race. The Mediterranean race originally is Hamitic, not Aryan, it is held by men competent to speak on that matter, and the known (presumably) Mediterranean prehistoric settlements in Turkestan, at Anau, are moreover obviously the settlements of a notably sedentary people following a characteristically peaceable mode of life. The population of these settlements might of course conceivably have presently acquired the nomadic and predatory habits reflected by the Aryan speech and institutions, but there is no evidence of such an episode at Anau, where the finds show an uninterrupted peaceable and sedentary occupation of the sites throughout the period that could come in question.

The population of the settlements at Anau could scarcely have made such a cultural innovation, involving the adoption of an alien language, except under the pressure of conquest by an invading people; which would involve the subjection of the peaceable communities of Anau and the incorporation of their inhabitants as slaves or as a servile class in the predatory organisation of their masters. The Mediterranean people of Anau could accordingly have had a hand in carrying this pastoral-predatory (Aryan) culture into the West only as a subsidiary racial element in a migratory community made up primarily of another racial stock.

This leaves the probability that an Asiatic stock, without previous settled sedentary habits of life, acquired the domesticated animals from the sedentary and peaceable communities of Anau, or from some similar village (pueblo) or villages of western Turkestan, and then through a (moderately) long experience of nomadic pastoral life acquired also the predatory habits and institutions that commonly go with a pastoral life on a large scale. These cultural traits they acquired in such a degree of elaboration and maturity as is implied by the primitive Aryan (or, better, proto-Aryan) speech, including a more or less well developed patriarchal system; so that they would presently become a militant and migratory community somewhat after the later-known Tatar fashion, and so made their way westward as a self-sufficient migratory host and carried the new material culture into Europe together with the alien Aryan speech. It is at the same time almost unavoidable that in such an event this migratory host would have carried with them into the West an appreciable servile contingent made up primarily of enslaved captives from the peaceable agricultural settlements of the Mediterranean race, which had originally supplied them with their stock of domestic animals.

Along with these new technological elements and the changes of law and custom which their adoption would bring on, there will also have come in the new language that was designed to describe these new ways and means of life and was adapted to express the habits of thought which the new ways and means bred in the peoples that adopted them. The immigrant pastoral (proto-Aryan) language and the pastoral (patriarchal and predatory) law and custom will in some degree have been bound up with the technological ways and means out of which they arose, and they would be expected to have reached and affected the various communities of Europe in somewhat the same time and the same measure in which these material facts of the pastoral life made their way among these peoples. In the course of the diffusion of these cultural elements, material and immaterial, among the European communities the language and in a less degree the domestic and civil usages and ideals bred by the habits of the pastoral life might of course come to be dissociated from their material or technological basis and might so be adopted by remoter peoples who never acquired any large measure of the material culture of those pastoral nomads whose manner of life had once given rise to these immaterial features of Aryan civilisation.

Certain considerations going to support this far-flung line of conjectural history may be set out more in detail: (a) The Aryan civilisation is of the pastoral type, with such institutions, usages and preconceptions as a large-scale pastoral organisation commonly involves. Such is said by competent philologists to be the evidence of the primitive Aryan speech. It is substantially a servile organisation under patriarchal rule, or, if the expression be preferred, a militant or predatory organisation; these alternative phrases describe the same facts from different points of view. It is characterised by a well-defined system of property rights, a somewhat pronounced subjection of women and children, and a masterful religious system tending strongly to monotheism. A pastoral culture on the broad plains and uplands of a continental region, such as west-central Asia, will necessarily fall into some such shape, because of the necessity of an alert and mobile readiness for offense and defense and the consequent need of soldierly discipline. Insubordination, which is the substance of free institutions, is incompatible with a prosperous pastoral-nomadic mode of life. When worked out with any degree of maturity and consistency the pastoral-nomadic culture that has to do with sheep and cattle appears always to have been a predatory, and therefore a servile culture, particularly when drawn on the large scale imposed by the topography of the centralAsiatic plains, and reenforced with the use of the horse. (The reindeer nomads of the arctic seaboard may appear to be an exception, at least in a degree, but they are a special case, admitting a particular explanation, and their case does not affect the argument for the Aryan civilisation.)

The characteristic and pervasive human relation in such a culture is that of master and servant, and the social (domestic and civil) structure is an organisation of graded servitude, in which no one is his own master but the overlord, even nominally. The family is patriarchal, women and children are in strict tutelage, and discretion vests in the male head alone. If the group grows large its civil institutions are of a like coercive character, it commonly shows a rigorous tribal organisation, and in the end, with the help of warlike experience, it almost unavoidably becomes a despotic monarchy.

It has not been unusual to speak of the popular institutions of Germanic paganism - typified, e.g., by the Scandinavian usages of local self-government in pagan times - as being typically Aryan institutions, but that is a misnomer due to uncritical generalisation guided by a chauvinistic bias. These ancient north-European usages are plainly alien to the culture reflected by the primitive Aryan Speech, if we are to accept the consensus of the philological ethnologists to the effect that the people who used the primitive Aryan speech must have been a community of pastoral nomads inhabiting the plains and uplands of a continental region. That many of these philological ethnologists also hold to the view that these Aryans were north-European pagan blonds may raise a personal question of consistency but does not otherwise touch the present argument.(b) A racial stock that has ever been of first-rate consequence in the ethnology of Europe (the Alpine, brachycephalic brunet, the homo alpinus of the Linnean scheme) comes into Europe at this general period, from Asia; and this race is held to have presently made itself at home, if not dominant, throughout middle Europe, where it has in historic times unquestionably been the dominant racial element.(c) The pastoral-nomadic institutions spoken of above appear to have best made their way in those regions of Europe where this brachycephalic brunet stock has been present in some force if not as a dominant racial factor. The evidence is perhaps not conclusive, but there is at least a strong line of suggestion afforded by the distribution of the patriarchal type of institutions within Europe, including the tribal and gentile organisation.

There is a rough concomitance between the distribution of these cultural elements presumably derived from an Aryan source on the one hand, and the distribution past or present of the brachycephalic brunet type on the other hand. The regions where this line of institutions are known to have prevailed in early times are, in the main, regions in which the Alpine racial type is also known to have been present in force, as, e.g., in the classic Greek and Roman republics. At the same time a gentile organisation seems also to have been associated from the outset with the Mediterranean racial stock and may well have been comprised in the institutional furniture of that race as it stood before the advent of the Alpine stock; but the drift of later inquiry and speculation on this head appears to support the view that this Mediterranean gentile system was of a matrilinear character, such as is found in many extant agricultural communities of the lower barbarian culture, rather than of a patriarchal kind, such as characterises the pastoral nomads. The northern blond communities alone appear, on the available evidence, to have had no gentile or tribal institutions, whether matrilinear or patriarchal. The classic Greek and Roman communities appear originally to have been of the Mediterranean race and to have always retained a broad substratum of the Mediterranean stock as the largest racial element in their population, but the Alpine stock was also largely represented in these communities at the period when their tribal and gentile institutions are known to have counted for much, as, indeed, it has continued ever since.

Apart from these communities of the Mediterranean seaboard, the peoples of the Keltic culture appear to have had the tribal and gentile system, together with the patriarchal family, in more fully developed form than it is to be found in Europe at large. The peoples of Keltic speech are currently believed by ethnologists to have originally been of a blond type, although opinions are not altogether at one on that head, - the tall, perhaps red-haired, brachycephalic blond, the "Saxon" of Beddoe, the "Oriental" of Deniker. But this blond type is perhaps best accounted for as a hybrid of the dolicho-blond crossed on the Alpine brachycephalic brunet. Some such view of its derivation is fortified by what is known of the prehistory and the peculiar features of the early Keltic culture. This culture differs in some respects radically from that of the dolicho-blond communities, and it bears more of a resemblance to the culture of such a brunet group of peoples as the early historic communities of upper and middle Italy.

If the view is to be accepted which is coming into currency latterly, that the Keltic is to be affiliated with the culture of Hallstatt and -La Tène, such affiliation will greatly increase the probability that it is to be counted as a culture strongly influenced if not dominated by the Alpine stock. The Hallstatt culture, lying in the valley of the Danube and its upper affluents, lay in the presumed westward path of immigration of the Alpine stock; its human remains are of a mixed character, showing a strong admixture of the brachycephalic brunet type; and it gives evidence of cultural gains due to outside influence in advance of the adjacent regions of Europe. This Keltic culture, then, as known to history and prehistory, runs broadly across middle Europe along the belt where blond and brunet elements meet and blend; and it has some of the features of that predatory-pastoral culture reflected by the primitive Aryan speech, in freer development, or in better preservation, than the adjacent cultural regions to the north; at the same time the peoples of this Keltic culture show more of affiliation to or admixture with the brachycephalic brunet than the other blond-hybrid peoples do.

On the other hand the communities of dolicho-blond hybrids on the shores of the narrow Scandinavian waters, remote from the centers of the Alpine culture, show little of the institutions peculiar to a pastoral people. These dolicho-blond hybrids of the North come into history at a later date, but with a better preserved and more adequately recorded paganism than the other barbarians of Europe. The late-pagan Germanic-Scandinavian culture affords the best available instance of archaic dolicho-blond institutions, if not the sole instance; and it is to be noted that among these peoples the patriarchal system is weak and vague, - women are not in perpetual tutelage, the discretion of the male head of the household is not despotic nor even unquestioned, children are not held under paternal discretion beyond adult age, the patrimony is held to no clan liabilities and is readily divisible on inheritance, and so forth.

Neither is there any serious evidence of a tribal or gentile system among these peoples, early or late, nor are any of them, excepting the late and special instance of the Icelandic colony, known ever to have been wholly or mainly of pastoral habits; indeed, they are known to have been without the pastoral animals until some time in the neolithic period. The only dissenting evidence on these heads is that of the Latin writers, substantially Caesar and Tacitus, whose testimony is doubtless to be thrown out as incompetent in view of the fact that it is supported neither by circumstantial evidence nor by later and more authentic records. In speaking of "tribes" among the Germanic hordes these Latin writers are plainly construing Germanic facts in Roman terms, very much as the Spanish writers of a later day construed Mexican and Peruvian facts in mediaeval-feudalistic terms,-to the lasting confusion of the historians; whereas in enlarging on the pastoral habits of the Germanic communities they go entirely on data taken from bodies of people on the move and organised for raiding, or recently and provisionally settled upon a subject population presumably of Keltic derivation or of other alien origin and inhabiting the broad lands of middle Europe remote from the permanent habitat of the dolicho-blond.

Great freedom of assumption has been used and much ingenuity has been spent in imputing a tribal system to the early Germanic peoples, but apart from the sophisticated testimony of these classical writers there is no evidence for it. The nearest approach to a tribal or a gentile organisation within this culture is the "kin," which counts for something in early

Germanic law and custom; but the kin is far from being a gens or clan, and it will be found to have more of the force of a clan organisation the farther it has strayed from the Scandinavian center of diffusion of the dolicho-blond and the more protracted the warlike discipline to which the wandering host has been exposed. All these properly Aryan institutions are weakest or most notably wanting where the blond is most indubitably in evidence.

Taking early Europe as a whole, it will appear that among the European peoples at large institutions of the character reflected in the primitive Aryan speech and implied in the pastoral-nomadic life evidenced by the same speech are relatively weak, ill-defined or wanting, arguing that Europe was never fully Aryanised. And the peculiar geographical and ethnic distribution of this Aryanism of institutions argues further that the dolicho-blond culture of the Scandinavian region was less profoundly affected by the Aryan invasion than any other equally well known section of Europe. What is known of this primitive Aryan culture, material, domestic, civil and religious, through the Sanskrit and other early Asiatic sources, may convincingly be contrasted with what is found in early Europe. These Asiatic records, which are our sole dependence for a competent characterisation of the Aryan culture, shows it to have resembled the culture of the early Hebrews or that of the pastoral Turanians more closely than it resembles the early European culture at large, and greatly more than it resembles the known culture of the early communities of dolicho-blond hybrids.(d) Scarcely more conclusive, but equally suggestive, is the evidence from the religious institutions of the Aryanised Europeans. As would be expected in any predatory civilisation, such as the pastoral-nomadic cultures typically are, the Aryan religious system is said to have leaned strongly toward a despotic monarchical form, a hierarchically graded polytheism, culminating in a despotic monotheism.

There is little of all this to be found in early pagan Europe. The nearest well-known approach to anything of the kind is the late-Greek scheme of Olympian divinities with Zeus as a doubtful suzerain, - known through latter-day investigations to have been superimposed on an earlier cult of a very different character. The Keltic (Druidical) system is little known, but it is perhaps not beyond legitimate conjecture, on the scant evidence available, that this system had rather more of the predatory, monarchical-despotic cast than the better known pagan cults of Europe. The Germanic paganism, as indicated by the late Scandinavian - which alone is known in any appreciable degree -was a lax polytheism which imputed little if any coercive power to the highest god, and which was not taken so very seriously anyway by the "worshipers, if Snorri's virtually exclusive account is to be accepted without sophistication. The evidence accorded by tile religious cults of Europe yields little that is conclusive, beyond throwing the whole loose jointed, proliferous European paganism out of touch with anything that can reasonably be called Aryan. And this in spite of the fact that all the available evidence is derived from the European cults as they stood after having been exposed to long centuries of Aryanisation.

So that it may well be held that such systematisation of myths and observances as these European cults give evidence of, and going in the direction of a despotic monotheism, is to be traced to the influence of the intrusive culture of the Aryan or Aryanised invaders, - as is fairly plain in the instance of the Olympians.(e) That the languages of early Europe, so far as known, belong almost universally to the Aryan family may seem an insurmountable obstacle to the view here spoken for. But the difficulties of the case are not appreciably lessened by so varying the hypothesis as to impute the Aryan speech to the dolicho-blond, or to any blond stock, as its original bearer. Indeed, the difficulties are increased by such an hypothesis, since the Aryan-speaking peoples of early times, as of later times, have in the main been communities made up of brunets without evidence of a blond admixture, not to speak of an exclusively blond people. (There is no evidence of the existence of an all-blond people anywhere, early or late.)

The early European situation, so far as known, offers no exceptional obstacles to the diffusion of an intrusive language. Certain mass movements of population, or rather mass movements of communities shifting their ground by secular progression, are known to have taken place, as, e.g., in the case of the Hallstatt-La Tène-Keltic culture moving westward on the whole as it gained ground and spread by shifting and ramification outward from its first-known seat in the upper Danube valley. All the while, as this secular movement of growth, ramification and advance was going on, the Hallstatt-La Tène-Keltic peoples continued to maintain extensive trade relations with the Mediterranean seaboard and the Aegean -on the one side and reaching the North-Sea littoral on the other side. In all probability it is by trade relations of this kind - chiefly, no doubt, through trade carried on by itinerant merchants -that the new speech made its way among the barbarians of Europe; and it is no far-fetched inference that it made its way, in the North at least, as a trade jargon. All this accords with what is going on at present under analogous circumstances.

The superior merit by force of which such a new speech would make its way need be nothing more substantial than a relatively crude syntax and phonetics - such as furthers the dissemination of English to-day in the form of Chinook jargon, Pidgin English, and Beach la Mar. Such traits, which might in some other light seem blemishes, facilitate the mutilation of such a language into a graceless but practicable trade jargon. With jargons as with coins the poorer (simpler) drives out the better (subtler and more complex). A second, and perhaps the chief, point of superiority by virtue of which a given language makes its way as the dominant factor in such a trade jargon, is the fact that it is the native language of the people who carry on the trade for whose behoof the jargon is contrived. The traders, coming in contact with many men, of varied speech, and carrying their varied stock of trade goods, will impose their own names for the articles bartered and so contribute that much to the jargon vocabulary,- and a jargon is at its inception little more than a vocabulary. The traders at the same time are likely to belong to the people possessed of the more efficient technology, since it is the superior technology that commonly affords them their opportunity for advantageous trade; hence the new or intrusive words, being the names of new or intrusive facts, will in so far find their way unhindered into current speech and further the displacement of the indigenous language by the jargon.

Such a jargon at the outset is little else than a vocabulary comprising names for the most common objects and the most tangible relations. On this simple but practicable framework new varieties of speech will develop, diversified locally according to the kind and quantity of materials and linguistic tradition contributed by the various languages which it supplants or absorbs.

In so putting forward the conjecture that the several forms of Aryan speech have arisen out of trade jargons that have run back to a common source in the language of an intrusive proto-Aryan people, and developing into widely diversified local and ethnic variants according as the mutilated proto-Aryan speech (vocabulary) fell into the hands of one or another of the indigenous barbarian peoples,- in this suggestion there is after all nothing substantially novel beyond giving a collective name to facts already well accepted by the philologists. Working backward analytically step by step from the mature results given in the known Aryan languages they have discovered and divulged - with what prolixity need not be alluded to here - that in their beginnings these several idioms were little else than crude vocabularies covering the commonest objects and most tangible relations, and that by time-long use and wont the uncouth strings of vocables whereby the beginners of these languages sought to express themselves have been worked down through a stupendously elaborate fabric of prefixes, infixes and suffixes, etc., etc., to the tactically and phonetically unexceptionable inflected languages of the Aryan family as they stood at their classical best. And what is true of the European languages should apparently hold with but slight modification for the Asiatic members of the family. These European idioms are commonly said to be, on the whole, less true to the pattern of the inferentially known primitive Aryan than are its best Asiatic representatives; as would be expected in case the latter were an outgrowth of jargons lying nearer the center of diffusion of the proto-Aryan speech and technology.

As regards the special case of the early north-European communities of dolicho-blond hybrids, the trade between the Baltic and Danish waters on the one hand and the Danube valley, Adriatic and Aegean on the other hand is known to have been continued and voluminous during the neolithic and bronze ages, - as counted by the Scandinavian chronology. In the course of this traffic, extending over many centuries and complicated as it seems to have been with a large infiltration of the brachycephalic brunet type, much might come to pass in the way of linguistic substitution and growth.

Chapter 5
An Early Experiment in Trusts

According to Much,[62] following in the main the views of Penka, Wilser, De LaPouge, Sophus Móller, Andreas Hansen, and other spokesmen of the later theories touching Aryan origins, the area of characterization of the West-European culture, as well as of that dolicho-blond racial stock that bears this culture, is the region bordering on the North Sea and the Baltic, and its center of diffusion is to be sought on the southern shores of the Baltic. This region is in a manner, then, the primary focus of that culture of enterprise that has reshaped the scheme of life for mankind during the Christian era. Its spirit of enterprise and adventure has carried this race to a degree of material success that is without example in history, whether in point of the extent or of die scope of its achievements.

Up to the present the culminating achievement of this enterprise is dominion in business, and its most finished instrument is the quasi-voluntary coalition of forces known as a Trust. In its method and outward form this enterprise of the Indo-germanic racial stock has varied with the passage of time and the change of circumstances; but in its spirit and objective end it has maintained a singularly consistent character through all the mutations of name and external circumstance that have passed over it in the course of history. In the earlier, more elemental expression this enterprise takes the form of raiding, by land and sea. A shrewd interpretation might, without particular violence to the faces, find a coalition of forces of the kind which is later known as a Trust in the Barbarian raids spoken of as the Volkerwanderung. Such an interpretation would seem remote, however, and not particularly apt. The beginnings of a bona fide trust enterprise are of a more businesslike character and have left a record more amenable to the tests of accountancy. A trust, as that term is colloquially understand, is a business organization.

Now, the line of enterprise, of indigenous growth in the north-European cultural region, which first falls into settled shape as an orderly, organized business is the traffic of those seafaring men of the North known to fame as die Vikings. And it is in this traffic, so far as the records show, that a trust, with all essential features, is first organized. The term "Viking" covers, somewhat euphemistically, two main facts: piracy and slave-trade. Without both of these lines of business the traffic could not be maintained in the long run; and both, but more particularly the latter, presume, as an indispensable condition to their successful prosecution, a regular market and an assured demand for the output. It is a traffic in which, in order to get the best results, a relatively large initial investment must be sunk, and

---

[62] MATTHAEUS MUCH, Die Heimat der Indogermanen.

the period of turn-over - the "period of production" - is necessarily of some duration; the risk is also considerable. Further, certain technological prerequisites must be met, in the way particularly of shipbuilding, navigation, and the manufacture of weapons; an adequate accumulation of capital goods must be had, coupled with a sagacious spirit of adventure; there must also be an available supply of labor. There appears to have been a concurrence of all these circumstances, together with favorable market conditions, in the south-Baltic region front about the sixth century onward; the circumstances apparently growing gradually move favorable through the succeeding four centuries.

The Viking trade appears to have grown up gradually on the Baltic seaboard, as well as in the Sound country and throughout the fjord region of Norway, as a by-occupation of the farming population. Its beginnings are earlier than any records, so that the earliest traditions speak of it as an institution well understood and fully legitimate. The well-to-do freehold farmers, including some who laid claim to the rank of jarl, seem to have found it an agreeable and honorable diversion, as well as a lucrative employment for their surplus wealth and labor supply. From such sporadic and occasional beginnings it passed presently into an independently organized and self-sustained line of business enterprise, and in the course of time it attained a settled business routine and a defined code of professional ethics.

Syndication, of a loose form, had begun as early as the oldest accounts extant, but it is evident from the way in which the matter is spoken of that combination had not at that date - say, about the beginning of the ninth century - long been the common practice. It was not then a matter of course. The early combinations; were relatively small and transient. They took the form of "gentlemen's agreements," pools, working arrangements, division of territory, etc., rather than hard and fast syndicates. In those early days a combine would be formed for a season between two or more capitalist-undertakers, for the most part employing their own capital only, without recourse to credit; although credit arrangements occur quite early, but are not very common in the earlier recorded phases of the trade. Such a loose combine, say about the middle of the ninth century, might comprise from two to a dozen boats. What may be called the normal unit in the trade at that time was a boat of perhaps thirty tons' burden, with an effective crew of some forty men. Boats and crews gradually increase both in size and efficiency for a century and a half after that time.

Syndication, of an increasingly those texture and increasingly permanent effect, appears to have rapidly grown in favor through the ninth and tenth centuries. The reasons for this movement of coalition are plain. The volume of the trade, as well as its territorial extension, increased uninterruptedly. The technique of the trade was gradually improved, and the equipment and management were improved and reduced to standard forms. The tonnage employed at any given time can, of course, not be ascertained with anything like a confident approximation; but its steady increase is unmistakable. Year by year the boats and crews increase in average size as well as in number, until by the middle of the tenth century the number of men and ships engaged, as well as the volume of capital invested in the trade, are probably larger than the corresponding figures for any other form of lucrative enterprise at that time.

It is, at that time, altogether the best organized line of enterprise in the West-European region in respect of its business management, and the most efficient and progressive in respect of its equipment and technology. At a conservative guess, the aggregate number of ships engaged about the middle of the tenth century must have appreciably exceeded six hundred, and near have reached one thousand; with crews which had also grown gradually larger until they may by this time have averaged seventy or eighty men. There was consequently what would in modern phrase be called an "overproduction" of piratical craft - overinvestment in the Viking trade and consequent cut-throat competition. The various conditions came into violent conflict, and many of them went under, with great resultant loss of capital, impoverishment of well-to-do families, hardship and demoralization of the entire trade.

Added to these untoward conditions within the trade was the open disfavor of the crown, in each of the three Scandinavian kingdoms. The traffic had long passed out of the stage at which it had offered a lucrative opening for farmers' sons who were tired of the farm and eager to find excitement, reputation, and creature comforts in that wider human contact and busier life for which the tedium of the farm had sharpened their appetites. The larger capitalists alone could succeed as organizers or directors of a Viking concern under the changed conditions. The common run of well-to-do farmers had neither the tangible assets nor the "good-will" requisite to the successful promotion of a new company of freebooters. At the best, their sons could enter the business only as employees and with but a very uncertain outlook to speedy promotion to an executive position. On the other hand, as the trade became better organized in stronger hands, with a larger equipment, and as the competition within the trade grew more severe, the blackmail from which much of the profits of the trade was drawn grew more excessive and more uncertain both as to its amount and as to the manner and incidents with which it was levied. As competition grew severe and the small Vikings practically disappeared, and as the demoralization that goes with cut-throat competition set in, the livelihood of the common people, at whose expense the Vikings lived, grew progressively more precarious, and even their domestic peace and household industry grew insecure. Popular sentiment was running strongly against the whole traffic.

So much so, indeed, as to threaten the tenure of courts and sovereigns if the popular hardship incident to the continuance of the trade were not abated.The politicians, therefore, made a strenuous show of effort to regulate, or even to repress, the Viking organizations. Outright and indiscriminate repression was scarcely a feasible remedy, certainly not an agreeable one. The Viking companies were a source of strength to the country, both in that they might be drawn on for support in case of war and in that they brought funds into the country. The remedy to which the politicians turned, by preference, therefore, was a regulation of the companies in such a manner as to let "the foreigner pay the tax," to adapt a modern phrase. If the freebooters of a given state could be induced, by stringent regulations, to prey upon the people of the neighboring states, and particularly if they worked at cross-purposes with similar companies of freebooters domiciled in such neighboring states, it was then plain to the sagacious politicians of those days that the companies might be more of a blessing than a curse.

On trial it was found that this policy of control gave at the best but very dubious results, and consequently the repressive hand of the authorities perforce fell with increasingly rigorous pressure on the Viking organizations, particularly on the smaller ones which were scarcely of national importance. The competition in the trade was too severe to admit of a consistent avoidance of excesses and irregularities on the part of the Vikings, and these irregularities obliged the authorities to interfere.

Under these circumstances it is plain that no Viking combine could hope to prosper in the long run unless it were strong enough to take an international position and to maintain a practical monopoly of the trade. "International" in these premises means within the Scandinavian countries. In the days of its finest development the Viking trade was domiciled in the Scandinavian countries, almost exclusively. This means the two Scandinavian peninsulas, with Iceland, the Faroes, Orkneys, Hebrides, and the Scandinavian portions of Scotland. To this, for completeness of statement, is to be added a stretch of Wendish seaboard on the south of the Baltic and a negligible patch of German territory. The trade, so far as regards its home offices, to use a modern phrase, gathered in the main about two chief centers: the Orkneys and the south end of the Baltic. Outlying regions, such as the Norwegian fjord country and the Hebrides, are by no means negligible, but the two regions named above are after all the chief seats of the traffic; and of these two centers the Baltic - chiefly Danish - region is in many respects the more notable. Its Viking traffic is better, more regularly organized, is carried on with a more evident sense of a solidarity of interests and a more consistent view to a long-term prosperity.

As one might say, looking at the matter from the modern standpoint, it has more of a look of stability and conservative management, such as belongs to an investment business, and has less of a speculative air, than the trade that centers in the western isles. Perhaps it is just on this account, because of its greater stability of interests and more conservative animus, that the traffic of this region responds with greater alacrity to the pressure of excessive competition and political interference, and so enters on a policy of larger and closer coalition. It may be added that many of the great captains of adventure in this region are men of good family and substantial standing in the community. As may often happen in a like conjuncture, when the irksomeness of this competitive situation in the Baltic was fast becoming intolerable, there arose a man of far-seeing sagacity and settled principles, of executive ability and businesslike integrity, who saw the needs of the hour and the available remedy, and who saw at the same glance his own opportunity of gain.

This man was Palnatoki, the descendant of an honorable line of country gentlemen in the island of Funen, whose family had from time immemorial borne an active and prudent part in the trade, and had been well seen at court and in society. He was a man of mature experience, with a large investment in the traffic, and with a body of "good-will" that gave him perhaps his most decisive advantage. During the reign of Harald Gormsson, about the middle of the tenth century, Palnatoki seems to have cast about for a basis on which to promote an international coalition of Vikings, such as would put an end no headlong competition in the trade and would at the same time be placed above the accidents of national politics. To this end it was necessary to find a neutral ground on which to establish the home office of the concern. Such a mediaeval-Scandinavian New Jersey was the Wendish kingdom at the south of the Baltic. Jomsborg (on the island of Wollin, at the mouth of the Oder) seems to have been a resort of Vikings before Palnatoki organized his company there and strengthened the harbor, which may have been fortified by three who held it before him.

Here the new company was incorporated under a special franchise from the Wendish crown, with the stipulation that it was to do business only outside the Wendish territories. The tangible assets of the corporation were the harbor and fortified town of Jómsborg, together with the ships and other equipment of such Vikings as were admitted to fellowship; its intangible assets were its franchise and the good-will of the promoter and the underlying companies. Its by-laws were very strict, both as to the discipline of the personnel and as to the distribution of earnings. The promoter, who was the first president of the corporation, was given extreme powers for the enforcement of the by-laws, and throughout his long incumbency of office be exercised his powers with the greatest discretion and with a most salutary effect. This neutral, international corporation of piracy rapidly won a great prestige. In modern phrase, its intangible assets grew rapidly larger.

Backed by the competitive pressure which the new corporation was able to bring upon the smaller companies and syndicates, this prestige, of the JomsVikings; brought a steady run of applications for admission into the trust. The trust's policy was substantially the same as has since become familiar in other lines of enterprise, with the difference that in those early days the competitive struggle took a less sophisticated form. Outstanding syndicates and private firms were given the alternative of submission to the trust's terms or retirement from the traffic. There was great hardship among the outstanding concerns, especially among that large proportion of them that were unable to meet the scale of requirements imposed on applicants for admission into the trust. The qualifications both as to equipment and personnel were extremely strict, so that a large percentage of the applicants were excluded; and the unfortunates who failed of admission found themselves in a doubtful position that grew more precarious with every year that passed. Practically such concerns were either frozen out of the business or forced into a liquidation which permanently wound up their affairs and terminated their corporate existence.

The accounts extant are of course not reliable in minute details, being not strictly contemporary, nor are they cast in such modern terms as would give an easy comparison with present-day facts. The chief documents in the case are JomsVikingasaga, Saxo Grammaticus, Heimskringla, and Olafssaga Tryggvasonar; but nearly the whole of the saga literature bears on the development of the Viking trade, and characteristic references to the JomsViking trust occur throughout. The evidence afforded by these accounts converges to the conclusion that toward the close of the tenth century the trust stood in a high state of prosperity add was in a position virtually to dictate the course of the traffic for all that portion of the Viking trade that centered in the Baltic. Its prestige and influence were strong wherever the traffic extended, even in the region of the western isles and in the fjord country of Norway. It had even come to be a factor of first-rate consequence in international politics, and its power was feared and courted by those two sovereigns who established the Danish rule in England, as well as by their Swedish, Norwegian, and Russian contemporaries. It is probably not an overstatement to say that the Danish conquest of England would not have been practicable except for the alliance of the trust with Svend, which enabled him to turn his attention from the complications of Scandinavian politics to his English interests.

The extent of the trust's material equipment at the height of its prosperity is a matter of surmise rather than of statistical information. Some notion of its strength may be gathered from the statement that the fortified harbor of Jomsborg included within its castellated seawall an enclosed basin capable of floating three hundred ships at anchor. In the great raid against the kingdom of Norway, whose failure inaugurated the disintegration of the trust, the number of ships sent out is variously given by different authorities. The JomsVikingasaga says that they numbered one long hundred. This fleet, however, was made up of craft selected from among the ships that were under the immediate command of four of the great captains of adventure. The fleet, as it lay in the Sound before the final selection, is said to have numbered 185, but the context shows that this feet was but a fraction of the aggregate JomsViking tonnage. Of this disastrous expedition but a fraction returned; yet various later expeditions of the JomsVikings are mentioned in which some scores of their ships took part. The trust having become an international power, it undertook to shape the destiny of nations and dynasties, and it broke under the strain. It, or its directors, took a contract to bring Norway into subjection to the Danish crown. Partly through untoward accidents, partly through miscalculation and hurried preparations, it failed in this undertaking, which brought the affairs of the trust to a spectacular crisis. From this disaster it never recovered. With the opening of the eleventh century the Viking trust fell into abeyance, and in a few years it disappeared from the field. There are several good reasons for its failure. On the death of its founder the management had passed into the hands of Sigvaldi, a man of less sagacity and less integrity as well as of more unprincipled personal ambition, and somewhat given to flighty ventures in the field of politics. It was Sigvaldi's overweening personal ambition that committed the corporation to the ill-advised expedition against Norway.

The trust, moreover, being supreme within its field, the discipline grew lax and its exactions grew arbitrary, sometimes going to unprovoked excesses. As one might say, too little thought was given to "economies of production," and the charges were pushed beyond "what the traffic would bear." But for all that, in spite of its meddling in politics, and in spite of jobbery and corruption in its management, the trust still had a fair outlook for continued success, except that the bottom dropped out of the trade. For better or worse, the slave-trade in the north of Europe collapsed on the introduction of Christianity, at least so far as regards the trade in Christians; and without a slave market the Viking enterprise had no chance of reasonable earnings. At the same time, the risk and hardships of the traffic - the "cost of production" - grew heavier as the countries to the south became better able to defend their shores. The passenger traffic failed almost entirely, and the goods traffic was in a disorganized and unprofitable state. The costs were fast becoming prohibitive, even to men so enterprising and necessitous as the Norwegian freebooters. The situation changed in such a way as to leave the trust out.

Some show of corporate existence was still maintained for a short period after the trust's great crisis, but there was an end of discipline and authoritative control. The minor concerns and private establishments that had once formed part of the trust continued in the trade on an independent footing, but with decreasing regularity and with diminishing strength. As the equipment wore out it was not replaced, and the trade lapsed. The great captains of the industry, like Sigvaldi, Thorkel Haraldson, Sigurd Kapa, and Vagn Akason, turned their holdings to the service of the dynastic politics which were then engaging the attention of the northern countries. Much of this body of enterprise and wealth was exhausted in working out the imperialistic schemes of expansion of Svend and Knut the Great; and what was left over shared the fortunes of the other available forces of the Scandinavian countries, being dissipated in political dissensions, extortionate government organizations, and the establishment of a church and a nobility.

Chapter 6

As to a Proposed Inquiry
into Baltic and Cretan Antiquities

The problem on which my interest in prehistoric matters finally converges is that of the derivation and early growth of those free or popular
institutions which have marked off European civilization at its best from
the great civilizations of Asia and Africa. These characteristic free institutions of the Western culture comprise the decisive traits of the domestic
and religious life as well as those of the civil and political organization. It is
conceived that the underlying forces to which this scheme of free institutions owes its rise and its sustained and peculiar growth are to be looked
for (a) in the peculiar native endowment of the races (or race) involved in
the case, and (b) in the material (economic) circumstances under which
the Western peoples have lived, particularly in early times. The centers of
this cultural growth, as first known to history, have been the Aegean or
East Mediterranean region on the one hand and the North Sea-Baltic region on the other hand. Within these regions, again, exploration has latterly thrown Crete, with its cultural neighbors and ramifications, into the
foreground as the early center of growth and diffusion of the Aegean-
Mediterranean culture, while it has similarly centered attention on the
shores of the narrow Scandinavian waters as the most characteristic center of early culture in the North Sea-Baltic region. And (c) quite recently
the Pumpelly explorations in Turkestan have brought to light a culture (at
Anau) of a very striking character and showing features that argue for a
degree of relationship - racial, economic, and institutional - to these European centers, such as should merit close inquiry.

There is apparently reason to look for (a) a racial connection in prehistoric (Neolithic) times between the peoples of the Aegean (Crete, etc.) and
the peoples centering about the south shores of the Baltic, and (b) a sustained cultural connection, resting on trade relations, between the same
regions and running through the Neolithic and Bronze Ages of northern
Europe. It is believed that a sufficiently attentive canvass of the evidence
will bring out a consequent similarity of character in the institutions under which the peoples of these two regions lived; which would argue that
these two sources of what is most characteristic in later Western civilization are in great measure to be traced back to a common origin, racial and
economic. And it is conceived that the late-known culture of Anau will
come in as a complementary factor to round out this scheme of cultural
growth by supplying elements which have hitherto seemed lacking in any
attempted system of European prehistory. The "Aryan" explanation of this
community of institutions, it may be added, is no longer tenable.

A study of other primitive cultures, remote and not visibly related to this
early European civilization, shows a close correlation between the materi-

al (industrial and pecuniary) life of any given people and their civic, domestic, and religious scheme of life; and it shows, further, that the myths and the religious cult reflect the character of these other -especially the economic and domestic - institutions in a peculiarly naive and truthful manner.

An inquiry looking to the end here proposed, therefore, must have recourse to such industrial and pecuniary facts as are reflected by the available archaeological sites and exhibits, on the one hand, and to such indications of myth and religious cult as are afforded by the same explorations. These will have to be the main lines of approach, and it is along these lines that it is here proposed to review the evidence pertinent to the case - with the stress falling on the economic forces involved. A very considerable body of material is now available for such a study in this field of European prehistory, but little has been done toward exploiting it for the purpose here indicated. Nor has the material hitherto been canvassed in any comprehensive manner with such a question in mind.

While much of the material to be drawn on has been published in excellent shape, its publication has been under the hand of students and scholars animated with other interests than those here spoken for - more particularly has the economic (industrial and pecuniary) bearing of the materials exhibited received relatively scant attention. The men who have canvassed and edited the published materials have necessarily seen those materials in the light of their own interest, and so have brought out chiefly those features of the material upon which the light of their own interest would fall most strongly. Any student who approaches the material from a new quarter, therefore, and requires it to answer questions that were not present or not urgent in the minds of those earlier students, must see and review the sites and exhibits for himself and make such use as he can of these materials, with the help of other men already engaged in the general field which he enters. It is no less requisite to come into close personal contact with the men engaged than it is to make first-hand acquaintance with the available materials; for it is a most common trait of scientists, particularly when occupied with matter that is in any degree novel and growing, that they know and are willing to impart many things that are not primarily involved in the direct line of their own inquiry and many things, too, to which they may not be ready to commit themselves in print.

The evidences of the peculiar technological bent characteristic of Western civilization run very far back in the North Sea-Baltic culture, and the later explorations in Crete and its cultural dependencies suggest a similar aptitude for technological efficiency in the prehistoric Aegean culture. It is believed that a patient scrutiny of the available material for the two regions will go far to show (a) in what degree the two civilizations are to be correlated or contrasted on this technological side of their growth, (b) how far this technological peculiarity is to be traced back to racial or to environmental factors, and (c) what is the nature and force of the correlation, if any, between this peculiar development of technological efficiency and the early growth and character of that scheme of free institutions which today is as characteristic a trait of Western civilization as is its preeminence in point of technological efficiency.

It will be seen, therefore, that such an inquiry as is here had in view would require time and would involve a somewhat extended itinerary. At the outset, it is believed, a visit should be made to two or three of the less sophisticated Indian Pueblos of the Southwest, as the best available outside term of comparison by which to check certain features of the European evidence and particularly certain of the facts shown in the explorations at Anau.

The next move should, presumably, be to the sites and museums of Denmark and Sweden, with a side excursion of a somewhat detailed character to the British Museum and to certain archaeologists and ethnologists in England whose information and speculations must necessarily be drawn on. The Scandinavian scholars have the archaeology of their own region excellently well in hand, and their exhaustive acquaintance with the culture of later Germanic-Scandinavian paganism is likewise indispensable to a comprehensive survey of the question. Certain men and exhibits in Germany and Austria must also be seen and made use of, though this will presumably require less time and attention than the earlier and later stages in the proposed itinerary. The sites and exhibits of the Hallstatt and La Tène culture should also be visited, with more or less painstaking attention; and certain localities of northern Italy, marking one of the cultural areas that once in prehistoric times maintained trade relations with the Baltic, should likewise be seen and appreciated. There are also Italian students in this field whose aid is expected to be of first-rate value, both in the ethnology and the archaeology of the case.

More detailed study as well as a greater allowance of time would necessarily be given to the several sites in the Aegean, with Crete as the central and most important point; where a somewhat protracted residence would be desirable if not indispensable, and from which excursions might profitably be made to Sicily, southeastern Asia Minor, Cyprus, and perhaps Transcaspia, as well as to several localities in the Aegean territory proper. These excursions outside of the Aegean lands seem, at this distance at least, less requisite than a residence of some months in Crete and the visits to Aegean sites supplementary to the study of Crete. The residence in the Aegean here spoken of, with the allowance of time which it would involve, is desirable in part on account of the very appreciable mass of printed material bearing on the case, and which could most expeditiously and effectively be acquired, assimilated, and checked by a person living within striking distance of the sites with which the descriptive material deals.

It is believed that, in point of time, the inquiry so had in view should advantageously consume not less than three years.

Index

www.ingramcontent.com/pod-product-compliance
Lightning Source LLC
Chambersburg PA
CBHW061309220326
41599CB00026B/4804